D0397789

CONFLICT OF DUTY

JEFFERY M. DORWART

CONFLICT
OF DUTY

THE U.S. NAVY'S INTELLIGENCE DILEMMA, 1919–1945

NAVAL INSTITUTE PRESS
Annapolis, Maryland

Copyright © 1983
by the United States Naval Institute
Annapolis, Maryland

Third printing, 1984

Library of Congress Cataloging in Publication Data

Dorwart, Jeffery M., 1944–
  Conflict of duty.

  Bibliography: p.
  Includes index.
  1. United States.   Office of Naval Intelligence—
History—20th century.   I. Title.
VB231.U54D667 1983   359.3'432'0973   82-22515
ISBN 0-87021-685-6

Printed in the United States of America

To the memory of
Major Harold "Hal" Lewis,
killed while on a secret mission
in the Iranian desert,
25 April 1980

CONTENTS

PREFACE

In its most fundamental sense the mission of the United States Office of Naval Intelligence (ONI) between 1919 and 1945 was to collect, synthesize, and distribute information about foreign naval and maritime technology, strategies, and policies for the United States Navy. These data were gathered by a variety of methods, including the open accumulation of news by naval attachés, clandestine interception and decryption of coded radio communications, and through secret operations by spies and informers. Once raw information was assembled in ONI's Washington headquarters, it had to be sorted, classified, and analyzed before it became intelligence; and then in order to be of value to the navy, it had to be distributed to those who could use the intelligence for war planning in peacetime and for tactical and strategic operations in time of war.

However, there was another less clearly defined, subsidiary mission of naval intelligence from the end of World War I to the closing days of the Second World War in 1945. This secondary aspect of ONI duty was to provide security to the naval establishment and to the nation against foreign or foreign-inspired espionage, sabotage, and subversion. Theoretically this duty complemented the fundamental mission by employing naval information to identify and locate potential enemies of the navy and threats to the nation. But this function posed a far more difficult task for the professional line officers who directed and carried out this side of the navy's intelligence mission. While most could adjust to the larger question of processing strategic and technical naval data collected overseas, measures to afford internal security, counterespionage, and surveillance required investigative, political, and even legal expertise well beyond the scope of a naval officer trained at the U.S. Naval Academy in weapons technology, seamanship, and perhaps a smattering of strategy. The security side led to secret conduct, domestic operations, and snooping—often within the United States itself—that might violate the constitutional obligations and freedoms that every naval officer had pledged to uphold and defend. More dangerous from the navy's perspective, concentration on the security function might interfere with ONI's primary obligation to provide the freshest possible data about foreign military technology and war plans.

It is this agonizing contradiction between the informational and security aspects, which I call the United States Navy's intelligence dilemma, that provides the central theme of this study of ONI between 1919 and 1945. And while inasmuch as communications and combat intelligence at times become a part of the intelligence dilemma, I have chosen to leave these largely separate issues in the more competent hands of authors such as W. J. Holmes, David Kahn, and the host of writers now immersed in revealing the secrets of ULTRA. Yet as they are rewriting the battle history of World War II, perhaps a study of the navy's intelligence dilemma can help enhance an understanding of the more static, but equally important, side of the intelligence story.

Numerous individuals and organizations assisted in the research and writing of this book. Generous research grants were provided by the Rutgers University Research Council and by the American Philosophical Society. Captain Clyde J. Roach, USN, Captain Reinhold A. Dorwart, USNR (Ret.), Rear Admiral Cecil B. Coggins (MC), USN (Ret.), and Admiral Thomas B. Inglis, USN (Ret.), provided information and advice about the navy's intelligence history. Admiral Edwin T. Layton, USN (Ret.), allowed me to cite his Oral History, as did Mrs. Henri Smith-Hutton for her husband's Oral History. The Forrestal estate permitted me to use material in the Forrestal Papers deposited at Princeton University. I am indebted to the staff of the Old Army and Navy Branch of the National Archives, the Saturday crew in the Library of Congress Manuscript Reading Room, and the archivists at the Franklin Delano Roosevelt Library at Hyde Park for their assistance. I wish to thank especially Dr. Dean Allard, head of the Operational Archives of the Naval History Division, and Benis Frank, head of the Oral History Collection in the United States Marine Corps Museum and Library for both their scholarly guidance and personal friendship. And finally, the entire Naval Institute Press staff, but most notably editor Carol Swartz and designer Beverly Baum, displayed a genuine enthusiasm and meticulous professionalism during the entire production of this book. However, any errors and interpretations found in this study are solely my responsibility.

CONFLICT OF DUTY

PART ONE

THE INTERWAR YEARS
1919–1938

CHAPTER ONE

INTELLIGENCE DILEMMA

In 1930 the president of the United States authorized the burglary of private property for strictly personal reasons, and a United States Navy officer on active duty with the Office of Naval Intelligence (ONI) carried out the criminal act. His presidency paralyzed by the worst economic depression in American history and reeling from vicious political attacks, Herbert Hoover had become overly excitable and sensitive to any opposition or criticism. Thus, when he received a confidential report alleging that the Democrats had accumulated a file of data so damaging that if made public it would destroy both his reputation and his entire administration, Hoover determined to gain access to the material.[1]

Lifting such a file might prove tricky business, and the president needed a trusted intermediary. He found such an agent in former private secretary Lewis Lichtenstein Strauss, now a wealthy Wall Street banker. Strauss was no stranger to intrigue, and in fact his closest partner at Kuhn, Loeb and Company in New York was Sir William Wiseman, notorious head of British Intelligence in the United States during World War I. Moreover, as a naval reserve officer Strauss maintained close contact in New York City with Third Naval District Intelligence Officer (DIO) Paul Foster. Undoubtedly Foster convinced the banker to employ naval intelligence sleuths for the president's covert operation rather than the more experienced, but perhaps talkative, government men from the Justice or Treasury Departments. It was Foster, also, who brought new DIO Glenn Howell to meet Strauss in late May, at which time the three men, closeted in a secluded office at 52 William Street, conspired to carry out instructions from the White House. "Strauss told me that the President is anxious to know what the contents of the mysterious documents are," Howell recorded in his secret diary. "And Strauss is authorized by the President to utilize the services of any one of our various government secret services."[2]

Apparently Howell's credentials satisfied the banker, and he looked no further. Unlike most naval officers, the young lieutenant commander loved intelligence duty and as a DIO had participated already in several undercover operations—including the breaking and entering of offices occupied by local Communist party and Japanese consular agents. When not wandering about New York's seedy waterfront disguised as a common sailor, Howell sat at his desk in Third District headquarters dreaming up plans for an agency in which "the various intelligence units of the government be left intact exactly as they are now but that they may be considered as spokes of a wheel, the hub of which is a Central Intelligence."[3]

Yet despite his evident skill, Howell grew uneasy about the possible ramifications of the unlawful mission. He knew that district detectives had pursued legally questionable measures before, including the surreptitious entry and burglary of documents from the New York office of the Japanese Imperial Railway. But while this mission had been directed against suspected alien agents considered threats to the navy and the nation, Howell recognized that Hoover's politically motivated mission had nothing to do with naval questions, the national security, or with the DNI's primary obligation to gather information for ONI. Ultimately, if anything went awry, Howell might embarrass the president and the Navy Department and incidentally ruin his own professional naval career. But how could he resist a presidential request? "I am going to tackle it, of course, but it's a devilish awkward job, and I may very readily find myself in a hell's brew of trouble," Howell observed somewhat melodramatically.[4]

Finally, after several weeks of preparation, Howell and civilian assistant Robert J. Peterkin, a former police inspector, broke into the targeted Democratic Party office. "It was shortly after dawn, and we had been waiting several hours until the building was absolutely quiet," Howell recalled. After all the planning and expectations, though, the two secret agents found the mysterious chamber completely empty, not even a piece of furniture. Undismayed, Howell and Peterkin tracked down the former tenant, a political operator and propagandist named O'Brien. "We shadowed him for a bit and then I came to the conclusion that no President of the United States need be afraid of a ham-and-egger like this O'Brien," Howell noted. He discovered nothing incriminating and doubted the party hack's ability to discredit anyone. "All these beliefs I duly retailed to Lewis Strauss who transmitted them to Larry Richey (Hoover's private secretary and a former Justice Department detective) who informed the President," Howell recorded in his diary on 25 June 1930, concluding that Hoover "told Larry to tell Lewis to tell me to call off my watch and to consider the case closed."[5]

The operation had proceeded smoothly despite Howell's anxieties. No leaks occurred, and details about the president's initiation into political surveillance and abuse of presidential power remained locked in Howell's secret logbook until long after the deaths of both men, while ONI restricted access to the Third Naval District records during the 1930s by instructing that "in no case should they ever be supplied to the National Archives or any other agency to which the general public has access." Nevertheless, at the time, the incident raised some disturbing doubts, if not about the larger legal and constitutional questions, at least about the perplexing nature of intelligence duty, which had become in Howell's own theatrical expression "a devilish awkward job." Moreover, the burglary bothered his senior officers in ONI, since shortly after the mission, the Director of Naval Intelligence (DNI) cautioned his agents "that it is not their duty to pry into the private lives of others except in so far as their actions bear upon questions of our own defense."[6]

Whether or not the naval intelligence officers realized the full implication of their situation, they confronted a dilemma particularly American in nature. In order to defend a free and open society, sometimes U.S. intelligence had to pursue secret operations inimical to that very freedom. Moreover, once crossing the line between lawful conduct and extralegal measures, it became difficult to stop short of criminal activity. On its part, naval intelligence faced its own version of the dilemma. During the First World War, ONI had spawned an apparently inherent and irreconcilable conflict between the bureau's work for the Navy Department and its function as a government intelligence agency. Its primary mission was to provide strategic and technical data for naval war planners, and secondarily to secure the navy against internal and external threats—often by secret methods. These latter activities might have naval interest, but as in the case of Howell's adventure, might just as likely lead to unrelated and even illegal acts. The more ONI wandered into peripheral areas, the more it neglected strategic information; by the same reasoning, the harder it pursued its traditional mission, the more it ignored security questions. This dilemma intensified as the navy's worldwide mission and strategic responsibilities increased. To keep pace with larger and more complex requirements for information and security, ONI expanded, but this expansion diverted the office from its appointed mission and led to entanglement in non-naval matters. At the same time, augmentation of positive intelligence required, theoretically, a commensurate obligation to deny information to others and to counter efforts to carry out espionage, surveillance, or secret operations against the U.S. Navy. By leading ONI irresistibly away from its strategic naval mission, this perplexing negative function added dramatically to the ongoing intelligence dilemma.

The origin of this dilemma lay partly in ONI's early history and doctrine. Founded by routine departmental order in 1882, the office existed casually for over a decade as an informal branch of the Bureau of Navigation, where it operated without either congressional legislation or appropriations. The dozen junior officers in ONI followed a series of directives, commands, and memoranda to collect, collate, and distribute information. Basically, the Navy Department expected its intelligence bureau to stimulate interest in naval expansion by spreading news about the superiority of foreign technical advances among officers, lawmakers, and the general public. At the same time, ONI's handful of overseas naval attachés mailed home blueprints, articles, and specimens of European naval expertise in order to assist the navy in its conversion from a fleet of decrepit wooden sailing ships into a new navy of steel and steam-powered warships. In this, ONI succeeded spectacularly. "Without the information gathered by it, we should not have been in the position to build as we have built," former naval attaché French Ensor Chadwick asserted in 1902. "I think the Navy should remember that this change was the work of naval officers and largely the work done through and by the Office of Naval Intelligence, which has been a force in upbuilding the Service which has not been fully appreciated."[7]

Whether appreciated or not, ONI facilitated the construction of a modern force capable of smashing the out-classed Spanish Navy in 1898 and rivaling the world's leading fleets a decade later. The independent-spirited and reform-minded officers in naval intelligence believed that they were responsible largely for this great naval renaissance and grew bitter when credit went elsewhere. Moreover, as American sea power and diplomatic intrusions in the world increased, so too did ONI's responsibilities to gather information to prepare the U.S. Navy for possible conflict with the navies of other expanding industrial, military, and imperial powers. Since future confrontation would most likely occur on the seas, ONI assumed added importance and raised the estimation of its own value to the service. Not only did the office receive formal legislative mandate and an independent budget in 1899, but it joined the next year with the Naval War College and the Secretary of the Navy's new advisory body, the General Board, to form a primitive office of naval operations. Then for a short time, aggressive navalist Theodore Roosevelt boosted ONI's expectations of its place in the naval bureaucracy by consulting it daily on important military and diplomatic matters.[8]

ONI's moment of glory was short-lived, however, as recognition bred neglect and internal inertia, while institutionalization diminished earlier independence. For nearly a decade after TR's presidency, ONI languished. No one seemed interested in peacetime intelligence, nor since naval modernization, any longer wanted the latest technical data from abroad. Isolated and ignored, ONI rationalized its existence and importance in terms of traditional values. By stirring awareness of foreign menaces, the office could still contribute as a spokesman for preparedness as it had in the 1880s. As veteran intelligence officer Lyman A. Cotten insisted in 1911: "The influence of the navy upon public opinion must ever be ready to point the way, or sound the cry of warning as may be necessary, to the unprofessional opinion of naval affairs."[9]

When the European war broke out in 1914, ONI rushed to the forefront of a conservative naval establishment to sound "the cry of warning." Joining with insurgent naval officers such as Bradley Fiske, ONI staffers urged military preparedness and the formation of an office of naval operations to direct policy. The actual creation of such an office in 1916 and the attachment of ONI to it led to disappointment within the office staff and insurgent ranks, however. Instead of becoming the voice of a powerful naval general staff, ONI nearly disappeared into an office subordinated tightly to civilian direction. The office became a conduit to provide others with information so that they might direct policy and make strategic decisions.[10]

Thus, as the United States plunged into World War I in April 1917, its naval intelligence office was a tiny, insignificant organization, harboring a strong sense of tradition and a sense of its own importance and mission to protect the nation and the navy from potential enemies. America's entry into war tore away restraints and catapulted ONI into the complicated and murky world of secrecy, international espionage and counterespionage, code breaking, deception, surreptitious entry, eavesdropping, and domestic surveillance. This transformation was consistent with the dark side of an enlarged government involvement in American life manifested during the preceding decades of peacetime progressive reformism. Increasingly amenable to government regulation, Americans acquiesced when the Woodrow Wilson administration constructed a massive wartime effort to prevent internal opposition and to mobilize public opinion by passing alien, sedition, and espionage regulations.

Wilson's wartime legislation enabled the government to confiscate property, wiretap, search and seize private possessions, censor news, intercept and open mail, prevent public gatherings, and unleash hoards of federal sleuths, snoops, and informers. Naturally, agencies responsible for American security adopted and pursued the legal methods allowed under war emergency laws, but since many aspects of these new statutes remained vague and opened avenues to overly zealous enforcement, temptations developed to stretch government operations to the limit. This was true especially in the case of the U.S. Office of Naval Intelligence, which used the war crisis to rationalize expansion and resurrect lost influence in the Navy Department. Most of its efforts related directly to protecting the naval establishment, but sometimes slipped across nebulous guidelines into affairs devoid of naval interest.[11]

For the first time, ONI manifested a sinister side, materializing as elitism, anti-Semitism, illegal conduct, and repression of divergent opinions and civil rights. These aberrations resulted partly from wartime hysteria, fear of radicalism, and the general curbing of individual freedoms, and from the enrollment during the war of nearly three thousand reserve officers, volunteers, and enlisted personnel, who tended to view intelligence with less restraint than regular officers. Over five hundred worked in the Branch Intelligence Office in New York City alone. Hundreds more maintained Washington headquarters and carried on local intelligence in the recently created naval districts. ONI directed these people to gather information not only of naval interest but also about the labor unrest that threatened factories and yards doing contract work for the Navy—radicals undermining morale and spreading subversive thought, and the potential violence or sabotage to private property. Clearly the latter duties, while of legitimate naval interest, brought ONI fully into domestic security work and entwined naval intelligence in the expanding surveillance of Americans by agents of the Military Intelligence Division of the U.S. Army (MID or G-2), Justice and Treasury Departments, local police forces, and even private detective agencies.[12]

Once introduced to other dimensions of the intelligence business, ONI increasingly paid less attention to strategic information. During actual fighting, when combat or operational intelligence on the spot assumed more importance than long-range planning back in Washington, the navy hardly noticed this transformation in its intelligence office. But when war ended and the national crisis at home receded, the shadows of wartime intelligence lingered on. ONI found it impossible—and perhaps undesirable—to curb spying, surveillance, and secret operations and to return to a constricted office intent upon collecting strategic and technical data for some theoretical future war. To continue its expanded wartime role, its staff, and appropriations, ONI needed to remain an action agency, not a library to store attaché reports, maps, and old photographs. However, as much as the wider definition of intelligence appealed to most postwar DNIs, they grew uncomfortable at times with the tendency of their offices to wander off into matters unrelated to the interests of the U.S. Navy. Whether or not they realized the full implications of the naval intelligence dilemma, they agreed with Howell's admonition that duty in ONI had become "a devilish awkward job."

CHAPTER TWO

BOLSHEVIK MENACE

The future looked grim on 1 May 1919 as Rear Admiral Albert Parker Niblack assumed direction of ONI. Newspapers that morning blared out headlines about a sensational plot to assassinate Attorney General A. Mitchell Palmer, Postmaster General Albert S. Burleson, Judge Kenesaw Mountain Landis, industrialist John D. Rockefeller, and thirty-two other prominent Americans. This was merely the latest and most explosive development in a rapidly worsening atmosphere of terrorist bombings, labor violence, and hysteria that gripped the United States in the wake of the First World War. Nor were prospects overseas much brighter. Revolutionary violence, murder, and anarchy swept through Russia and Europe, while stirrings of nationalism destablized Latin America, China, and the Near East. At the peace conference in Paris, victorious powers squabbled over territory, reparations, and security rather than agreeing to treaty terms that would end at last the European War of 1914–1918. In the midst of this cauldron wandered a dazed President Woodrow Wilson pursuing his internationalist crusade for a league of nations with which to solve all the world's troubles.

Never before had such widespread domestic unrest and international disorder confronted an incoming naval intelligence director. Fortunately, Niblack possessed four decades of intelligence experience. Once while naval attaché in Germany during the 1890s, he had purchased weapons secretly to arm the American Fleet for war with Spain, and another time reportedly had rifled the German Kaiser's desk looking for battleship blueprints. Later Niblack had ventured in civilian dress through the Philippine Islands in search of the best site for an advanced naval base. Between 1910 and '11 he had chased about Latin America as the first permanent U.S. naval attaché in the Western Hemisphere, and finally on the eve of World War I had returned to Germany as naval attaché to monitor affairs.[1]

Despite a career devoted to intelligence, though, Niblack held no ambition in 1919 to head ONI. Exhausted after two wartime years as commander of American naval forces at Gibraltar, he wished to close his career as the second chief of naval operations (CNO), succeeding outgoing Admiral William S. Benson to the most prestigious post in the service. "Not that I am dissatisfied with Naval Intelligence," he told Secretary of the Navy Josephus Daniels, but he preferred the other billet "because Operations are based on Information and no other officer has wider contact with international affairs." Unmoved, Daniels selected instead Robert Coontz, a more diplomatic and even-tempered administrator.[2]

Though he would not admit it, Niblack considered the intelligence assignment too taxing at this point in his career. He had been away from such detailed work for five years, during which time radical changes had occurred in ONI. Moreover, his ability to recall facts and his powers of concentration had slipped to a level where one officer observed that the aging Niblack could neither ask coherent questions nor pay attention to related answers. Though this judgment of unpopular Niblack was too harsh, that of veteran intelligence officer Edward Breck was more important. Breck contended in a letter to wartime intelligence director Roger Welles in May 1919 that Niblack presented not one new idea about naval intelligence nor about how to run an office in the postwar era.[3]

After six months of apparent drift, Niblack decided to restore the prewar naval intelligence structure and doctrine. "The present endeavor is to get back to the old organization and the old system which has worked so well for us for so many years," he cabled naval attachés in January 1920. The outdated officer recalled those halcyon days before the Great War when duty in ONI meant the collection and distribution of strategic and technical information and an occasional exercise in war planning. At that time, a few dashing officers attached to U.S. diplomatic missions in glamorous foreign capitals provided data, gathered mostly through casual observation of local scenery, interviews over drinks and dinner with foreign officials, or by skimming easily accessible technical journals. And back in Washington, a dozen methodical junior officers and a few underpaid but diligent clerks kept this information on file, ready for any inquisitive naval bureau, board, or officer. Mostly these data were employed to prepare monographic studies on possible enemies for naval war planners at the Naval War College in Newport or for the General Board in Washington. Before World War I, such exercises had focused almost routinely on Japan, Germany, Great Britain, Mexico, and for a moment upon tiny Nicaragua. For each, ONI compiled information on the potential opponent's military and economic resources and estimated steps necessary for the U.S. Navy to carry out successful operations.[4]

Now that the war was over, Niblack expected to resume this type of work, directing a crew of industrious young officers, loyal clerks, and hardworking stenographers who would put together strategic scrapbooks of newspaper clippings, statistical sheets, and attaché reports. He would no longer employ the odd assortment of cable censors, detectives, safe crackers, informants, and wealthy society figures collected by Welles during the war. "I am not one of those people who associate themselves definitely with specialists," he wrote a friend, "and have always taken the run of the mill." Employment of such specialists implied the pursuit of tasks that Niblack considered outside the scope of naval intelligence. Referring to the then popular literary term for detective work, Niblack announced that his office aimed to avoid "anything savoring of 'gumshoe' methods."[5]

Painfully Niblack recognized that his vision of intelligence no longer existed. The office crawled with remnants of the wartime organization, some utterly incompetent or troublesome. One obnoxious ensign, appointed because of the influence of Senator John Sharp Williams of Mississippi, was "a nuisance in every respect," while another reservist allegedly accepted a bribe from Latin American businessmen for special favors. Senior clerk Nellie Huff displayed little clerical acumen, but intrigued constantly to discredit other clerks and flaunted her political connections. And then, ONI abounded with the specialists so despised by Niblack, but now seemingly essential to postwar operations. The furtive Dr. Emerson J. Haworth locked himself in a tiny office and poured over intercepted Japanese coded messages, while Edward Wales read other people's mail and A. B. Legare planned counterespionage adventures.[6]

New demands prevented a return to Niblack's conception of intelligence duty. State Department investigator Frank Polk urged the admiral to cooperate with the new division of political affairs and in addition to the usual naval material, to collect information about political developments abroad. Even his own department forced Niblack into areas repugnant to his view of naval intelligence, such as an investigation of homosexuality among naval personnel in Newport. Moreover, the majority of information currently flooding into his office concerned not the familiar ship dimensions, armor specifications, or gun designs, but suspected subversives, radicals, and undesirable aliens.[7]

Domestic subversion dominated Niblack's office from the beginning. When he assumed the intelligence billet in May 1919, the United States had fallen into the grips of a full-blown Red Scare, stimulated by the Bolshevik Revolution of 1917 in Russia, the formation of the Third International to promote Communist propaganda, and the general disintegration of international conditions. Government agents from the Justice, State, and War Departments infiltrated meetings of suspected radical organizations such as the Socialist Party, Communist Party of America, International Workers of the World (IWW), and the American Jewish Congress. Directed by politically ambitious Attorney General Palmer, government men searched for undesirable and dangerous subversives by breaking into offices without search warrants, seizing records and correspondence, tapping telephone lines, and arresting and sometimes deporting suspects.[8]

Nor was ONI immune to this hysteria. During the war, naval intelligence had vigorously pursued the IWW, a radical labor organization believed disruptive to shipbuilding efforts in Seattle and other U.S. ports. In addition, ONI sleuths had tailed socialist John Reed around New York City, eavesdropping on his wife and their close comrade Morris Hillquit. During this operation, naval operatives grabbed documents about the Bolshevik Revolution from Reed. Similar activity continued after the Armistice of 1918, and shortly before leaving as DNI, Welles had assured Secretary of the Navy Daniels that ONI would maintain contact with other agencies in an ongoing investigation "of the Marine Transport Workers and the alleged threatened combination between them and the Bolsheviki and Sinn Feiners." At the same time, Welles's assistant George W. Williams and the CNO's war planner Captain Harry Ervin Yarnell pressed for increased ONI participation in purging America of the sinister Bolshevik influence. The United States ought to declare war on the "Bolsheviki Government of Russia" and hold treason trials for American sympathizers, Yarnell advised the CNO. "It is considered that this subject is becoming a real menace in the United States," he warned, "and that it requires immediate and radical steps for its suppression."[9]

Similar forebodings emanated from ONI representatives overseas. Veteran naval attaché Captain John A. Gade, USNR, raised the spectre of creeping Bolshevism in his plea for appointment of the first permanent peacetime naval attaché to Scandinavia. "There is no better point of vantage from which to observe Russian conditions and report upon and counteract Bolshevism, as well as study the Russian press," Gade cabled. Other reports revealed Bolshevik intrigues throughout Europe and as far away as Afghanistan and "the Mohammedan world." One naval intelligence observer in the Baltic Sea noted that two hundred Russians manned the Soviet mission to Riga, prompting Latvians to fear being absorbed by their gigantic Bolshevik neighbor.[10]

Though skeptical of the strident anti-Bolshevism, Niblack forwarded to departmental policy makers each new bit of information about Bolshevism's various domestic and international manifestations. His interest in the menace culminated in December 1919, when after studying data sent over by MID, he prepared a summary for the department on an alleged nationwide terrorist plot led by Alexander Berkman, Emma Goldman, Mollie Steiner, Jake Abrams, and "several other Anarchists." According to the "reliable" source cited by Niblack, the expected terrorist campaign would be perpetrated by a combination of German and Russian Jews, Mexican bandits, IWW subversives, and a Japanese master spy named Kato Kamato. "The Terror will surpass anything that ever happened in this country, and the brains of the plot are already on the Pacific Coast, but it may be January or February before anything will be attempted," the DNI concluded.[11]

Whether or not he believed the contents of this incredible report, Niblack tired of the Bolshevik question by the spring of 1920. Thus, in April when State Department counselor William L. Hurley sent him three elaborate maps supposedly pinpointing Bolshevik cells around the world, Niblack returned the maps at once. "As this office is not making any special effort to keep up with the trends of Bolshevism, it was not thought necessary to copy them," the DNI responded impatiently.[12]

Caught unwittingly in the emerging naval intelligence dilemma, Niblack chafed at his government's continual emphasis on domestic radicals and Bolshevism. He wished to focus on areas of strategic naval importance instead. At the moment, turmoil in Asia and the Near East appeared far more ugent to Niblack than spying on a bunch of local Reds. In the Eastern Mediterranean, Admiral Mark Bristol carried out extensive intelligence gathering, reporting how the breakup of the Ottoman Empire and the emergence of Turkish nationalism threatened American property and access to local oil resources now needed for a U.S. fleet converted recently from coal to petroleum fuels. At the same time, commander of U.S. naval forces in Asiatic waters, Admiral Albert Gleaves, inundated ONI with information about Eastern Asia, the stirrings of Chinese nationalism, and Japanese machinations that endangered American interests and traditional open door policy in the Far East. Even the State Department stopped hounding Niblack about Bolsheviks long enough to request assistance in gathering news from China. "The political situation at Shanghai at present is unusually complicated and the Naval Intelligence officers could be of great value in keeping the Consul General fully informed concerning political affairs," Secretary of State Robert Lansing insisted.[13]

More important, Niblack's office focused on the constant flow of strategic information received about Japanese adventures in Siberia, Manchuria, and the Pacific Ocean, made more critical by growing tensions over naval building policies, racial equality clauses, and the treatment of Japanese in California. Gleaves sounded the warning from his Asian station. "Unless there is a great change in our relations with Japan," the ONI pioneer wrote in 1920, "she will aggravate the United States beyond the point of tolerance, and we will be forced to deliver the ultimatum; then she will strike without further warning."[14]

On his part, Niblack worried about Japan's seizure and retention during the past war of strategically vital former German islands in the Pacific Ocean. Long an advocate of America's own insular defensive perimeter, Niblack warned the department about Japanese efforts to create their own barrier. When rumors reached him in early 1920 concerning Japan's threat to cut a transoceanic cable on tiny Yap Island, the DNI sent an urgent memorandum to departmental war planners. "In view of the rapidly grow-ing trade between the United States and the Netherland East Indies," he cautioned, "it is vitally important not to let the control of the Yap-East Indies Cable fall into the hands of any power not interested in the open door."[15]

In order to keep pace with these strategic concerns and at the same instant continue domestic surveillance, Niblack realized at last that ONI must expand. But as he overcame his own doubts, he confronted postwar demobilization, which drained personnel, funds, and programs. On Armi-stice Day, ONI had boasted 306 officers in Washington alone; however, by 1 July 1920 just forty-two remained, and many of these faced imminent detachment. The DNI fought to maintain an enlarged organization. First, he discovered $450,000 unexpended from a million-dollar wartime secret fund, funneling some of it to ONI personnel. "Before the expiration of the fiscal year, I distributed among the various Naval Attachés about a hundred thousand dollars to be regarded as a Secret Fund," Niblack explained. Next, he testified before several congressional committees in an attempt to raise an additional $240,000 for peacetime intelligence in East Asia and Latin America. "I went before the Naval Appropriations Committee yesterday, and soaked them," he bragged to former Naval Academy room-mate William Sims. "I told them, in reply to questions . . . that for the price of one battleship we [ONI] could make Guam-Midway-Honolulu secure and for the price of another one could make the Pacific ours."[16]

Inevitably Niblack considered his budget too small. He ordered naval attachés to record all monies expended routinely under "Fund A," a general intelligence account, and under "Fund B," the confidential information fund. The latter troubled him most. "As the fund is not large, it required considerable manipulation from this end to make it cover work in all parts of the world," he informed naval attachés. The intelligence budget grew tighter still, restricting even the traditional collection of information. Nib-lack's inability to meet the basic demands of the attaché system led to disillusionment and a relapse into earlier paralysis over how to run the organization. The DNI became obsessed with petty details, ordering his staff to guard against anyone stealing the ONI messenger's bicycle "for joy riding." The fumbling old officer apologized for lack of leadership and warned his staff not to stir up trouble, because "this is no time to get things and it is well to let well enough alone."[17]

At the moment of deepest pessimism, Niblack appeared before another congressional committee, this one investigating the conduct of the U.S. Navy in World War I. Chaired by stalwart Republican Senator Frederick Hale of Maine and manned by Republicans Lewis H. Ball of Delaware, Henry Keyes of New Hampshire, and Democrats Key Pittman of Nevada and Park Trammell of Florida, the subcommittee examined charges brought against the Navy Department by Rear Admiral Sims, U.S. Force Commander in Britain during the recent war. A brilliant and always controversial officer, Sims capped decades of reformist agitation to reorganize the department along general staff lines with a series of postwar accusations against Secretary Daniels and CNO Benson. Among the charges, Sims claimed that lack of war planning, antisubmarine warfare doctrine, and operational coordination had delayed victory and endangered American lives unnecessarily. His charges struck a responsive note throughout the service, whose members were displeased with years of strong and sometimes abrasive civilian direction. "From my personal experience, and what I hear from many sources," fellow insurgent William K. Harrison wrote Sims, "I should say that the Navy was practically solidly behind us who are trying to bring about a real reform this time."[18]

Though Harrison exaggerated sympathy with Sims's attack on the service, the admiral's bombshell occurred at a critical moment for both the fading Wilson administration and the confused postwar navy. Wilson had tied the future American naval program to a League of Nations security and peace-keeping framework, but his paralytic stroke, Senate defeat of the peace treaty, and public aversion to continued international obligations placed naval planners in a quandary about future programs and policies. At the same time, the service split into factions: should the navy turn to aircraft carriers or continue to rely mainly on a battleship fleet, build distant bases or concentrate on strengthening Pearl Harbor? There were other disagreements over tactics, doctrine, and equipment. At the center of the growing division within the navy lay a bureaucratic power struggle over who had responsibility for future war planning. The most important issue, intelligence officer George Baum wrote Sims in May 1920, was "whether in the future the General Board or the Planning Section of Operations is to prepare the Building Program and specify the military characteristics of vessels, and whether or not War Plans prepared by the Planning Section of Operations should be referred to the General Board for criticism before being submitted to the Secretary for his approval."[19]

This convoluted naval and political atmosphere surrounded Niblack as he assumed his seat before the five senators in Room 235 of the Senate Office Building. While waiting to testify, he confronted his own personal doubts. Forty years before, Niblack had been Sims's roommate and close comrade at the Naval Academy in Annapolis. Through the years "Nibs" and Sims had remained warm friends, especially as fellow naval attachés in Europe during the 1890s. They had shared common ideas about gunnery reform, doctrine, war planning, and naval intelligence until the First World War. But by 1920 something had gone sour, destroying the life-long friendship. Perhaps Niblack envied Sims's national reputation and more rapid advancement, or resented his own subordinate status during the war. More likely, by siding with Daniels Niblack hoped still to close out his career as CNO. Whatever the reason, Niblack sought to discredit his former roommate in front of the Senate subcommittee. "I am not here to defend any person," he announced, "but am defending the United States Navy, which is not under fire by its enemies but of its friends."[20]

Poor Niblack tried, explaining patiently that contrary to Sims's charges, the navy's war-planning mechanism, especially the General Board, had been adequate to prepare the fleet for war. He advocated minor reforms but ended on a laudatory theme. "The Navy Department does work all right and has worked all right. The bureau system is a splendid system, and has stood the test of war," he insisted. Subsequent hostile cross-examination by Republican Hale ruffled Niblack's composure, however. He lapsed into vindictive personal attacks on his old shipmate. Exchanges with the senators became more abrupt, and finally the DNI waved off further questions. "I am getting ready for the next war right now, and I am very loath to go into a postmortem of the last war, because my interest is in the next one," he almost shouted at the legislators.[21]

Niblack's strained testimony before the Hale subcommittee proved too much for an already fragmented Navy Department. Two months later Coontz shipped the DNI off to England as naval attaché and then to command U.S. naval forces in European waters. The unhappy officer had become an embarrassment around Washington, Admiral Hilary P. Jones, Commander in Chief of the Atlantic Fleet, observed, and everyone seemed "very well satisfied to have Nibs that far away from them."[22]

No such stigma surrounded Niblack's relief, Captain Andrew Theodore Long, a "polished, courtly gentleman." Immensely popular, Long was the perfect selection to regroup naval intelligence after a demoralizing year of Bolshevik-watching, demobilization, and internal rot. An even-tempered professional, he cared little for bureaucratic bickering or competition between divisions of the naval hierarchy. Long worked smoothly with CNO Coontz to adjust ONI to peacetime cutbacks, which included a departmental order to each commanding officer afloat to limit expenses for intelligence to $15 per month. Unlike indiscreet Niblack, Long expressed no public antipathy toward secret operations, quietly encouraging the employment of spies, informers, and other sources such as the assistant cashier of the National City Bank of New York. "You may feel free to give us such confidential information as you may see fit," Long wrote the banker.[23]

More importantly, Long understood that postwar ONI could not avoid entirely involvement in non-naval matters. "If the line be strictly drawn, this office is not required to keep abreast of the political movements," he advised naval attachés, "but from whatever cause those Departments most directly concerned have and do frequently ask the Navy Department for the latest developments, the responsibility for the answer finally falling on this office." He placed the political subject in perspective, though, suggesting that such information should not be accumulated "in any large quantity."[24]

Long was pursuing this expedient policy in early 1921 when the State Department requested the services of Lieutenant Commander Hugo W. Koehler as naval attaché in Warsaw to monitor Bolshevik affairs. As assistant attaché in Russia during the war, Koehler had traveled in disguise through Soviet territory, obtaining a unique understanding of the people, politics, and conditions. Sadly deficient in Russian experts, the diplomatic branch wanted the navy's man. "It seemed to us in the State Department that the special qualifications which he possesses for obtaining information regarding Russian affairs," Assistant Secretary of State Robert Woods Bliss told Long, "would make him most useful if he were assigned to the Legation at Warsaw at this time, when the relations between Poland and Soviet Russia are being established with the opening of trading posts along the frontier between the two countries." Despite lack of naval interest in Polish conditions, Long dispatched Koehler. But when State Department pressure subsided, ONI recalled the naval attaché from Warsaw.[25]

While accepting the realities of postwar intelligence, Long labored to preserve and strengthen traditional doctrine. After all, like Niblack he was a product of the old-time network, once serving as an intelligence officer in 1909 and as naval attaché in Rome during the Tripolitan War of 1911 where he had observed the first use of aircraft in combat. Later, Long had served as naval attaché in Paris. However, instead of resurrecting some long-dead image of ONI, Long determined to reconstruct the strategic objectives and informational network at the center of the enlarged postwar organization. Working closely with Coontz, the DNI pressed naval officers around the globe to gather data, while at the same time he provided these officers with updated packages of confidential publications. In his first month as director, Long dispatched twenty-eight separate ONI reports on everything from mine-sweeping techniques to coastal defenses to the commanding officer of battleships in the Atlantic Fleet. At the same time ONI assumed responsibility for distribution of all naval news to the general public through an Information Section. "This Section is not organized for purposes of propaganda," one Navy spokesman insisted, "but to furnish the public with correct information regarding the navy, its mission, and its use in peace and war." Whatever the definition, it suited Long's purpose by reviving the aspect of ONI's publicity role that had first projected naval intelligence's value to the service as a promoter of the New American Navy in the late nineteenth century.[26]

During his brief twelve-month tour, Long mastered the naval intelligence dilemma by balancing nicely between secret operations and traditional strategy and information. By invigorating the process of gathering and disseminating data, Long placed the emphasis on naval business, but at the same time he expedited postwar concepts and enlarged the definition of intelligence. His directorship provided a period of transition, bridging the disoriented and demoralized Niblack office with that of Captain Luke McNamee, who in September 1921 replaced Long and plunged headlong into the intelligence dilemma caused by the tumultuous and tawdry world of Warren G. Harding's administration.

CHAPTER THREE

FALSE INFORMATION

The return to "normalcy" under the handsome new President Harding defused the most intense postwar antiforeign feelings and diverted attention to more pleasant matters. New gadgets such as the automobile, radio, airplane, and moving picture entertained and fascinated the American public, while Prohibition challenged those who wished to buy alcoholic refreshments. Tired of constant moralistic crusades during the preceding decades of progressivism and world war, Americans appeared anxious to escape from domestic reform and international involvement. Congress and the administration reflected this mood, determining to pass few new laws, curb government spending, and ignore the League of Nations.

Politics of normalcy forced the U.S. military to retrench and budget declining resources. This process frustrated the navy, particularly in its effort to complete construction of a fleet second to no other as outlined in the naval bill of 1916. But after the war, neither the public nor the government shared the navy's eager quest to achieve parity with the top-ranked Royal Navy. Indeed, they were against building any ships at all. Instead, the Harding regime pondered eliminating existing naval units and taking other measures toward arms reduction and naval limitations. The president's interest in this question heightened when British officials, who confronted their own postwar revolt against expensive naval programs and an embarrassing alliance with Japan, suggested talks to prevent a mad naval race, and culminated in his invitation on 11 July 1921 to the world's naval powers to attend a conference in Washington.[1]

Harding's call for this conference resulted not only from a welter of postwar domestic and international concerns, but also from his own desire to prove political leadership. Since the United States had repudiated the Versailles peace treaty and turned its back on European security, the Washington gathering provided an alternative forum where the United States and the victorious Allied nations of World War I might iron out maritime and diplomatic differences. At the same time it reflected a popular revulsion to continued warship construction.

In the months following Harding's invitations, American Secretary of State Charles Evans Hughes organized the details of the forthcoming assembly. Most naval data came from ONI, which had been awaiting the call for some time. Back in January DNI Long had instructed the naval attaché in London to examine British attitudes toward naval holidays and disarmament, and the next month he ordered all attachés to collect local opinion concerning a possible naval limitations conference. Serious work began in July when the ONI staff prepared specifics on foreign naval expenditures, building programs, and existing warships. Long's assistant, Commander William W. Galbraith, coordinated operations, instructing naval attachés to prepare summaries of press commentary, parliamentary proceedings, and other indicators of public policy and opinion toward naval reductions. "In formulating a plan of action for the United States," Galbraith explained, "it is desirable to know, as far in advance as possible, the probable plan of action on the part of other representatives together with some insights into the instructions given the delegates by their governments."[2]

In response, the few attachés left after postwar demobilization scrambled to interview local officials, peruse public papers, and assemble newspaper clippings. The naval attaché's office in London mailed pages of press cuttings, marked appropriately with thick red and blue pencil lines underscoring relevant statements. At the same instant, former DNI Niblack managed an interview with the King of England, but characteristically found the conversation disappointing. "Personally I do not attach much importance to his views since the Prime Minister is the important factor in the coming conference," Niblack wired Washington. More insight was shown in naval attaché Commander F. Brooks Upham's correspondence from Paris, which included French disarmament data and photographs of prospective Gallic delegates. Concurrently, an ONI source in Berlin polled members of the Inter-Allied Control Commission, discovering a common fear of Japanese militarism. And finally from Japan, naval attaché Captain Edward Howe Watson tried to penetrate the secrecy surrounding Japanese intentions and proposals for naval limitation, forwarding bits of news to ONI.[3]

As the information accumulated on various intelligence desks, ONI began compiling and synthesizing the data for American statesmen slated to attend the conference. ONI's biographical file on Japanese delegates, although not necessarily of much value, nevertheless provided a few moments of good reading; it told more about U.S. naval intelligence than it did about the Japanese. According to ONI, Takei Daisube had "unusually high morals for a Japanese," while naval attaché Yoshitake Uyeda had "unusual reasoning powers for an Oriental." Uyeda fascinated naval intelligence particularly. Educated in the United States, he was a dashing figure about Washington. "He used to give gay cocktail parties in his apartment at the Benedict at which female clerks of the Navy Department were present," ONI noted for the enlightenment of U.S. officials.[4]

ONI's sheets of statistics, graphs, and charts were more helpful to an American delegation interested in the comparative tonnage of warships and strengths of navies. For the most part, ONI offered this information in a mechanical, straightforward manner, without commentary or analysis of the political and strategic implications. However, an occasional statement of concern crept in—such as one ONI statistician's warning that relative naval power between nations could not be measured in exact mathematical terms nor equitable naval ratios by simple formulas. Such reservations faded temporarily when on 12 November 1921 Secretary of State Hughes opened the Washington Conference with a sensational speech calling upon the world's naval powers to scrap thousands of tons of warships, place a ten-year building holiday on new battleships, and limit the size and armaments of all future warships.[5]

Not surprisingly, Hughes's proposals to destroy much of the world's naval hardware stunned foreign contingents. However, the almost universal public acclaim greeting the opening address left little opportunity for any delegation simply to walk out. Each country would have to swing the best terms it could out of the proposals. Thus, during the next weeks foreign representatives cabled home for instructions regularly while ironing out details. The Japanese flooded their home government with coded messages in order to determine whether they should accept an inferior ratio of battleship tonnage to that of Great Britain and the United States. Furthermore, they wished to clarify Tokyo's policy concerning larger diplomatic and security interests in the Pacific Ocean and the Far East. Meanwhile, the European delegates contacted their own governments about the extended ship ratios, diplomatic bargaining points, and the limits to which each might go in naval disarmament.[6]

Hectic communications between Washington and the foreign capitals provided American intelligence agencies with an unusual opportunity to gather inside information about another delegation's position before it was presented at the bargaining table. Access to such confidential data was made possible by wartime advances in wiretapping, message interception, and code breaking—mostly through the work of U.S. Army expert Herbert Osborne Yardley. After the war, Yardley established a secret decoding section in New York City for the State Department, known ominously as the "Black Chamber." At the same time ONI improved its own code-breaking capabilities by gaining covert access to several foreign code books. Thus, both before and during the Washington Conference, U.S. agents were able to intercept and read secret foreign communications. Undoubtedly they eavesdropped on the various delegations, and ONI forwarded intercepted wireless communications regarding the conference to U.S. policy makers at least as early as 18 July 1921.[7]

Whether or not communications intelligence influenced the final outcome of the Washington Conference, by February the parties had accepted Hughes's basic position outlined in the opening speech. Final arrangements included a naval arms limitations pact, a proscription against the use of submarines and noxious gases, a treaty clarifying the status of insular possessions in the Pacific Ocean, and an agreement to stabilize the Far East and uphold China's territorial integrity. The Washington treaties offered hope that many outstanding postwar international differences might be resolved by peaceful means, and that naval races might be slowed indefinitely. On the other hand, the treaties satisfied no one, left more questions unanswered than they solved, and raised some disturbing new issues concerning public complacency toward possible treaty violations by the signatories.

This last issue most distressed the naval officers in ONI, who during the next few years determined to warn the public about apparent dangers to U.S. security and the government about expected foreign violations of treaty terms and attempts to deceive the United States. No sooner had the delegates to the historic conference left than new DNI McNamee expressed concern for the future. "The Conference has adjourned with general rejoicing," he wrote naval attaché Raymond D. Hasbrouck in Rome, "and apparently Congress thinks it is now free to abolish the Army and the Navy." Watson voiced similar cynicism from his Tokyo attaché post, warning that while American politicians planned to shoot the U.S. Navy to pieces, the Japanese would secretly strengthen their fleet and gain a critical advantage over the emasculated American navy. "In their characteristic clever way," he confided to McNamee, "they will doubtless arrange so as to maintain their Navy in a more prepared condition than any other—in spite of the Washington Conference and any other circumstances."[8]

These naval intelligence officers believed that the euphoria surrounding the conference blinded Americans to the need for continued naval defenses, concluding that ONI must be the vehicle to spread the warning. Such a crusade had to begin at once. "The ignorance of the public, even the educated classes, of what the navy stands for is, as you know better than I, deplorably dense," retired intelligence officer Breck told Admiral Sims in March 1922. Current ONI personnel agreed, some devoting spare time to lectures and articles designed to counteract anti-navy sentiment. "We are making a big fight against the pacifists," McNamee wired Hasbrouck, "and I am enclosing you a speech that I made before their National Council, which seems to have done considerable good." In the same vein, intelligence officer Captain Charles Lincoln Hussey debated pacifist Norman Thomas at the Foreign Policy Club in Philadelphia, stating the navy's case.[9]

As in the late nineteenth century, ONI spokesmen found an outlet during the 1920s for their opinions in the pages of the U.S. Naval Institute *Proceedings*, a monthly journal published by this organization founded at Annapolis in 1873 to promote knowledge about the U.S. Navy. In the May 1923 edition of the *Proceedings*, McNamee presented naval intelligence's line in defense of naval preparedness. Resurrecting arguments used by Alfred Thayer Mahan and other late-nineteenth-century navalists, while at the same moment appealing to the business world of the twenties, the DNI explained how a strong navy protected American commerce and opened avenues of trade in Asia and Latin America. According to figures cited by McNamee, the U.S. Navy's Special Service Squadron in the Caribbean curbed local revolutions that threatened to deprive American businessmen of $500 million worth of trade in bananas, sugar, and petroleum products, while the Yangtze River patrol in China defended another $100 million annual business. And yet according to McNamee, "pacifists and little Navy men" at the Washington Conference had employed "Alice in Wonderland reasoning" to strip the navy to the point where it could not protect this vital commerce. These same people, who must be under the influence of Bolshevism, planned to reduce the navy even further, the director insisted. "I am repeating no idle rumor, when I tell you that much of this propaganda has a sinister foreign source, its object the overthrow of our government and the ultimate dictatorship of the proletariat."[10]

Retired intelligence officer Captain Dudley Wright Knox, who would head ONI's naval library and historical archives for three decades and subtly influence every DNI and ONI policy, was even more blunt than his boss. In his essay for the *Proceedings*, Knox expanded McNamee's thesis about a sinister foreign influence burrowing into American life, spreading pacifism, subversion, and undermining naval preparedness. "From what has been set forth it is clearly indicated that large sums of money are being spent by many powerful organizations in which foreigners play a prominent role to propagandize the country through the press, the church, the stage, the movie, the schools and colleges, the lecture platforms and virtually every agency of communication," Knox claimed. He appealed to the navy to "successfully indoctrinate the country along sound naval lines."[11]

On his part, Knox assumed the lead in this indoctrination of the American public both as a promoter of Navy Day celebrations and as naval editor of the American *Army and Navy Journal*. Always drawing freely from the wealth of data readily available in ONI and from his own personal files, the studious, serious-minded naval officer wrote essays, lobbied with congressmen, and corresponded with religious and political leaders in an attempt to spread the navy's perspective on arms limitations. Knox's major effort to teach the public occurred in 1922 when he published *The Eclipse of American Sea Power*. Reminiscent of his idol Mahan, Knox wanted his book to stimulate the kind of interest eventually accorded Mahan's *The Influence of Sea Power Upon History*. Knox sought to present "a professional interpretation" rather than a propaganda tirade on how the Washington Conference led to the eclipse of American sea power by Great Britain and Japan. "Only by superior efficiency in keeping up its 'Treaty Navy'," the progressive historian contended, "can America hope to nullify even partially the disproportionate sacrifices imposed upon her by the agreements she subscribed to at the Conference."[12]

Unfortunately for Knox, the tract was neither good history nor sensational revelations and never made the desired impact. Partly the seemingly academic tone and ponderous style limited the audience, while simultaneous publication of Hector C. Bywater's more colorful *Sea-Power in the Pacific* overshadowed the pedantic work by the scholarly, bespectacled naval officer. Ironically, though, like Mahan's earlier classic, Knox's book stirred up more debate in Britain. Assistant naval attaché in London, Lieutenant Thaddeus Austin Thomson Jr., wrote Knox in December 1923 about the considerable ripple his *Eclipse of American Sea Power* had caused among British naval authorities. "Until the time of its appearance, the British Government in general and the Admiralty in particular were laughing up their sleeve at having put it over us," Thomson confided. "In my opinion they are very anxious at the re-action that might take place if American public opinion were adequately educated as to the results of the treaty."[13]

Undiscouraged, Knox continued his crusade to educate public opinion in the United States, while his colleagues in ONI assisted by publishing information pamphlets "for a correct understanding of the treaty for the limitation of armaments." Naturally these pamphlets described the navy in glowing terms. Not only was the service portrayed as an indispensable agency to defend trade and commerce, but also as a positive moral factor and reforming force in the world. "The Navy has aided the Governments of Haiti and Santo Domingo to install order, sanitate their towns, and improve conditions generally," one ONI tract explained. Probably the impact of such a moralistic approach suffered from coincidental reports about a scandal surrounding the Navy Department's illegal leasing of its oil reserves at Teapot Dome and Elk Hill. In any case, no ONI publication could alter the indifference or outright skepticism with which the public greeted efforts to promote U.S. naval preparedness in the years following the popular Washington Conference.[14]

Perhaps a better method to bring the American people to their senses, McNamee thought, might be to unearth and reveal foreign treaty violations. The DNI expected that such evidence would be easy to obtain, since he assumed that all signatories would circumvent the settlement and try to deceive the other powers. Though personally inclined toward Anglo-American cooperation, he suspected that Britain would cheat on treaty obligations. "The policy of keeping equality with Great Britain has made all the information in regard to her Navy of vital importance," McNamee warned naval attaché Hussey in London. Hussey confirmed these fears. British officials not only obstructed the collection of treaty information but released false or misleading data on gun elevation, ship modernization, and fleet equality. Moreover, British intelligence infiltrated the American Embassy to learn about U.S. secrets. "While we have Americanized the office," Hussey insisted, "I am not by any means sure that there are not 'leaks' which enable the Admiralty to know the contents of the reports made from this office."[15]

In order to avoid leaks, McNamee flirted for a time with the notion of employing as his intelligence and counterintelligence operation in Europe a secret organization formed by the persistent Niblack. When the department had exiled the former director to Europe, he had discovered that the State Department and MID intelligence networks in Europe had dried up after the war. Niblack had determined to have one last fling with his career-long obsession by organizing a band of secret agents in London, Paris, and Berlin. In January 1922, he asked the Navy Department for money to run the show. "The Secretary of the Navy can by a stroke of a pen set aside this sum of money [£6,000] from the appropriation 'Pay Miscellaneous' and the whole matter should be explained secretly to Congress as I explained it when I got the original allowance," Niblack insisted.[16]

Without waiting for a reply from Washington, Niblack plunged ahead with his scheme and recruited secret agents. The irrepressible intelligence officer found an unemployed former military intelligence sleuth named Whepley wandering about London pedaling his dubious skills and hired him as chief agent. In France, the U.S. admiral employed professional detective and man-about-town Louis Thenoz to direct Paris espionage. Apparently forgetting his earlier disgust with such people, Niblack declared that these men were experts in their fields. "Whepley contemplates going all through Germany and on into Russia, where he has very good connections, to get at the bottom of Germany's economic conditions and military resources, and also Germany's understanding with Russia." Somewhat unconvincingly he maintained that Whepley was more than just an unsavory detective. "The kind of information Whepley gets is somewhat rarified and a little over the heads of the ordinary gumshoe artist because he deals with international relations."[17]

Niblack's conversion to undercover methods almost convinced the usually pragmatic McNamee. However, at the last moment Acting Secretary of the Navy Theodore Roosevelt, Jr., intervened and ordered Niblack to disband his impromptu network. "Under the present policy of rigid economy, a policy which has been inaugurated since you left Washington," Roosevelt advised, "it does not appear justifiable to maintain a small espionage organization in Europe." Niblack knew this was the end. His mercenary agents would go elsewhere in search of money, hiring out to some other foreign intelligence agency. Bitterly he wrote Washington that already his people had traced evidence of astounding Japanese secret purchases of war material from European arsenals and shipyards. The department ignored him. At last the tired naval officer admitted that after nearly four decades of pushing intelligence, he had lost enthusiasm. "I am through with the whole business," he conceded to McNamee. "I had my trick at the wheel and you can spend your money the way you like."[18]

Unknown to Niblack, McNamee had little money to spend. For the first time since 1916, annual appropriations for ONI slipped below $150,000. McNamee searched for ways to save or gain pennies, including a requirement that naval attachés certify that poor drinking water at their posts necessitated the purchase of expensive mineral water. The director saved some money by cutting back the length of intelligence reports, which he believed no one read anyway. In a positive sense, the economy forced him to streamline methods and improve sources of information. He ordered attachés to cultivate newspaper correspondents, businessmen, consular officials, and commercial attachés, pumping them for news about the reliability of reports on foreign technical developments. He needed especially to know how far foreign warships sailed each year and what ports they called on around the world, "in order to show Congress the relative amount of cruising done by principal navies." And finally, the DNI borrowed a technique recently employed by the U.S. Army, holding periodic attaché conferences for the evaluation of information. "The Navy Department has been placed in a most embarrassing position by inaccurate information from abroad," he told his naval attachés.[19]

Despite false and misleading data from Europe, that from Japan existed hardly at all. The mist that obscured Japanese naval activities became more impenetrable in the wake of the Washington Conference. Little news arrived in ONI about the development of bases or fortifications on Japan's Pacific Island possessions, about experiments with new weapons, or the scrapping of ships in compliance with treaty obligations. Japanese submarine construction was a complete mystery to ONI. "With its present information," McNamee admitted, "ONI is unable to determine definitely classes, numbers in each class, and characteristics of Japanese submarines built or building." Even the U.S. State Department hid data about Japan from ONI. Naval attaché Commander William F. Halsey, Jr., in Berlin, complained that the diplomatic office withheld from him documents on the petroleum situation and general treaty conditions in the Far East.[20]

Commander William F. Halsey, U.S. naval attaché in Germany in 1923 (standing second from left), complained that he was given incomplete information about the Washington Naval Conference. Vice Admiral Philip Andrews, CinCUSNavEur (seated right) is the other identifiable officer in this embassy setting.

Knowledge about conditions in Japan was clouded further when Lyman Atkinson Cotten replaced the popular Watson as naval attaché in Tokyo. Not that Cotten was incompetent. On the contrary, he had served successfully in the same post before World War I, but in 1922 he arrived in poor health, found his assistant Garnet Hulings abed with tuberculosis, and confronted extreme official secrecy. Ironically, years before in an essay on the Russo-Japanese War of 1904–05, Cotten had praised "Japan's strategy of absolute secrecy at every stage of the war" which "may well be considered by us, belonging as we do to a press-ridden country, always clamoring for the publication of military information however valuable to an enemy it may be." Now, not only did this same secrecy hinder Cotten's collection of treaty information, but the controlled Japanese press attacked him as an evil spy. "This matter has been reported to the American Ambassador, but there seems to be nothing that can be done to stop such publications," Cotten cabled McNamee in December 1922.[21]

The American ambassador, Cyrus E. Woods, failed to press Cotten's complaint very vigorously, since for some reason he was determined to discredit the naval attaché. Boss of the Western Pennsylvania Republican political machine, corporation lawyer, and Harding crony, Woods had already received the reputation in ONI as being nothing more than a "political jackal." Earlier as ambassador to Spain, Woods had forced the recall from Madrid of the navy's best attaché, David McDougal LeBreton. "I believe that he is jealous of anybody in his office who has independent dealings with another Department of the Government, and, being of a naturally suspicious nature, he probably thinks that they are reflecting on him," McNamee warned Cotten.[22]

Despite these many obstacles, ONI demanded immediate data from Cotten. "We are preparing now for the shock of the next Congress and you cannot send in too much information about the Japanese Navy," McNamee cabled his beleaguered attaché. The DNI lacked details on Japanese treaty strengths, future construction programs, and current gun elevation specifications on Japan's biggest battleships. Incredibly, as Cotten prepared to collect this information, a terrible earthquake rocked the area and interrupted his work. Moreover, the catastrophe resulted in Cotten's recall when Ambassador Woods accused him of hiding in the mountains during the crisis rather than lending assistance in the supervision of Red Cross operations. In a related and mysterious development, ONI lost another key operative who had information about the Japanese mandated islands when he died in the earthquake's rubble at a local hospital.[23] (See chapter 4.)

Thus decimated, the naval attaché office forwarded little news of value to ONI. Only convalescing assistant naval attaché Hulings acquired useful data, when early in 1924 he tricked a Japanese officer into revealing the tonnage of a new submarine. "He became embarrassed, his face got red;" Hulings gloated, "he had said too much and after some stuttering and hesitation he said 1500 tons." More commonly, U.S. naval intelligence relied on rumor or accepted misleading and false information, causing several dangerous misestimations of Japan's warmaking potential. This was true especially in ONI's analysis of Japanese naval aircraft and aircraft carrier developments. Perhaps reflecting the bias of many senior officers in the U.S. fleet against aircraft carriers and toward battleships, no intelligence officer seemed anxious to promote air power and risk career advancement. Thus one respected attaché told McNamee in 1923 that Japan could neither build nor fly aircraft effectively. "She dreads aerial warfare and seeks to limit its scope for she will not use it to advantage aggressively," the attaché concluded. Later McNamee incorporated such arguments in an article for the *Proceedings* in which he minimized the value of aviation for the navy.[24]

False and misleading information pervaded other ONI reports about Japan as well. "These people have no ability and no principles capable of sustaining them alone and unsupported," one intelligence officer observed about the Japanese in 1922. "They are remarkably curious," according to another naval attaché report. "Like children, they wish to touch everything they see and it is unsafe to allow them access to any piece of machinery with which they are unfamiliar." Study of Japanese responses to the earthquake reinforced the racial and psychological stereotype that stressed regimentation, subservience to rules, and overall lethargy. Such information supported the evaluation of a Marine Corps expert on amphibious doctrine and intelligence, Major Earl H. Ellis, who insisted that in any future combat the United States could easily defeat Japan. "Our advantages over the enemy will be those generally common to the Nordic races over the Oriental— higher individual intelligence, physique and endurance," Ellis concluded. Nevertheless, these supposedly inferior Orientals might be a tricky foe if allowed to build bases and fortifications on a string of islands in the middle of the Pacific Ocean, and Ellis determined to travel secretly to the area and gather information to correct ONI's most dangerous gap in true and accurate data—details about Japan's mysterious islands.[25]

THE MYSTERIOUS ISLANDS

Scattered about in thousands of miles of Pacific Ocean between the Hawaiian and Philippine islands lay the coral atolls and volcanic islets of the Caroline, Marshall, and Mariana Islands. Since early in this century these islands attracted both Japanese and American interest because of their strategic location across the heart of the Pacific. If fortified, and sprinkled with naval bases and air strips, these picturesque islands might control the approaches to Southeastern Asia and the passage to the Indian Ocean. Japan acted first in 1914 by exploiting the world war to seize the insular possessions from their German colonial masters, and after the war retained them as League of Nations mandates. The United States objected for a time to this thinly disguised term for occupation and colonialism, especially the occupation of the vital cable station on Yap atoll in the Carolines that connected the United States and the Dutch East Indies. Eventually, Americans gained equal access to radio and cable facilities on Yap, but Japan closed other mandated islands tightly to U.S. inspection.

After the Yap incident, the American public and government lost interest in the issue. Not so naval intelligence, which considered Japan's insular chain of vital interest to the United States. Possession of the islands, or at least free access to the area, had become a central part of ONI's strategic doctrine during the nineteenth century, and various intelligence officers had presented this view to departmental planners. During the war, ONI had warned that Japanese acquisition posed an immediate danger to American policies. Later at the Paris peace conference, U.S. naval intelligence people monitored Japanese communications regarding the possession of former German colonies in the Pacific Ocean. During the Yap controversy, even usually muddled Niblack presented a clear, incisive argument to the General Board for the retention of an American presence on the islands. Apparently persuaded, Coontz ordered the intelligence office to prepare a booklet on the distant region. "In the event of a Pacific Campaign," the

CNO advised Niblack, "a detailed knowledge of all harbors in the Pacific possessed by the United States, and other nations, will be indispensable."[1]

Such data became more critical as ONI files began to fill with rumors and gossip about supposed sightings of fortifications, dockyards, airfields, and boatloads of Japanese laborers in the mandated islands. In one case, two wandering American marines and their native girl friends beached on the Carolines in 1920, and though hustled away by Japanese authorities, they succeeded in learning from a local native about huge new gun emplacements under construction on one of the coral islands. Though unverified, the information impressed ONI, largely because its files contained no other information from visitors to these mysterious mandates. Most material had been accumulated prior to the world war, and during the conflict, CNO Benson had proscribed clandestine probes and reconnaissances. And, of course, after the war sensitive political conditions precluded the U.S. Navy from steaming openly into these coral-formed harbors. When aggressive assistant naval attaché Lieutenant Ellis Mark Zacharias cabled from Tokyo in 1920 that he had wangled an invitation from local officials to visit Jaluit, Ponape, Truk, Saipan, and other remote Japanese island outposts, the Navy Department ordered him to decline the offer.[2]

Thus, confronted with demands for fresh data to update an exercise against Japan known since 1906 as War Plan ORANGE, and at the same time restricted from traditional sources, ONI searched for alternative means to gain strategic information. One appeared in early 1920. A California college professor and former missionary to Japan asked the navy for aid in locating and marking graves of U.S. sailors lost in the Pacific during Commodore Matthew C. Perry's famous expeditions to open Japan to Western contact in the 1850s. Niblack jumped at the opportunity, appealing to Coontz to ask the Secretary of the Navy for permission. The DNI envisaged packing such a grave-marking expedition with ONI personnel. "Information that would indicate the existence or nonexistence of fortifications on Okinawajima and Amani-o-shima," Niblack insisted, "is the most important single intelligence item which the Office of Naval Intelligence lacks." Outgoing Secretary Daniels agreed, urging the State Department to arrange with the Japanese government for such a ceremonial visit.[3]

Politely Japan granted permission for the U.S. Navy to stop at the unimportant Okinawan ports of Naha and Kirun to hold services over already known gravesites, but refused to allow Americans to probe other islands in search of lost relics of the Perry voyages. Undiscouraged, new intelligence director Long believed that permission to visit Okinawa had set a precedent that could be exploited more fully in the future. "If it is thought desirable to continue this idea further it is possible that there are other graves of American seamen in nearly all the islands in which the United

A visit to these tombstones on Naha, Okinawa, that mark the graves of Admiral Matthew C. Perry's casualties in 1854 was part of an elaborate gravemarking ruse dreamed up by ONI in the early 1920s to penetrate the secrets of Japan's mysterious islands. (Courtesy U.S. Army)

States is now interested," he advised Coontz in October 1920. The Japanese would be sympathetic to such overtures, the DNI predicted, because of their deep reverence for ancestor worship and ceremony.[4]

American scientific excursions into the Pacific Ocean offered more promise. In May 1921 Rear Admiral Edwin A. Anderson recommended the hiring of a renowned U.S. scientist to head a biological or zoological survey of the Japanese mandates on board a Fish Commission steamer such as the *Albatross*. Carefully trained intelligence agents posing as the famous scientist's research assistants would man the spy ship. "It is not thought that the Japanese Government would, or could, seriously object to the proposed expedition, if the scientific character of the work was widely advertised and its primary object carefully concealed," Anderson contended somewhat naively. The admiral suggested further that after the mission uncovered evidence of fortifications and advanced Japanese bases, it could collect enough specimens of legitimate scientific value to defray the cost of the trip through the sale of publications that revealed the natural history of the region.[5]

ONI rejected the contrived and complicated ruse, relying instead upon an actual scientific enterprise to cover an investigation of Japanese islands. An opportunity appeared conveniently in 1921 in the person of famed University of Michigan geologist William Herbert Hobbs. No one could suspect Hobbs of spying. He was an internationally respected expert on coral reefs, volcanoes, glaciers, and earthquakes; he also carried a special introduction from Baron Shidehara, Japan's ambassador to the United States, to officials on all Japanese islands requesting full cooperation in the study of volcanic formations and coral growth. Though anxious to use Hobbs, ONI hesitated to contact him directly, preferring to go through the office of University President M. L. Burton. "Should any letter showing that the Office of Naval Intelligence was interested in his activities fall into the hands of the Japanese," McNamee warned Burton, "it might seriously compromise his standing and interfere with his investigations." The Ann Arbor administrator agreed not to inform his employee about ONI's interest in the trip.[6]

Next, ONI bypassed the University of Michigan by contacting officials of the U.S. Geological Survey in order to obtain copies of Hobbs's reports. No luck here either, since the Interior Department informed ONI that Hobbs was not their man and would not forward his research findings to them directly. An Interior Department assistant secretary added a little friendly advice. "As Professor Hobbs is a loyal American citizen," the civilian bureaucrat confided to ONI, "I am sure that he would be glad to send directly to the Navy Department any information that he may acquire in his investigations." Apparently ONI gave up this scheme.[7]

Grave markers and geologists proved of limited value, and ONI turned to other sources for information about the increasingly secret island groups. Long wrote the U.S. Shipping Board to encourage merchant ship captains to navigate closer to the mandates in order to pick up any data of military value. At the same time, naval intelligence reported that it had placed an agent at the meteorological station on Yap. But like the rest, these avenues failed to uncover the secrets of the mandates.[8]

ONI realized that it must plant its own spies in the Pacific Ocean to pursue clandestine operations and to collect secret data. There seemed to be adequate personnel for such undertakings, and assistant intelligence director Robert Henderson listed a number of "live wires" for this work, including a reserve officer proficient in the Japanese language. There may have been others considered for secret missions to the mandates, but only one agent ever penetrated those islands during the 1920s—Marine Corps Major Earl Hancock Ellis. "Pete" Ellis's mission for ONI was (and still is) some-

Lieutenant Colonel Earl H. "Pete" Ellis died under mysterious circumstances while on a naval intelligence mission to discover whether the Japanese had fortified their Pacific mandates.

thing of a puzzle. "It was always a mystery about Ellis at ONI," fellow USMC intelligence expert William A. Worton recalled years later. "Any time you worked at Hush-hush Section, the name Ellis always came up because we did a tremendous amount of translating of Japanese codes in those days," and former missionaries used as code breakers "knew much about Ellis and the stories about Ellis."[9]

ONI interest in Ellis as a postwar agent surfaced in September 1920 when Niblack contacted Marine Corps Commandant John A. Lejeune about using the skilled, but reportedly unstable, officer for intelligence duty. From the outset, ONI's involvement with Ellis was ambiguous, a harbinger of the later mystery surrounding his travels and death in the Pacific. At first Niblack asked this veteran of several Latin American intelligence operations to review ONI's monographs on that region, but then the DNI informed Lejeune in ungainly prose that "the main object of his coming to the Office of Naval Intelligence is preparatory to intelligent intelligence work along the lines that O.N.I. desires information." Of course, Niblack knew that Ellis was adequately prepared to do "intelligent intelligence work!" What the director meant became clearer four days later when he informed the General Board that ONI now had the services of a trained observer to accompany U.S. scientific and photographic expeditions voyaging about the Pacific Ocean.[10]

In the months after Ellis's apparent attachment to the intelligence office, he shuttled back and forth between a secluded office at Lejeune's headquarters (not in ONI) and a local hospital, where he underwent constant treatment for a severe nervous disorder. All that time Ellis was working on a secret project. Drawing on information available in Niblack's office, he constructed the first war plan for advanced base operations in Micronesia. Although primitive by later standards, the exercise outlined tactics for reducing Pacific island defenses and forecast amphibious doctrine by discussing troop mobilization and delivery methods. "The following study of Advanced Base Operations in Micronesia," Ellis suggested, "has been made for the purpose of crystallizing ideas as to future operations in that area."[11]

After completion of his paper, Ellis disappeared deep into the Pacific posing as a merchant for the Hughes Trading Company of New York. After several efforts to penetrate the Japanese mandated islands by way of Australia, Ellis surfaced next in Yokohama, where in August 1922 a U.S. Navy doctor hospitalized him for severe nervous exhaustion and probably acute alcoholism, although fellow intelligence officer Lieutenant Sidney Mashbir, USA, claimed that the "act of being drunk" was only a cover. Seemingly unaware of his secret mission and certainly convinced that he had become an alcoholic, ONI's representatives in Japan monitored his movements and because of his boasts that he worked for U.S. naval intelligence, recommended that he be returned at once to the United States. Ellis slipped away, however. In early 1923 naval attaché Cotten, learning that Ellis had died of unknown causes on Palau, Caroline Islands, dispatched Chief Pharmacist Lawrence Zembsch to the islands to recover Ellis's remains and, of course, to have a look around. Several months passed before Zembsch returned. He had an urn containing Ellis's ashes but was in a stupor and suffered from amnesia, apparently drug-induced. Hospitalized, the intelligence agent gradually recovered. Before ONI could learn anything from him, however, the terrible earthquake of 1 September 1923 destroyed the hospital, killing the only person who could provide the answers about the Ellis affair.[12]

While awaiting word about Ellis, ONI launched another mission that proved to be the most successful operation in the 1920s against these Japanese islands. Learning that the new scout cruiser, the *Milwaukee*, would make a shakedown cruise near the islands, McNamee requested permission to equip the warship with intelligence gear and personnel. Data on the island groups, he informed the CNO, remained sketchy despite years of intensive efforts by ONI to explore the region. "This office has exhausted every possible source of information (domestic and foreign, including German) and has been unable to obtain any information of military value," McNamee admitted. "The only way the information can be obtained is by sending a man-of-war to the locality to get it."[13]

Receiving necessary approval, McNamee directed elaborate preparations. The *Milwaukee*'s two scout planes offered a unique opportunity to take aerial photographs of the atolls and harbors, and the DNI ordered installation of special cameras suitable for long-distance photography. "It is believed at such places as Taongi, Rongelap, Eniwetok, etc.," the DNI explained, "that the presence or absence of shoals within the atoll can be definitely and quickly determined by observation from planes." Further, the director indoctrinated the *Milwaukee*'s navigator prior to the shakedown cruise about what information already existed in ONI and what data the General Board and Plans Division desired. The *Milwaukee* returned with a collection of excellent pictures and data that indicated extensive harbor dredging by the Japanese but no construction of fortifications or gun emplacements. For the first time, ONI seemed satisfied with its information about the islands.[14]

The *Milwaukee*'s successful mission ended for a time ONI's urgent search for exotic means to penetrate the mandates. Throughout the remainder of the decade, the collection of data from that strategic region became a routine part of the periodic revisions of War Plan ORANGE. Thus, in March 1927 Colonel Richard M. Cutts, USMC, revising Ellis's Micronesian plan,

The new light cruiser *Milwaukee*, on its shakedown cruise in the mid-Pacific in 1922–1923, was carefully prepared by DNI Luke McNamee to collect intelligence on the Japanese mandated islands.

investigated the Tawitawi island group. Cutts's version prescribed measures to seize and defend two atolls in the Marshalls as subsidiary bases from which U.S. forces could defend lines of communications to the Philippines. The new plan still relied on aerial reconnaissance and outdated information, however, and was based on the very dangerous assumption that "there is at present no known Orange force in the Marshall Islands."[15]

Despite intensive activity throughout the 1920s, ONI had learned less about the Japanese mandates than about treaty violations by all the signatories of the Washington pact. Traditional methods of gathering information through attachés, routine reconnaissance, or special intelligence missions had led often to incomplete, misleading, or false data. To provide accurate news about increasingly secretive and militarily powerful Japan, something more was needed, and ONI directors began to resort more frequently to clandestine surveillance and secret operations—some of which skirted or transcended legal limits. Old-fashioned intelligence was no longer sufficient, McNamee told a class at the Naval War College in late 1922. "The fact that we have never had brought home to us the need of a real intelligence service in operation against a first-class naval power," he argued, "has given us in this respect a false sense of security."[16]

But Japan had become a first-class naval threat. In the years ahead ONI would try to counter this threat by becoming "a real intelligence service," employing every weapon available in its undeclared war against Japan, including eavesdropping and surreptitious entry.

CHAPTER FIVE

SURREPTITIOUS ENTRY

Luke McNamee held a broad interpretation of intelligence. Though recently at odds with his wartime mentor, Admiral Sims, over the value of aircraft to the navy, he still reflected that retired officer's concept that an intelligence office was the core of strategic planning, operations, and security. In order to coordinate responsibilities, McNamee hoped to expand ONI, utilizing fully all sources of information—including spying, domestic snooping, clandestine measures, and electronic surveillance. The last particularly impressed McNamee, who later headed a wireless company after retirement from the navy. "Direction finders will give the key to the probable source of despatches," he insisted. McNamee found value as well in aerial reconnaissance, photographic espionage, surreptitious entry, and the recruitment of businessmen, journalists, and college professors for undercover assignments. Moreover, he dipped freely into non-naval matters in order to secure data, even working closely with William J. Burns, chief of the Justice Department's Bureau of Investigation, to collect files on *The Negro World*, an allegedly subversive publication.[1]

Yet the naval intelligence dilemma haunted McNamee. Publicly the professional naval officer declared that ONI never ventured into areas unrelated to the navy's strategic interests nor participated in covert operations. "During the war we necessarily had thousands of agents whose business was to guard against spies and traitors," he wrote in one magazine article. "This was a war condition under which the just suffered with the unjust, for of course many ludicrous mistakes were made by amateur agents." Consequently, ONI faltered between 1917 and the end of the fighting, McNamee admitted, "but now in peace time, all that work in the United States is handled by the Department of Justice."[2]

Contrary to his official disclaimer, between 27 September 1921 and 19 December 1923 McNamee's office actually expanded wartime surveillance and secret operations despite congressional restraints, lack of funds, and public chagrin over gumshoe methods. Did the DNI lie deliberately?

Searching for justification, he rationalized that ONI's pursuit of such work was necessary to national defense and provided the navy with much-needed strategic information about dangerous potential enemies. McNamee never placed ONI within the context of illegal conduct or suppression of civil rights and liberties. After all, other agencies of the government protected Americans from gangsters, bootleggers, or enemy agents through undercover detection and eavesdropping. For McNamee, ONI was only fulfilling its legal duty to protect the navy and the nation from any menace—Bolshevik, Japanese, or whatever; it was acting as a real intelligence service using realistic methods.[3]

If necessary, McNamee could further justify this view by drawing upon ONI's history. Secret operations against Japan had begun long before World War I, at least as early as 1902 when as a result of the Anglo-Japanese alliance, ONI considered infiltrating secret agents into Japan. Serious thought about such methods began after the Russo-Japanese War, and in 1906 ONI, the General Board, and the Naval War College initiated war planning against Japan. The suggested plans included securing lists of possible espionage agents, setting up confidential cable codes and security and counterespionage measures for the Hawaiian Islands. Throughout World War I, ONI spied on its counterparts in Japan, Latin America, and East Asia, where naval attaché Irvin van Gorder Gillis constructed an espionage network to follow Japanese intrigues in China, Manchuria, and Siberia. All the while special agents, such as Harry Catlin, a salesman for the Nicholson File Company of Rhode Island, filtered into the Far East. Catlin employed aliases and false post office drops for communications with ONI about Japan. ONI even undertook a covert operation against Japan in Mexico that the U.S. State Department considered of questionable legality.[4]

McNamee continued and expanded the earlier surveillance of the Japanese. But in 1922 such secret operations differed substantially from previous experiences, because they evolved largely within the United States itself. McNamee set the tone in February when he gleaned information furtively from the private bank account of the Henry A. Hitner Company of Philadelphia in order to discover whether the American company sold scrap metal to Japanese buyers. His office jumped more fully into domestic detective work a few months later in response to a warning that a Japanese spy had entered New York City intent upon stealing secrets about the U.S. Navy's aeronautical program. Instantly, the DNI ordered Third District intelligence personnel to counter the spy's progress. Employing familiar wartime techniques, district intelligence officer Clarence Lamont Arnold instructed his people to break into private offices and ransack luggage in search of the mysterious Oriental agent. In March 1923, Arnold sent ONI's counterespionage chief Royal E. Ingersoll photocopies of correspondence taken surreptitiously from a steamer trunk belonging to Eike Takeuchi, a Japanese officer visiting New York City. Possibly the haul included a code book, since Ingersoll recalled later that the operation led to the first break in Japanese codes. In the process of examining suitcases, apparently ONI sleuths mistakenly rifled the luggage of an American college professor, although Arnold's report failed to specify the circumstances surrounding this search.[5]

Arnold's team attempted next to crack the big safe at the office of the Japanese consul at 165 Broadway, thinking it possibly contained code books and details of Japanese espionage in the United States. Several times the DIO broke into the private property, but failed to open the vault. "Our efforts at 165 will be discontinued," Arnold informed Ingersoll, "as I am satisfied that the safe man is unable to open the safe without possible damage which might lead to our detection." Nevertheless, ONI forged ahead with other covert operations against Japanese agents in New York City, San Francisco, South America, and the Panama Canal Zone, and in late 1923 the office informed the CNO that it had broken a Japanese spy ring on the East Coast.[6]

Just as McNamee's office showed signs of becoming a full-fledged intelligence organization, pursuing all aspects of such work, his tour as DNI ended abruptly when the department transferred him to London as naval attaché. Coming soon after his revelation to the CNO of ONI's covert activity, it seemed as though the department was expressing dissatisfaction with such conduct; in reality, routine personnel policy rather than any thought of interfering with intelligence policy governed the decision. Nevertheless, this regular rotation of officers saved McNamee from further entanglement in the intelligence dilemma, but at the same time, it deprived ONI of a most dynamic and effective director and threatened to undermine postwar security measures. Once again, there appeared to be an irreconcilable conflict between ONI's service to the navy and its evolution as an intelligence agency.

The department replaced McNamee with mild-mannered Henry Hughes Hough, recently returned from a pleasant two-year stint as naval governor of the Virgin Islands. Hough characterized the reserved atmosphere of the current Calvin Coolidge administration. Rushed into the presidency by the untimely death of Warren Harding in 1923, Coolidge pledged to run a government based on restraint, austerity, and additional limitations on spending for naval construction. As a contrast to the corruption and immorality of Harding's regime, the silent New Englander wrapped his administration in a mantle of morality, especially in the office of attorney general where Harlan F. Stone proscribed federal wiretapping and undercover operations. Confronted by this atmosphere, Hough needed to move cautiously in pursuing secret activities. To impatient intelligence

Ellis Mark Zacharias devoted a controversial career to naval intelligence, serving as a language student, code breaker, assistant attaché, district intelligence officer, deputy director of naval intelligence, but never as DNI, the post he most coveted.

officer Zacharias, for one, this careful approach meant simply that Hough was a timid and incompetent DNI, but in fact the new director expanded McNamee's work. No stranger to intelligence, Hough had served in ONI twice before between 1907–11 and as naval attaché to Paris and St. Petersburg from 1911 to 1913. As DNI he patiently pursued leads about Japanese espionage in the Philippine Islands, Hawaii, and the Canal Zone. Like Long and McNamee, he kept domestic surveillance intact, probably authorizing the burglary of the offices of the pacifistic, anti-navy Federal Council of Churches of Christ of America.[7]

Hough's major contribution lay in communications intelligence and eavesdropping. In early 1924 he instructed his people on the Pacific Coast and in the fleet to accelerate interception of Japanese radio traffic. "It is believed highly desirable that copies of all Japanese messages in code and all Japanese messages in plain Japanese addressed to government officers in Japan or the United States be sent to this office for examination," Hough explained. After examining the intercepts in ONI, Hough forwarded them to Director of Naval Communications Ridley McLean for further study by the code breakers, such as Lieutenant Commander Laurence W. Safford, in the code and signal section. When the naval communications office displayed early tendencies to restrict access to its product, Hough insisted that

McLean forward all decoded information to assist ONI in the indoctrination of intelligence personnel in Shanghai. Meanwhile, Hough's office monitored radio transmissions in the Mediterranean from both British and Italian ships, but expressed slight interest in young Justice Department sleuth J. Edgar Hoover's suggestion that Hough listen in on Soviet wireless transmissions.[8]

Increasingly convinced of the value of eavesdropping, Hough decided to contact commercial telephone and telegraph companies in order to gather information about Japan from them. Undoubtedly he knew that federal communication codes forbade release of cablegrams and messages, but he tried anyway. "It is impossible to get from the telephone or cable companies any Japanese messages, government or otherwise," Hough admitted at last. The director's search for information had dragged his office steadily toward increased domestic surveillance and perilously close to unlawful actions. Though apparently Hough avoided such violations, throughout the remainder of the decade his successors continued to focus on communications intelligence and eavesdropping. Between 1925 and 1927 ONI veteran W. W. Galbraith, first as DNI and then as assistant director, established a research desk in ONI for the study of wireless, cable, and telephone interceptions and created listening posts around the world. In the meantime, from his station on board the cruiser *Marblehead* in Asian waters, Zacharias monitored Japanese naval radio traffic during Japanese maneuvers and carrier training operations.[9]

The successes achieved by Galbraith and Zacharias in improving intelligence contributed partly to the latter's criticism of Hough, but actually, the two more colorful and aggressive intelligence officers had merely built upon Hough's work. There was one area, though, where Galbraith overshadowed his quiet predecessor—in counterespionage and information security. As early as 1921 while working in ONI, Galbraith had warned about the easy access civilian photographers and journalists had to the bombing trials and gunfire tests against both the radio-controlled *Iowa* and captured German warships such as the battleship *Ostfriesland*. In response, the Navy Department had done nothing more than give naval intelligence a general cognizance over the review and release of classified information. McNamee had tried in 1922 to secure a list of restricted data and a definition of ONI's power over security and censorship, but failed, and when Galbraith returned to the office on 9 October 1925, he discovered the same ill-defined policy as to the release of secret information to the public that he had criticized several years before.[10]

Soon Galbraith learned that leaks, loose talk, and the unauthorized release of classified information posed a greater problem than ever. His predecessor had failed to block the publication of photographs of a secret CN Drop Bomb or to stimulate departmental concern for security. And now Galbraith received news that two officers had handed over a secret intelligence report on British naval strength to notorious naval publicist and lobbyist William B. Shearer. He resolved to tighten security by circulating a list of subjects that ONI considered too sensitive to release to the press or the public. These included any data on torpedoes, mines, gun sights, direction and fire control systems, and most especially, information about the flight deck, catapults, arresting gear, and elevators on the powerful new U.S. aircraft carrier, the *Saratoga*. But ONI held advisory status only, and the various bureaus made their own rules and judgments, which were often contrary to ONI's definition of security. The great number of magazine and newspaper photographs that appeared during the late 1920s on every detail of the *Saratoga* underscored this issue. Despite Galbraith's best efforts, it would be well into the espionage-filled thirties before the Navy Department would support ONI's attempts to curb the release of secret data.[11]

While Galbraith pursued specialized aspects of intelligence, between July 1926 and December 1927 the department directed Arthur Japy Hepburn to serve as DNI and to concentrate almost exclusively on the preparation of information, statistics, tables, and charts, these data to be used for an upcoming naval disarmament conference to extend the Washington treaty ratios to smaller warships. On the surface this service merely duplicated

Scholarly, quiet Arthur J. Hepburn was appointed DNI in 1927 for the express purpose of preparing routine information for representatives to the upcoming arms limitations conferences, but he soon became attracted by the more exotic aspects of intelligence duty. (Courtesy Franklin D. Roosevelt Library)

work done earlier for the delegates to the Washington Conference in 1921. Hepburn's people collected attaché reports on foreign opinion concerning limitations and drew up comparative tables of naval strength and ship tonnage for the Coolidge government. But this time, several factors allowed the ONI to influence the outcome of disarmament talks. Instead of civilian leadership, naval officers would head delegations to the new conference. Moreover, ONI had grown used to functioning in a world of deception, eavesdropping, and surreptitious entry, and flirted with the idea of slanting information in order to sabotage the conference. This possibility was suggested by former naval attaché in London Hussey, the officer in charge of compiling statistics for ONI. Hussey fell under the influence of fanatical navalist and president of the U.S. Navy League, William Howard Gardiner. "Captain Hussey has done an enormous amount of work in selecting and collating data on the general lines outlined by you in your paper you left with me," Admiral Hilary P. Jones, who would serve as naval advisor in the upcoming conference, wrote Gardiner in 1925. "He has brought out some very interesting possibilities. Please consider this as entirely confidential as we are saying nothing outside about the work," Jones confided to Gardiner.[12]

Hepburn left details to Hussey and others, either ignoring or totally ignorant of Gardiner's influence on ONI. The respected, forthright, but very reclusive Hepburn expressed no intention of deliberately slanting information to wreck any conference or embarrass the Coolidge administration. However, like all his predecessors during the decade, he succumbed to the wider interpretation of intelligence. Thus, when ruthless lobbyist Shearer sent Hepburn confidential information about alleged British duplicity in order to sabotage preparatory naval limitations talks in Geneva, the DNI declared official distrust for any data sent by this unsavory character, but confessed privately that Shearer might be of value to ONI. "In fact it is the opinion of several officers who have known him personally that his interest in the Navy partakes somewhat of the nature of a mania which might possibly be turned to some account if the circumstances ever permitted to the employment of such an erratic and unusual type of character," Hepburn confided.[13]

Although appointed largely for the purpose of preparing the navy for limitations conferences, the scholarly Hepburn, once an intelligence officer on Admiral Bristol's staff in Turkey, became fascinated with other aspects of the intelligence business. In January 1927 he discussed the nature of confidential investigations with one naval attaché. Hepburn believed that from time to time ONI needed to pursue investigations of American businessmen, transients, and criminal elements, employing informants and detectives to assist with this domestic surveillance. "It must be clearly established that all investigations must be conducted under pretext," Hepburn insisted, "and with such discretion that other departments will not have reason to complain of activities trespassing on their provinces, and to prevent any general impression of strong O.N.I. activities getting abroad."[14]

Before being captivated completely by the intelligence dilemma, Hepburn left for sea duty, and on 1 January 1928 veteran intelligence officer and former naval attaché to Chile Alfred Wilkinson Johnson stepped in as the new DNI. While he familiarized himself with office routine at ONI headquarters in Washington, at the other end of town the Supreme Court rendered a decision that upheld the conviction of Seattle businessman and bootlegger Roy Olmstead for violation of Prohibition laws. Since the government's case had been based on evidence obtained by wiretapping and other clandestine methods, the Court seemed to settle the legality of eavesdropping, search, seizure, and surveillance. Though apparently unrelated to the naval intelligence business, the Olmstead case reinforced the tendencies of all federal security agencies to pursue domestic surveillance and secret operations. It was no coincidence that Johnson's naval intelligence organization carried on this line of work with more vigor and thoroughness than any ONI team during the 1920s.[15]

The major target of surreptitious entry under Johnson's directorship remained Japanese consular and business offices in New York City and on the West Coast. On five consecutive nights during September 1929, DIO Howell, two detectives, two photographers, a locksmith, and an enlisted lookout broke into and entered the office of the Japanese Inspector of Naval Machinery at the Metropolitan Tower, Number One Madison Square. Painstakingly, the ONI team cracked the big office safe, pulled the documents and code books for photostating, and then meticulously replaced them back in the vault. Among the photostated material lay copies of tables that revealed the latest Japanese military aircraft, photographs of shells, statistics on muzzle velocities of Japanese naval rifles, and a chart on the ranges of individual guns. "The grand thing about the whole performance," Howell wrote with his characteristic embellishment, "is that they haven't the slightest suspicion that we have this stuff, for they are still using the same old secret code, and of course we are getting first hand information as to what they are really thinking and saying and planning."[16]

Domestic surveillance in 1929 did not end with the Japanese. ONI agents, led again by Howell, who maintained a direct telephone link to Johnson's office in Washington, raided the headquarters of the Communist Party of America at 43 East 125th Street. Supposedly prompted by an investigation of Communist activity among naval enlisted men and sailors, the operation turned into an orgy of vandalism as the naval intelligence crew ransacked files, threw papers on the floor, busted open desk drawers and scattered the contents about the rooms, and forced open the door on the office safe. "We even swiped the check books and bank books to create even more trouble," Howell bragged. So that the trail would not lead to ONI, Howell planted false evidence to deceive the local Reds into thinking some other radical had vandalized their offices. These extreme measures seemed appropriate to Howell because of his personal disgust for Communists. "I have been following Communism for months, and I am convinced that it is the severest menace the United States have," he explained. "These damned skunks acting under the orders of Moscow presume to come over here and preach their sedition and overthrow the government."[17]

The burglary of Communist Party headquarters in New York provided a fitting climax to a postwar decade during which ONI developed all the techniques of what McNamee called a real intelligence agency. Howell's operation illustrated naval intelligence's use of espionage, secrecy, deception, undercover methods, and gumshoe measures. Simultaneously, it demonstrated clearly the navy's intelligence dilemma. Undertaken for limited naval objectives, the burglary manifested wider non-naval aspects and opened the door to even more exotic enterprises, such as Howell's political operations for President Hoover.

CHAPTER SIX

DANGER SIGNALS

The possibility that Herbert Hoover would resort to illegalities had seemed remote when the quiet Quaker took office as president in 1929. Except for minor farm relief problems, he had confronted no critical domestic issues, and Americans seemingly enjoyed a period of unprecedented prosperity. Internationally, the world basked in the euphoria of the recent Kellogg-Briand Peace Pact, which promised to outlaw war as an instrument of national policy. Perpetuating this spirit, the United States negotiated a series of bilateral arbitration treaties and improved relations with Latin America. Hoover expected to continue his party's programs of peace, prosperity, and international comity. He promised to withdraw U.S. forces from troubled Nicaragua and unstable Haiti, who were there to maintain order, and accelerated American participation in disarmament conferences. The former mining engineer planned an honest, efficient, and righteous government. Secrecy and subterfuge would assume no part in this blueprint, and as evidence of this good will Secretary of State Henry L. Stimson discontinued secret code-breaking operations in the "Black Chamber" with his famous admonition that "gentlemen do not read each other's mail."[1]

In pursuit of a policy of economy and peace, Hoover set out to limit and reduce armaments further than his two Republican predecessors. Helpful was the like-minded British government of Labor Prime Minister Ramsay MacDonald and Foreign Secretary Arthur Henderson. In June the pacifistic MacDonald expressed interest in a naval limitations conference. That same month, Hoover ordered the Navy Department to prepare statistics for such a conference, including tables on all classes of warships and charts on the tonnage, ages, and armament of American naval vessels. Once again this unpleasant duty fell on the Office of Naval Intelligence, and DNI Johnson instructed naval attachés assigned to the leading sea powers to prepare studies of the British, Japanese, French, and Italian navies. As these data arrived in Washington, Johnson introduced them to meetings of the General Board, where a group of senior officers struggled over ways to measure the relative naval power of nations for Hoover. "I know you have had to be at their beck and call a great deal of the time," naval attaché Arie Corwin wrote the DNI from Holland. "Perhaps they will realize more the value of Naval Intelligence."[2]

The General Board was too engrossed in agonizing over the creation of a realistic "yardstick" for naval disarmament to bother much with ONI's reputation. Moreover, even if such work enhanced the value of naval intelligence, it agitated Johnson, who abhorred civilian interference in naval affairs such as that pursued presently by the Hoover administration. Back in 1920, he had warned his commanding officer and inspirational leader Sims that when confronted with pressure to maintain a strong navy, civilian leaders often attempted to divide the service into squabbling cliques. "I fear that we are likely to be purposely led into a controversy among ourselves by Mr. Daniels so that he may escape in the smoke screen," Johnson had complained. And now Hoover followed the same path by appointing Admiral William Veazie Pratt, another Sims disciple of former days, as his personal selection to head the U.S. technical staff to the forthcoming London Naval Conference. Pratt supported Hoover's plans to eliminate 8-inch-gun cruisers from U.S. building plans, contrary to the advice of ONI and the General Board.[3]

Johnson confronted other troublesome questions concerning the compilation of figures for the disarmament conference. A recent scandal that surrounded efforts by leading American shipbuilders to use lobbyist Shearer to sabotage the naval limitations conference at Geneva during Coolidge's term and to influence congressional appropriations created suspicion toward any data published by the Navy Department. Senator Carl Hayden of Arizona had specifically questioned the accuracy of ONI figures that indicated U.S. naval inferiority. Johnson's office had to bend over backward to prepare careful statistical reports, and the information package prepared for Pratt was probably the most thorough yet attempted by ONI. One document contained a synthesis of fifty-five editorials from eighteen British publications in order to present an accurate evaluation of British public opinion toward naval limitations. Biographical sketches of foreign delegates to the London conference were compiled with far more painstaking detail and relevance than in prior exercises. Such thoroughness allowed ONI to contribute valuable insight into the character behind some of the leading delegates. ONI's sketches of MacDonald and Henderson revealed their personal idiosyncrasies, wealth, strengths, and weaknesses, while that of Admiral of the Fleet Sir Charles E. Madden underscored his potential as the most important figure at the gathering. "No man who has worked for Britain has ever lived behind such a thick veil of self-effacement," the intelligence office explained. "Yet for eleven consecutive years, much of it without any leave worth mentioning, he was in high command of squadrons afloat."[4]

Perhaps the major obstacle confronting Johnson was the apparent restriction against eavesdropping on conference participants. Stimson's sermon against reading other people's mail caused the DNI to hesitate to use clandestine methods to intercept communications about the London meeting. His reservations soon faded, however, and ONI intercepted foreign messages, including telegrams, to the Japanese delegation. The entire business of preparing the navy for the London conference, though, drained Johnson and his staff, making them all edgy. Only after the American delegation departed for Britain could the DNI write his friend Joseph K. Taussig at the Naval War College that the extreme tensions in ONI had at last eased.[5]

The respite was momentary. Soon news arrived that Britain, Japan, and the United States had signed a London Naval Treaty that limited the total size of fleets, defined ratios for cruisers and destroyers, and established parity in submarines. The pact presented ONI with many new and difficult problems, but Hoover insisted that this settlement would save millions of dollars without compromising the national defense, and he pressed hard for Senate confirmation. He considered passage of the London treaty the most important accomplishment of his administration, perhaps looking for a bright spot in what had become suddenly a tarnished and desperate American government. While the preliminary preparations and final negotiations had absorbed the attention of both the executive and naval establishments, the Wall Street stock market had crashed in October 1929, gradually ushering in the worst economic depression in history and unraveling the flimsy postwar structure of reparations, loans, and war debts. Soaring unemployment, misery, and financial dislocation soon overshadowed his disarmament accomplishments. Opponents smeared him unmercifully for his failure to alleviate suffering and stem the disintegration of the economy. Hoover fought back, pushed limited government programs, urged voluntary conservation, and curbed government spending. All to no avail. Rapidly losing his grip on affairs, the president lapsed into moments of paralysis and panic, undoubtedly accounting for his authorization of the Howell burglary in June 1930.

By the spring of 1930 an atmosphere of pessimism and gloom settled over the nation plagued by bank failures and long bread lines of destitute workers. Depression settled into the Navy Department as well. Final ratification of the London Naval Treaty added to the feeling of frustration and helplessness. The General Board, ONI, and many naval officers considered the treaty harmful to naval security, and with deepening gloom feared that Hoover would use the pact as an excuse to make further cuts in men and materiel. They were right. The president pared personnel, laid up ships, curbed fleet maneuvers to save expensive fuel, furloughed officers without pay, and reduced the salaries of others. A disconsolate CNO Charles F. Hughes resigned early to make way for his replacement, Admiral Pratt, the officer considered most responsible for the navy's surrender to Hoover's disarmament mentality. The depth of feeling against Pratt appeared later when his successor, William H. Standley, accused him of making deals with the Hoover administration, leading to the "definite loss of overall naval efficiency."[6]

Contrary to Standley's opinion, Pratt slaved to improve fleet efficiency and streamline bureaucracy. In order to provide the same services with diminished resources, the CNO searched for better ways to do the same job—especially through recommendations made by his new planning section. Nowhere was Pratt's crusade for economy and efficiency more evident than in steps taken by DNI Johnson in early 1930 to eliminate marginal and unnecessary duties in ONI. Primarily, the director sought to advance methods for gathering, sorting, and storing information. In the days before computers and data processing, this meant installing better typewriters, duplicating and filing machines, and teaching attachés and naval officers the fundamentals of preparing concise and clear intelligence reports. Johnson's attempts to cut down paper work took on something of a crusade but led ironically to a flood of new memoranda on how to improve efficiency in the routing and disseminating of information. Apparently the contradiction escaped the bureaucrat, as he ordered the condensation of reports but at the same instant instructed that "when this is done, make sufficient copies for all interested parties and don't forget that the Service afloat, or outside of Washington, may also be interested."[7]

Meanwhile, Johnson revised the ten-year-old instruction sheet for the duties of naval attachés, hoping to eliminate overlapping functions and improve quality. He urged attachés to stick to naval matters, avoiding the seduction of undercover operations that took time and energy away from basic duties. The ONI instruction for naval attachés in 1930 warned against other kinds of seduction as well. "The use of immoral women as agents is regarded as being very precarious. A woman that will sell herself is usually willing to sell her employer," ONI cautioned. "In addition, women of this type exert a very demoralizing effect upon the men under whom they are placed," the office punned unintentionally.[8]

Despite several clumsy steps to adjust ONI to the depression, Johnson recognized that too much information, poorly analyzed, obscured important signals from abroad. In January 1930 he explained how the pile of data from the various intelligence agencies and offices of the government inundated ONI, which could not process this material since "no additional officer or clerical assistance can be obtained." The hard-pressed director begged naval attachés to be selective in what they reported, avoiding extraneous matters such as lists of dinner guests or repetitive data. The DNI only desired information about submarines, radio communications, and fleet tactics, material of direct and unquestionable naval interest.[9]

Fearful that his people would be unable to keep pace with the demands of intelligence while the government pared resources, Johnson turned to volunteers for assistance. He believed that the DIOs should mobilize volunteer agents and reserve intelligence officers, but expected ONI to contact civilians in all walks of life for information as well. To this end, Johnson communicated with the likes of W. K. Vanderbilt, William Vincent Astor, and aircraft designer Grover Cleveland Loening. Naval intelligence briefed wealthy yachtsman Astor about what data it needed from him during his upcoming pleasure cruise to the West Indies. Two months later, Johnson invited Loening to Washington to discuss whether he would collect aircraft material for ONI. "Much of the information received from abroad on aviation, I feel is not thoroughly reliable," the DNI noted, "and it is of distinct value to have such information as you have furnished us to amplify or check up on what we already have."[10]

Before Johnson could complete further modifications, though, the department ordered him to Nicaragua as president of the National Board convened to monitor sensitive elections in that unsettled country. For the past six months he had battled, along with his boss, Admiral Pratt, to increase efficiency despite depression, disarmament, and disillusionment. "I also feel that, although actual accomplishment may have fallen somewhat short of anticipation," he wrote naval attaché Corwin in June 1930, "we have made some progress and that the Office of Naval Intelligence is constantly increasing its value to the service."[11]

At least Johnson had balanced the worst aspects of the intelligence dilemma, leaving secret operations to Howell and other local intelligence operators. This allowed some freedom for the Washington office to concentrate on strategy, especially as related to the London Naval Conference. His final estimation of international conditions for department war planners underscored the strategic emphasis. In this memorandum, Johnson insisted that Senate ratification of the London agreement assured that Japanese aggression in the Far East would go unchecked, especially by an eventual invasion of Chinese territory. "This treaty certainly increases the probability of Japan taking such action," he estimated, "and although it does not endanger the territory of the United States it does appear to bring us nearer to, instead of further from, another expensive war."[12]

On the surface Johnson's final evaluation of world conditions seemed yet another negative response to naval limitations and congressional parsimony, with the severe depression making the DNI's judgment more brooding than normal. Thus, if anyone in Hoover's administration bothered to read this ONI report, which was doubtful, they dismissed it as familiar rhetoric from an office noted more for propaganda than predictions. Unfortunately, this time ONI's warning of danger signals in the Far East had been based on careful and thorough analyses of data and exhaustive study of developments in Asia by Japanese expert Zacharias and in ONI by Yangtze Patrol veteran Roscoe Schuirmann, years later a DNI during World War II. Moreover, ONI had excellent information to work with gathered recently by the navy's enlarged intelligence operations in China. Since 1927, when the Asian giant had exploded into near civil war between the Nationalist faction under Chiang Kai-shek and Mao Tse-tung's Chinese Communist Party, ONI had increased the news sources from the Far East by attaching additional assistant naval attachés to both the Peking and Tokyo posts and by improving liaison with the expanding regimental intelligence office of the 1,250-man 4th Marine Regiment in Shanghai. In addition, the navy maintained seven gunboats and destroyers on the Yangtze River and off the South China coast, all busily gathering information. The ungainly gunboat *Panay* at Hankow proved the most effective, but all observed and reported the impending anarchy in the Far East that forecast an Asian war. "The political situation is a complicated puzzle," naval attaché Charles C. Hartigan summarized from Peking in November 1929. "The Nationalist Government [Kuomintang or KMT] is experiencing its worst struggle for existence since it was established."[13]

Consistently, naval intelligence warned that China's disintegration would hasten Japanese penetration of mainland social, political, and economic life. One report noted Japan's monopoly over coal and shale oil industries in Manchuria, while another revealed the construction of fortified blockhouses along Japan's South Manchurian Railroad concession. At last, in June 1931 ONI received the long-expected news that Japanese troops were mobilizing in Manchuria. It came as no surprise when barely a year after Johnson's warning, elements of the Japanese Army under the pretext of bandit suppression seized Manchuria. Perhaps with a certain satisfaction, naval intelligence prepared "a politico-military estimate of the Manchurian situation," reminding about earlier ONI predictions. "A survey of the recent Japanese occupation of all strategic points in or near the South Manchurian Railway zone indicates that it was carried out according to a preconceived plan, and was the culmination of a series of incidents stretching back over a number of years," the ONI paper concluded in September 1931.[14]

The invasion of Manchuria shattered Hoover's dream of world disarmament—weakened already by economic crisis. Japanese aggression, the collapse of postwar treaty arrangements, and financial framework marked an end to the brief period of peace and pointed toward a future filled with danger. With the deepening depression and rising militarism, Hoover's early faith was replaced by paranoia. Enemies seemed all about, fed by greed, political ambition, and alien ideologies that were nurtured by joblessness and disillusionment with American life and values. Consequently, when unemployed veterans of World War I formed a Bonus Army and marched to Washington to lobby for relief, the president ordered them removed, acquiescing in General Douglas MacArthur's ruthless employment of tanks and bayonets to disperse what he called Communist anarchists and revolutionaries.[15]

Not surprisingly at this moment of governmental fear and overreaction, ONI became more active in domestic surveillance. Captain Hayne Ellis, who took command of ONI in June 1931 after an ineffective eleven-month tour by sickly Harry A. Baldridge, intensified the observation of reputedly radical and pacifistic groups, including Bonus Marchers, the Communist Party of America, the National Council for Prevention of War, the National Federation of Churches, and the Women's League for Peace and Freedom. Ellis mobilized every available source—especially district intelligence officers, retired officers, volunteer informants, vigilante-style societies, and professors of naval science on college campuses. Of the last, he asked those at Yale, Harvard, Georgia Tech, Northwestern, and several West Coast universities to spy on "ultra-pacifist" students and faculty. At the same moment, the DNI instructed naval district commandants to develop programs to counteract the antinavy influence of historian Charles Beard's best-selling book *The Navy: Defense or Portent?* and "insidious propaganda of a similar nature with which pacifistic organizations are flooding the country."[16]

With social unrest, suspicion, and radicalism spreading each passing month, ONI became more concerned than ever with secrecy and security. There were legitimate grounds for improving both. In January 1932, the office's head of security, Commander Walter K. Kilpatrick, informed Ellis that someone had entered Room 2722 of the Navy Department building after hours and had tampered with the lock on a confidential filing cabinet. "As secret information which might have considerable sales value is on file in the various rooms occupied by the Office of Naval Intelligence," Kilpatrick cautioned, ONI needed to improve security. In a similar fashion, the office asked the Justice Department to assist in a case where someone had attempted to purchase secret naval data from a department employee.[17]

In tightening internal security, ONI confronted the perennial riddle of how to restrict classified information when the Navy Department failed to designate exactly what constituted classified material. Despite Galbraith's endeavors in 1925 to clarify the situation, no firm rules or regulations yet governed the release of confidential or even secret data. At last confronted by worsening security leaks, CNO Pratt asked the General Board in 1932 to review the subject, even though the DNI no longer sat as an ex-officio member. Ellis, his assistant William Baggaley, and Kilpatrick represented

ONI at the hearings, where Kilpatrick explained that after surveying existing practices and interviewing bureau chiefs, he had found no departmental consensus on the definition of secret information nor on methods to secure such material. Kilpatrick recommended publishing precise instructions governing the nature of confidential and secret data. At the same session, however, Ellis testified that even this measure would not stop leaks unless the entire navy became security conscious. "The service must be indoctrinated to intelligence," the ONI director averred. "We are so prone to brag about everything we do that everybody wants to write an article or take a picture of it." The appearance of naval officers before congressional committees presented an even more dangerous breach of security, Ellis contended, because "we are too prone in these open hearings to disclose confidential matter."[18]

More important were the attempts by ONI to preserve the integrity of the Navy Department's codes and code-breaking capability. This task became urgent after Secretary of State Stimson closed Yardley's "Black Chamber," and the bitter cryptographer aired his grievances in public, revealing long-kept secrets. In January 1932 Assistant DNI Baggaley warned one naval officer not to attend Yardley's lectures and to ignore his contention that ONI and the Office of Naval Communications had made slight progress in code breaking since the first world war. "The cryptographic activity of the Navy is not a matter of discussion among Naval Officers," Baggaley warned, "and must not be referred to much less discussed among civilians." Known somewhat less than affectionately as "Bill the Bastard," Baggaley concluded that Yardley "should be hanged at the yardarm." In a similar case, Ellis warned another naval officer not to publish his account of the U.S. Navy's interception of wireless messages from the German-owned Sayville station on Long Island during the past war, because the topic was too sensitive at the moment. In addition, the DNI cabled all naval attachés, warning them that the over-use of top-grade naval codes for routine business could compromise security by giving foreign code breakers too much material to study. Finally in February 1932, Ellis sent the attachés brand new "cylindrical cipher devices" to speed encoding and decoding and improve communications security.[19]

The constant concern with security and secrecy, though, threatened to paralyze ONI rather than stop leaks. Johnson had warned earlier that with an overemphasis on secrecy "it is not hard to let the 'chipmunk' instinct work and hide [information] away under lock and key where it will never do anyone any good." Apparently just such paralysis crept into ONI by late 1931 when Baggaley hesitated to tell Captain William Satterlee Pye, head of the U.S. naval mission in Peru, which was under ONI's cognizance, anything about conditions back in Washington. "This is an uncertain world we are living in here at the present time, and there is no telling so far as the

Navy is concerned what the picture will be next year," he apologized obliquely. At the same instant, Ellis incredibly told Pye to make his own decisions without consulting ONI, because Ellis could not (or would not) take responsibility for explaining official policy toward naval missions in Peru.[20]

It was the Navy Department's request for fresh strategic information with which to revise War Plan ORANGE that gradually stirred Ellis and his crew of eighteen naval and marine officers and thirty-eight civilians to forge ahead with the intelligence business. The London naval ratio of 1930 no longer assured the U.S. Navy a 25 percent superiority in all classes of warships in the Pacific Ocean, while the Manchurian invasion clearly indicated Japan's warlike intentions. Both required a hasty rethinking of American naval strategy for the Far East and Pacific, and a simultaneous revamping of naval intelligence. Consequently, Ellis undertook the most exhaustive revision of the intelligence section of the ORANGE Plan since World War I, and by January 1932 informed one district commandant that the arrangements were 100 percent completed, except for the writing in of names to fill mobilization billets. Two months later, Ellis contacted reserve and retired naval officers for inclusion in his war slate, including former DNI Galbraith, wartime cable censor David W. Todd, and ex-naval attaché Gillis.[21]

War planning against ORANGE kept ONI too busy during 1932 to trouble about the implications of the depression for the navy. Ellis's people cooperated with commanders of forces engaged in the annual Fleet Problem, which in 1932 focused on the defense of the Hawaiian Islands and Pacific Ocean against a hostile carrier fleet. During this practice ONI mobilized West Coast DIOs to connect Fleet intelligence with the Washington center, pointing toward development of an operational intelligence and coastal information system. At the same time, Ellis ordered an aerial reconnaissance of the Aleutian Islands to search for a Japanese presence, instituted surveillance against Japanese visitors in the United States, and searched for Japanese language experts in American universities. The DNI wrote naval attaché John H. Magruder at the Hague to cooperate with Dutch informants. "I hope that through your contacts you will be able to soon be sending us something about the activities of the *Orange* in the East Indies," Ellis wrote. The director wanted most to learn about Japan's purchases and shipments of oil from the Netherlands East Indies, a certain sign of war preparations. To supplement Magruder, Ellis mobilized civilian informants with the Standard Oil Company of California to report on tanker traffic and trans-Pacific oil shipments.[22]

The post-Manchurian activity in ONI revived interest in the mandated islands once again. In January 1932 the General Board held hearings on the entire situation, inviting the testimony of Harvard University international legal expert, George Grafton Wilson. During the course of Wilson's visit, the question of Japanese control over their Pacific mandates was raised and concern expressed for lack of League of Nations inspection of the area. "There must be some funny business going on," DNI Ellis observed, "and naturally we would like to find out what it is." Like Niblack and McNamee, Ellis became obsessed with the mysterious islands and considered dispatching private yachts or a scientific expedition to the Marshalls, Carolines, and Marianas. However, Ellis proved no more successful than his predecessors in solving the riddle.[23]

Inevitably, the harder Ellis and ONI focused on War Plan ORANGE, the more convinced they became that Japan had developed a master plan or blueprint for conquest. "Unquestionably the Japanese are simply carrying out a pre-determined policy and plan," Baggaley insisted, "and nothing that the League or the United States will do will have the slightest effect." Ellis agreed, citing the so-called "Tanaka Memorial," a tract written by Baron Gi-ichi Tanaka, outlining Japanese imperial aims in East Asia as evidence of an exact time table for expansion and war. The DNI mailed his copy of the memorial to an officer at the Army War College. "I understand that our friends are working on the schedule outlined in this article," Ellis wrote. The director disagreed with Baggaley's contention that the U.S. could not respond, however. At the very least, the Hoover government could prepare for war by establishing mobilization plans and a network of informants to watch Japan. In March 1932 Ellis tried unsuccessfully to interest other branches of the government in his ideas, but the State Department explained that in peacetime it was not necessary to develop a wartime information system.[24]

Instead of preparedness, the Hoover administration pursued policies of moral sanctions, nonrecognition of any territories seized by force, and cooperation with a League of Nations investigation of the Manchurian incident. Confronted by an isolationist public, deepening economic paralysis, and reluctant philosophically to provoke hostilities, Hoover responded cautiously to international crisis. For a moment in January 1932 after Japan attacked some Chinese troops near Shanghai, the president considered stronger measures but settled at last on the dispatch of more marines and a few ships to the region in order to protect American lives and property. Perhaps the president could do no more, but to the intelligence officers in ONI, intent on war planning and monitoring danger signals, Hoover's apparent timidity and cowardice resulted from blind pacifism and refusal to recognize reality. "The coming year promises to be one of general international unrest with war threatening on every horizon," Ellis predicted, and the DNI resolved to push vigilance, war planning, and preparedness in the face of isolationist public opinion and the paralyzed, pacifistic administration. "Under such conditions," he concluded, "it behooves this office to be prepared for the storm if and when it comes by concentrating all effort on the completion of the monographs of the major powers."[25]

In updating these monographs, it became evident that "the storm" might break out in places other than Manchuria or Shanghai. Danger signals appeared everywhere that naval intelligence looked. In Italy the Caproni factory and other arms makers cranked out warplanes and weapons at a maddening pace. At the Skoda Works in Czechoslovakia, an ONI report noted that 18,000 men worked three consecutive shifts to produce trench mortars, tanks, machine guns, and munitions. Since even during peak production in World War I, Skoda employed only 12,000 laborers, the current figure seemed an ominous portent to analysts in ONI. Moreover, the office collected data on secret German rearmament in violation of the Versailles treaty, with naval attaché Corwin observing the feverish activity of German engineers and military types in the Netherlands. "To my mind they are the people to be watched," Corwin reported from The Hague, "for as they themselves say, they are the only people of all those countries in Europe in the world war who are putting that experience into a study of and the manufacture of war materials." The growth of National Socialism added urgency to the observation of German activities, and in 1932 Baggaley ordered naval attaché Kenneth G. Castleman in Berlin to finish his study of the Nazi party for ONI's German monograph. The assistant DNI instructed Castleman to contact ONI's informant with the U.S. Shipping Board in Hamburg for additional information about the National Socialists.[26]

For Hayne Ellis and the others in ONI, all information pointed unmistakably toward world war in the near future. But then that was their job, and whether during peacetime or actual fighting, those in ONI necessarily possessed a more intense, and at times narrow, understanding of world conditions. In some ways, ONI was always at war. But for other Americans in 1932, local bank failures, growing bread lines, and endemic unemployment appeared far more important than events in far-distant Manchuria, Italy, or Central Europe. Yet either way, the United States required fresh leadership to restore optimism and revive economic and military strength, and many turned for direction to the dynamic, charming, former Assistant Secretary of the Navy Franklin Delano Roosevelt.

CHAPTER SEVEN

NEW DEAL FOR NAVAL INTELLIGENCE

Roosevelt's election in 1932 revived a somnolent U.S. Navy. Skilled yachtsman and lover of ships and the sea, he seemed the ideal civilian administrator to many naval officers. As Assistant Secretary of the Navy during Wilson's presidencies, FDR hovered around navy society both in Washington and at Annapolis and cultivated the friendship of numerous young officers who by 1932 had reached senior positions in the service. Thus, new CNO William Standley had been the president's golfing partner in the years before his crippling polio attack, while future CNOs Leahy and Stark had known FDR well. More importantly, Roosevelt shared many of their basic assumptions about international affairs, military preparedness, and sea power. "Those of us who knew FDR," Standley confided, "recalled that he was a serious student of Admiral Mahan's writings, a believer in a strong Navy as our 'first line of defense,' a man with unbounded faith in the value of sea power, and that he had acquired considerable naval knowledge and experience as Assistant Secretary of the Navy." Though less effusive, other officers agreed that Roosevelt provided a favorable contrast to his Republican predecessor. "Thank goodness Mr. Roosevelt did not follow in the footsteps of pacifist Hoover," Admiral Yarnell sighed.[1]

Roosevelt was never quite as enthusiastic about a big navy as many officers believed, however, and in any case support for increased naval construction was eclipsed by more pressing needs in 1933. During the first one hundred days of his presidency, FDR's energies went toward constructing a monumental New Deal program for relief and recovery from the great depression. A responsive Congress passed legislation designed to meet emergencies confronted by nearly every segment of American society—from impoverished farmers to bankrupt business tycoons. Often hastily conceived and motivated by clever politics, nevertheless New Deal measures provided needed relief, restored faith in U.S. institutions, and engendered a forgotten optimism in the unhappy nation. Those in the naval establishment were no exception, as FDR discovered $238 million in public works emergency funds for the support of naval projects and personnel, and from time to time diverted funds to the navy under the National Industrial Recovery and other New Deal acts. Moreover, in contrast to his unpopular predecessor, Roosevelt pledged to hire additional personnel, reopen facilities, and order more ships. As evidence of his intentions to enlarge the navy, he ordered Secretary of the Navy Claude A. Swanson to have the department study new types of warships and sites for additional naval bases.[2]

Early momentum continued the following year when Congress passed a naval authorization bill introduced by Georgia Congressman Carl Vinson and Senator Trammell of Florida. FDR was quick to point out that the Vinson-Trammell Act merely outlined a possible building program for 102 ships and did not appropriate funds for actual construction. "I have to do that because I have had so many appeals from pacifist organizations which do not understand it," Roosevelt told some newspaper reporters in March 1934. Despite the president's cautious political statements in the face of continued powerful isolationist and pacifist sentiment, the Navy Department assumed correctly that the Vinson-Trammell Act marked the end of an era of naval limitations and the start of an administration commitment to bring the U.S. Fleet up at least to the strength permitted under the Washington and London naval treaties.[3]

New life surged through the entire naval establishment as it awaited additional measures from its friend in the White House. The navy seemed important once more and morale soared. Nowhere was this infectious attitude more evident than in the navy's intelligence office, singled out at once by the new president for a number of special tasks, including observation of reported Japanese mystery ships off the Central American coasts. "Let me know if O.N.I. hears anything," FDR urged the department in October 1933. Not since Theodore Roosevelt's days had a president displayed such daily interest in ONI, following its routine and operations through his aide and ONI staff officer, Lieutenant Lucien Ragonnet. He kept in touch with naval intelligence work on collecting treaty data, on the security of naval facilities and factories doing confidential naval contract work, and on attempts to gather information about Japanese islands in the Pacific. From time to time, he recommended individuals for special tasks, supporting the appointment of assistant naval attaché Roscoe Hillenkoetter as a diplomatic courier so that he could wander freely about Europe observing military conditions. "The President was delighted by the idea," Special Assistant Secretary of State William C. Bullitt observed in late 1933, "and will, I am convinced, keep this service going unless it works out badly."[4]

Not surprisingly, the Navy Department strengthened its intelligence organization with some of the most capable officers ever to serve under ONI. On 4 June 1934 popular, articulate, and aggressive Captain William

Dilworth Puleston replaced Ellis as DNI. One admiring junior officer recalled that Puleston "was a man who was the ideal planner, who, though always intolerant of stupidity and inaction, inspired his subordinates with the enthusiasm which filled him too, and showed the way to considerable achievement by his own ingenuity, energy, and devotion to duty." A student of world history and foreign relations, the new director had recently completed a visit to the Imperial Defense College in Britain and recommended the creation of a similar national war college in the United States, lecturing on the subject at the U.S. Army War College. Puleston's studies led to his publishing a major biography on Alfred T. Mahan and a monograph later on the role of sea power during World War II. But now in 1934, Puleston brought some of his ideas to the intelligence office, including a firm conviction in the value of the Naval War College's studies and estimates on the world situation and its war plans exercises. His expertise, combined with a genuine enthusiasm for the intelligence billet, led to what one intelligence officer called the greatest years in ONI's history, and to what another believed was the office's most direct period of influence over naval policy.[5]

Captain William Dilworth Puleston leaving the *Mississippi* in 1934 to assume command of ONI.

Puleston's supporting cast between June 1934 and April 1937 was impressive as well. Among the twenty-two officers in ONI's Washington headquarters were Zacharias, Arthur H. McCollum, Paul Bastedo, Samuel A. Clement, Jonas H. Ingram, John T. G. Stapler, and Maurice G. Holmes. Russell Willson, Harold Medberry Bemis, and future DNI Walter S. Anderson served as naval attachés overseas. More important still were the younger officers who learned the intelligence business under Puleston's tutelage. These included future DNI Leo Hewlett Thebaud, future central intelligence director Hillenkoetter, Assistant DNI Howard D. Bode; naval attachés Ben Wyatt and Henri H. Smith-Hutton; Fleet Intelligence Officer Edwin T. Layton; language specialists William A. Worton and Bankston T. Holcomb Jr.; and reserve intelligence officers Andrew Wylie and Al Hindmarsh.[6]

Puleston employed as well seven civilian assistant naval research analysts funded in 1935 by a $16,200 congressional appropriation. "One of the prime functions of the position is to provide continuity of experienced personnel which otherwise would be lacking due to the changes regularly made in officer personnel," CNO Standley explained. Attracted by the prospect of steady salaries in depression-era America, highly trained and qualified specialists applied for a job that in reality was that of a glorified typist and filing clerk. The original analysts included a Ph.D. from the University of Pennsylvania, a graduate of Georgetown University's Foreign Service School, the curator of a leading museum, a former postal official, and one woman—Mary S. Abernathy. Later additional funding of $10,000 under the NIRA led to the hiring of six junior clerk stenographers and translators.[7]

Along with money for fresh personnel came new funds for little details such as a telephone for the head of the Latin American desk and new furniture and bookcases. Although not plentiful by later standards, the $121,000 for the collection of information provided an encouraging contrast with that allocated by parsimonious Republican administrations during the late 1920s and early 1930s. Puleston became more liberal in doling out cash for creative projects. He sent $4,000 to the DIO in Seattle to develop counterespionage against suspected Japanese agents and other radical and subversive suspects. Another $250 went to the DIO in San Francisco to investigate foreign-owned tuna-fishing boats suspected of spying on U.S. naval maneuvers. Overseas, Puleston forwarded $650 to the naval attaché in Rome, Commander Francis Cogswell, to investigate the North African coastline for signs of naval and air bases, and $200 for an assistant naval attaché in the newly opened naval attaché office in Moscow.[8]

With additional funding and personnel, Puleston's people were prompted to pursue with uncharacteristic vigor and enthusiasm the most mundane and routine tasks. Revisions of dreary monographs filled with clippings pasted together by earlier indifferent intelligence officers proceeded rapidly. Soon these loose-leaf books became useful summaries of conditions overseas, including as always data from naval attachés, but also data from many other departments and offices of the government. "If there was anything affecting us in any way," McCollum insisted, "we got it." Thus, between 1935 and 1937 ONI published a number of important monographs covering everything from censorship methods to procedures for espionage, counterespionage, and passport control. Three publications focused on sailing directions for the Japanese mandates, revealing details on the geography, hydrography, population, and possible fortifications. The last concerned ONI most, and sailing directions for the Caroline Islands claimed that fortifications existed on Ponape, Kusaie, Truk, and Yap, while similar studies of the Mariana and Marshall Islands noted possible strongholds on Jaluit and Bikini. Meanwhile, ONI moved ahead on a monograph for the strategically vital and oil-rich Netherlands East Indies, nearly completing the study when Puleston left in April 1937.[9]

In preparing strategic data, Mahan enthusiast and war college lecturer Puleston gravitated toward the Naval War College, directing the closest collaboration between ONI and the Newport school since Mahan's own days as college president during the 1880s. The DNI corresponded frequently with current college president Admiral Edward C. Kalbfus, forwarding intelligence material to the officer and asking for advice in return to assist ONI in preparing estimates of the international situation. "I have in mind bringing up to date, for our office, tactical studies of the Japanese fleet as a fighting machine," Puleston wrote Kalbfus in February 1935, and "I know the War College has done considerable work along this line." The war college forwarded results of their work, and intelligence officer Zacharias, for one, insisted that his Far Eastern desk examine every study with considerable care and thought, especially those on economic subjects.[10]

Analysis and study led Puleston's staff away from mere compilation of facts and into the field of actual strategic projections and at times of relatively sophisticated estimations of foreign conduct. Lieutenant Commander Ward P. Davis studied the entire postwar naval treaty system within the larger framework of reparations, war debt payments, and economic depression, predicting a complete collapse. Meanwhile, Zacharias revised earlier silly estimates about Japanese inability to operate aircraft effectively from carriers at sea, while Layton prepared a study of Japanese industry and a "strategic power grid." As a result, Puleston could assure the department that not only were Japanese naval pilots efficient fliers but also were quite capable of launching predawn air strikes from their aircraft carriers. "Japanese aviators are as good and probably better than U.S. aviators in instruments and night flying," the DNI warned the CNO in late 1934.[11]

Mostly, this type of information was employed by officers on the General Board or in Operations to update War Plan ORANGE and several less compelling efforts, such as War Plan TAN for intervention in Cuba and a proposal to save Brazil from possible German or Italian aggression. At the same time congressmen and the president looked at ONI material. Puleston wanted his organization to be more than an office of static information for policy makers, however, and he forecast the later emphasis on operational intelligence by stressing the publication of tracking charts of foreign tankers, merchantmen, and warships, speed curves of latest men-of-war, and ship-recognition manuals based on the silhouettes of actual scale models. The "idea of ONI being an outfit to serve the fleet in outlying areas was a thing that was elaborated and established by Captain Puleston," intelligence officer McCollum contended. [12]

Collecting action data required novel methods, and Puleston cultivated several ingenious sources. He cooperated with the State Department in the employment of Hillenkoetter as a diplomatic courier to carry dispatches over a route connecting Berlin, Warsaw, Moscow, and Prague. The young officer's primary obligation was, of course, to accumulate information for the navy. Meantime in Asia, Puleston operated without State Department aid to establish a coast-watcher system and espionage network that included as agents Andrew Wylie, a member of the Asiatic Primate Expedition, and Al Hindmarsh, a Harvard exchange professor at the Imperial University in Tokyo. [13]

In addition, Puleston asked Marine Corps Commandant John C. Russell for the services of Chinese language officers Major Worton and Captain Charles C. Brown for "certain urgent work" in the Far East. Worton agreed to undertake a secret mission in northern China for ONI. In preparation for the clandestine (and still classified) mission, Worton resigned temporarily from the Marine Corps, assumed a fictitious identity, and traveled on a phony passport. No one except Puleston, Russell, and Standley knew about Worton's mysterious secret undertakings. "I didn't realize it at the time, but I suppose if I had been killed like Ellis," Worton recalled years afterward, ". . . my wife would never have received any benefits or anything else." [14]

While Puleston searched for novel methods to gather data, the international situation provided constant incentives to further the expansion of naval intelligence. In 1935 Fascist Italy invaded Ethiopia, and the next year Spain exploded into a civil war with most European nations providing some kind of military and economic assistance to one side or the other. Both conflicts stimulated U.S. naval intelligence operations overseas. In fact, ONI dispatched Lieutenant Colonel Pedro A. del Valle, USMC, as the sole neutral naval observer to accompany Benito Mussolini's legions into Eastern Africa. As CNO Standley observed, the Italian government made del

Valle an "extraordinary invitation to embark on vessels of the Italian Navy, an invitation rarely extended to any one." Shortly thereafter Puleston urged other personnel to observe the fighting that had just broken out on the Iberian peninsula, particularly since both the legal republican government and the rebels led by General Francisco Franco employed some of the latest weapons developed after the last world war. "The most important mission of your office at the present time," Puleston advised naval attaché Cogswell, "is the obtaining of information concerning Spain, with particular reference to the performance of aircraft, aircraft bombs, and both aircraft and anti-aircraft ordnance."[15]

While European affairs heated up, Puleston maintained ONI's focus on the potentially dangerous situation in the Far East. Though the Sino-Japanese War began two months after he left ONI, Puleston read personally all he could on the turmoil in China. During this interval, ONI compiled a detailed list of possible agents among retired naval personnel now working in the Orient as ship pilots, engineers, telegraph operators, surveyors, or for the Firestone Tire and Rubber Company in India. The DNI emphasized as well the assignment in Peking and Shanghai of assistant naval attachés who were familiar enough with the Chinese language to collect data on the possible breakdown in political and economic conditions that might encourage Japanese intervention. "In dealing with the Chinese by diplomatic and commercial methods," he predicted, "the threat of summary military action by Japan will ever loom large in the background."[16]

For a moment the lingering vision of disarmament joined the increasing tempo of violence and warfare in the mid-1930s in absorbing Puleston's energies. In 1935 the last major attempt to slow naval races and avoid confrontations occurred at the London Naval Conference. Once again ONI accumulated data for the American delegation, but unlike earlier experiences, this time naval intelligence assembled the information without the usual office tensions or any thought of deception. Years of experience, combined with Puleston's efficient staff, shaped the smooth operation, as did the understanding that Japan would terminate the Washington Treaty in 1936 anyway and demand total naval parity—thus dooming further limitations. Consequently, ONI could carry out this unpleasant duty without the fear that somehow it was undermining naval preparedness. "We have about finished our work here in connection with the disarmament conference," intelligence officer Jonas Ingram wrote in early 1935, "as the Japs themselves about ended another of our altruistic experiments by walking out to suit their convenience."[17]

Preparing data on strategy, international affairs, or for peace conferences was easy for Puleston, as he moved quickly and effortlessly through the familiar strategic side of intelligence. Not so the more difficult and strange world of security, secrecy, and surveillance, which troubled Puleston. Growing evidence that Japanese, Russian, and German secret agents were spying in the United States forced the DNI's attention in this direction even while he pursued his strategic interests. Domestic operations had never ceased during previous directorships, but secret operations within the United States, including Howell's surreptitious entry, had been individual exercises without vigorous coordination from Washington headquarters. Puleston changed this approach by laying the foundation for centralized control and instructing DIOs never to act without consulting the DNI, but at the same time he gave them a greater latitude to gather information on radicals, subversives, ultrapacifists, and Communists through surveillance "and other surreptitious methods."[18]

The DNI's interest in naval district intelligence stirred activity at the local level as it had at the Washington establishment. Puleston's promise of additional funds and clerks encouraged the DIOs further. In the Thirteenth Naval District, former ONI officer Claude B. Mayo constructed an aggressive volunteer network of informants in the Seattle area to chart supposed Japanese secret agents in the Pacific Northwest. John Downes in the Ninth Naval District and Great Lakes Training station enrolled Dan Hanna, editor of the *Cleveland News*, and other prominent midwesterners in his reserve intelligence team. More importantly, Downes created an industrial intelligence service that infiltrated every factory or firm contracting work for the navy to inform on suspected labor radicals, spies, or saboteurs who might compromise the national defense or disrupt working conditions for management through labor organizations or strikes.[19]

The well-established DIOs in San Francisco and New York City expanded as well. In the Twelfth Naval District the DIO formed units composed of six reservists in several zone intelligence systems in order to follow both Japanese espionage and the Young Communist League activities in California. At the same moment the always active Third Naval District Intelligence Office enlarged domestic pursuit under forceful new DIO Captain Wallace Benjamin Phillips and Detective Peterkin, Howell's partner in the Hoover burglary, who carded all known Japanese residing in the New York area. "This was to be used in corralling the individuals for internment or breaking down any system of espionage or sabotage which may have been contemplated by these Japanese in the event of conflict with the United States," the DIO reported. Such work took on added importance when FDR expressed his support in 1936 for locating all Japanese for possible incarceration in a "concentration camp" during a crisis.[20]

Corralling Japanese espionage did not have to wait for a conflict, however, as Puleston's office found and unmasked Japanese suspected spies as well as two former U.S. Navy men spying for Japan. Though ONI had unearthed occasional acts of espionage throughout the previous decade, serious Japanese espionage against the navy began shortly after the Manchurian incident and led to collaboration by 1935 with the militant German spy organization in the Western Hemisphere. Ellis's office had suspected that the Japanese naval attaché's office in Washington directed spy operations throughout the United States, Central America, and in the Panama Canal Zone, and had learned about the employment of Japanese-owned commercial fishing boats for spying on U.S. fleet exercises off the California coast. In response, Ellis had instituted some countermeasures—including the tailing of Japanese students believed to be Imperial Navy officers enrolled at Harvard, Yale, and several West Coast universities—and had nabbed the Japanese assistant naval attaché Yoshiro Kanamoto for photographing the naval fuel oil reserve depot at Point Loma and for sketching the North Island Naval Air Station. The latter led to his expulsion.[21]

Puleston accelerated counterespionage against Japan, assigning an eager Zacharias to unearth the ruses employed by naval attaché Tamon Yamaguchi to cover Japanese spies in the United States. The director worried especially about the so-called language students who frequented American college campuses. "The personality and movements of Japanese language officers are matters of greatest interest to this office," Puleston insisted, "because experience in the past has shown that they engage in illegal activities." In fact Lieutenant (jg) Cecil H. Coggins (MC), a young medical officer at the Naval Dispensary at Long Beach who worked for the DIO in the Eleventh Naval District, suspected that these language students were turning U.S. seamen in California, exchanging cash for secrets. Specifically, Coggins reported that a former yeoman named Harry Thomas Thompson had sold top-secret engineering, gunnery, and tactical information about the U.S. Pacific Fleet to an agent of the Japanese Imperial Government. A largely self-taught intelligence enthusiast, Coggins worked with Pacific Fleet Intelligence Officer Lieutenant Commander Joseph John Rochefort, local police, and the FBI zone office to discover Thompson's contact man, who turned out to be, as Coggins suspected, a Japanese language student and naval officer, Toshio Miyazaki. Now greatly agitated, Puleston assigned Zacharias and ONI's counterespionage man Commander Samuel Averett Clement to the case, simultaneously dispatching McCollum to the Branch Hydrographic Office in San Pedro to provide liaison. Finally, the office's first true counterespionage operation led to Miyazaki's flight and to Thompson's arrest by the FBI, conviction under the Espionage Act of 1917, and imprisonment at the McNeil Island Federal Penitentiary.[22]

Puleston's greatest feat as spy catcher occurred by accident, when in the process of routinely investigating a missing confidential manual, he turned up unusual spending by former naval officer John Semer Farnsworth. Cashiered from the U.S. Navy in 1926 for begging money from enlisted personnel to support his high-living wife, Farnsworth reappeared suddenly

Extensive ONI surveillance against former naval officer John Semer Farnsworth (seen above in his naval academy yearbook photo) led to his arrest and conviction in 1937 on espionage charges, and convinced DNI Puleston to pursue domestic intelligence more vigorously.

around naval circles carrying pockets full of crisp, new, high-denomination bills. Naturally, the alert Puleston launched an investigation, which revealed that the Naval Academy graduate had been visiting old classmates and naval friends still on active duty, asking about new warship design, weapons, and tactics and casually borrowing code and signal books, blueprints, maps, and other secret and confidential Navy Department material. Though as yet unaware of his real motives, the director warned all bureaus and offices about Farnsworth's practice of calling on old shipmates and asking too many questions.[23]

Months of painstaking surveillance by both ONI and FBI failed to reveal anything, however. But the pressure on Farnsworth, who was indeed selling secrets to Japanese agents, caused him to panic. Drinking heavily, the traitorous ex-U.S. Navy officer spilled his tale of espionage to a local columnist, insisting that he was really a double agent. The journalist turned the unprincipled Farnsworth over to the government. For his spying, Farnsworth was convicted on 26 February 1937 of unlawfully disclosing information affecting the national defense to a representative of a foreign nation in violation of federal statute and was sentenced to a term of from four to twelve years in the Atlanta Federal Prison.[24]

During the Thompson and Farnsworth episodes, Puleston worried also about reports from San Diego, possibly from Lieutenant Coggins, that Japanese-American fishermen were really trained naval officers on active duty with the Imperial Japanese Navy. Allegedly, one Japanese diver had disappeared under the hulls of U.S. warships anchored in the harbor. Moreover, evidence suggested suspicious activity down the coast at Guaymas, Mexico, where Japanese fishing craft stopped often to visit a local bottling plant suspected of being a radio direction-finding station. Apparently reports convinced SecNav Swanson who told Secretary of State Cordell Hull on 19 January 1935 that Navy Department files showed conclusively that Japanese fishing vessels spied on the U.S. fleet. Perhaps Puleston made such a report to Swanson, but in a letter to the commandant of the Eleventh Naval District that same day, the DNI expressed a far less dogmatic interpretation of reports supplied by naval intelligence people in California. "While the information contained therein pertains only to the routine fishing operations of the vessels concerned," Puleston observed, "it is useful and valuable at this time in that it furnishes certain negative information, pending the results of further investigation of the activities of these vessels which should be undertaken to establish definitely whether or not these vessels are in any way directly or indirectly engaged in Orange intelligence activities." Nevertheless, he recommended that the Joint Army and Navy Board study the question more thoroughly and also favored legislation to restrict the operation of alien-owned fishing craft in U.S. waters.[25]

Puleston turned next to the question of plant security, an ONI duty neglected since the vigorous program pursued by DNI Welles in World War I. Encouraged by the Roosevelt administration to expand this line of work to keep pace with the increase in naval contracts with private factories, in October 1934 Puleston ordered all Inspectors of Naval Material to guard against foreign agents, who under the cover of foreign buyers hoped to take a peek at confidential defense equipment. The director encouraged as well the expansion of the industrial intelligence service so that patriotic informers and reserve intelligence officers would report all signs of radical or subversive action or labor unrest, and potential cases of sabotage and espionage. The DNI worked intimately with ardent anti-Communist businessmen and industrialists, such as the president of the Bendix Aviation Corporation, to coordinate measures for plant protection, anti-labor and anti-Communist propaganda.[26]

District personnel contributed to plant security, but with varying degrees of success. The DIO in the Fourth Naval District forwarded thor-

ough reports about Italian, Chinese, Russian, Dutch, and German visitors
to the Baldwin Locomotive works in Philadelphia and the Electric Storage
Battery Company and Radio Corporation of America factory across the
Delaware River in Camden, New Jersey. But district agents in San Diego
made a more casual observation of visitors to the Consolidated Aircraft
Corporation plant, reporting that Asians of "doubtful nationality were
observed in the crowd."[27]

Plant security, spy hunting, and domestic surveillance generally
brought ONI into close contact with other branches of federal and local
government. Puleston cooperated intimately with J. Edgar Hoover of the
Federal Bureau of Investigation in compiling lists of foreign-born employees at defense plants, fingerprinting people working on naval contracts,
and exchanging information on suspected radicals and subversives, especially alleged Japanese agitators among nonwhite Americans. The two
governmental security leaders established a regular program whereby ONI
personnel could attend the FBI training course for investigative officers,
and in October 1936 Puleston sent Commander Herman Edward Keisker,
USNR, over as the first ONI student.[28]

Puleston sought closer ties with both the War and State Departments,
urging naval attachés to develop a harmonious relationship with their
military counterparts and suggesting periodic attaché conferences to discuss common problems. "We are at present developing our relationship
with the Military Intelligence Division with the object of making the
alliance very close indeed," Puleston wrote naval attaché Laurance McNair
in Rome. The director moved more cautiously in overtures to the per-
petually aloof State Department, especially since they had rebuffed him in
his efforts to develop a joint espionage network in East Asia. In 1936 he
inquired about possible ONI participation in a radio broadcasting program
that sent information overseas, which the Office of Naval Communications
ran for the State Department. Puleston explained that his interest stemmed
from ONI's responsibility to spread the navy's "point of view" abroad in
times of strained relations. Aware of probable objections to interference in
the diplomatic business, he defended his proposal. "Personally, I think the
Navy Department could very well assist the State Department in this
matter to the advantage of both Departments."[29]

Despite Puleston's appeal, no one in the diplomatic branch found closer
cooperation with naval intelligence very urgent in implementing the current peaceful and neutral foreign policies of the United States. Even the
initial positive reception by MID faded. As Puleston wrote McNair, "A
real combination of the two services cannot now be effected." Nevertheless,
he envisaged a unified American intelligence agency for the future and
made some movement in this direction, foreseeing the attempts in 1938 to
make ONI, MID, and the FBI the three agencies responsible for all

intelligence. Puleston's contacts with other intelligence organizations evolved naturally from his early work as DNI, which between 1934 and early 1937 promised to make ONI a dynamic and influential part of the naval bureaucracy. Puleston's leadership abilities overshadowed those of his predecessors in the desolate Hoover years. ONI personnel were of high quality, their intelligence product sound, and their morale and enthusiasm genuine.[30]

Because of the undoubted success and élan of the Puleston years, however, the achievements of ONI during the preceding decade were partially eclipsed, somewhat the way FDR's charisma and public relations efforts obscured the fact that at times he recast programs conceived by Hoover to meet the depression crisis—most notably the Reconstruction Finance Corporation. Puleston operated in the enriched atmosphere of the early New Deal; he had the promises of more money and added incentives from both the administration and the Navy Department to pursue intelligence duty. Naval intelligence directors Johnson and Ellis were not so fortunate. In fact, Puleston carried out and at times dressed up the many measures already set in motion during the first days of the depression—such as improved war planning, lists of informants, revived district intelligence, and streamlined procedures. Puleston fleshed out these programs, improved others, and added his own personal style and flair, but ultimately he built upon the framework provided by his less-publicized colleagues Johnson and Ellis. Like FDR's early legislative program, Puleston's new deal for naval intelligence soon ran into problems and slowed down, as his very success as an intelligence director now dragged ONI into the most severe and frustrating confrontation yet with the U.S. Navy's intelligence dilemma and thrust him into a relentless pursuit of domestic enemies, radicals, and subversives.

CHAPTER EIGHT

IN PURSUIT OF
DOMESTIC ENEMIES

Shortly before Puleston entered ONI, the then DNI Ellis had warned him about the complications and frustrations of the naval intelligence business. "We are doing our best with this office to try to preserve the few remaining secrets we possess," he explained in January 1934. "Only over our dead body will [the] Society of Naval Engineers publish complete information on any more trial trips," Ellis told Puleston. "Puley, when you sit here in ONI you will see our viewpoint." That viewpoint derived from ONI's conviction that only that office took the threats of espionage, sabotage, or subversion against the U.S. Navy seriously, and hence needed to become the agency to combat the navy's enemies whether at home or abroad. Indeed, security leaks, ill-defined and poorly enforced control measures, and unauthorized handouts of confidential data confronted Puleston. Despite the installation of better locks on filing cabinets, beefed up marine guards, and improved surveillance during Ellis's tenure, security deteriorated continually. Top secret data disappeared at an alarming pace, including a complete set of blueprints from the navy's experimental XF3F2 aircraft and even a copy of War Plan ORANGE.[1]

Naval codes were compromised, too. Naval attaché Commander Thomas M. Shock in Peking warned that "certain agencies were listening in on our traffic. One cannot be too careful in communicating." Similar problems appeared in Rome and within the district intelligence organizations at home where an administrative cipher employed exclusively for reports on persons under surveillance had been compromised by unknown parties. "Because of this fact and as a replacement," Stapler cabled one DIO, "the Code and Signal Section has devised a special intelligence code for use between the Division of Naval Intelligence of the Navy Department and the District Intelligence Officers." The breakdown in the integrity of confidential naval communications became more critical still when a fight between ONI and the Office of Naval Communications erupted over which bureau held cognizance for communications security, nearly paralyzing the entire system and forcing Puleston to ask the CNO to intervene and restore peace.[2]

Roosevelt's foreign policies promoted other security leaks. Shortly before Puleston became DNI, Roosevelt and Soviet Commissar of Foreign Affairs Maxim Litvinov had negotiated U.S. recognition of Josef Stalin's Communist regime, opening formal Russian-American diplomatic relations for the first time since World War I. Partly because he lacked confidence in the State Department, FDR expected the navy to set up some of the embassy machinery in Moscow, especially a radio transmission station and a naval attaché office to facilitate the exchange of information. Naturally, responsibility rested with ONI, and the office frantically searched for someone competent in the Russian language to head the naval mission. After rejecting Lieutenant Commander William J. C. Agnew, ONI selected Captain David Rowen Nimmer, USMC, one of the handful of U.S. officers stationed in Harbin since April 1930 to study the Russian language.[3]

By May 1934 Nimmer had sailed for Moscow with six assistants, including a radio code expert, store clerk, and several secretaries. On the 16th Nimmer registered his cable address ALUSNA Moscow and contacted A. I. Gekker, Chief of Foreign Liaison Section of the People's Commissariat for Defence of the U.S.S.R. Meanwhile, Puleston had taken over in Washington and routinely dispatched orders to Nimmer to forward information on Russian ships, diesel engine development, and chemical warfare. But Nimmer's response surprised Puleston. "As general practice," the attaché answered, "because of peculiar mental quirks amongst Russian officials, it was thought best, for the time being at any rate, to avoid seeking information directly from the Russian Admiralty as for every question put to them they would put twenty to us." In dealing with the Russians, the Marine Corps officer complained, "the complete accomplishment of any single item of business is de-energizing to say the least."[4]

Puleston discovered exactly what Nimmer meant when he met Russian naval attaché to Washington, Paul Yurevitch Oras, and his assistant, Alexander M. Yakimichev. The overbearing Soviet officers demanded free access to U.S. Navy yards, ships, bases, and civilian factories producing defense material. They wanted to see the Naval Air Station in San Diego. They wanted blueprints of the fast new battleship, the *North Carolina*. They wanted specifications on the aircraft carrier *Saratoga*. Like their comrades five decades later the Russians eagerly sought knowledge of every detail of U.S. technology and military developments. In June 1934, Oras, Yakimichev, and a Mr. Sokoloff of the notorious Amtorg Trading Corporation, the Russian cover for industrial and military espionage in the United States, invaded the Norfolk Navy Yard, demanding a limousine to travel around the facility. They wanted to see everything. The base intelligence officer informed ONI that the Russians were extremely rude and contentious.[5]

What could Puleston do? Personally, he considered the Russian attachés nothing more than agents of expansionist "Slavism" intent upon conquering the world. He felt duty bound to deny them anything of value for the modernization of the Soviet war machine. But on the other hand, Roosevelt advocated friendly relations with the Soviet Union, including the sale of American machinery and aircraft to the Russians. Consequently, Puleston decided to place tiny obstacles in the way of the Russians, advising the commanding officer of the *Saratoga* to hustle the visitors through the warship in a friendly but rapid manner so that they would see nothing. Despite his best efforts, however, the DNI failed to stop the Soviet agents from obtaining most all of the information they went after. CNO Standley described their success. "Russian attachés, military, naval, and commercial, picked up everything—copies of all technical and trade magazines and military and naval professional magazines, blueprints, and everything from nuts and bolts to washing machines, tractors and combine harvesters."[6]

Unhappy that his government was giving away so much and receiving so little in return, Puleston resolved to supplement Nimmer's sparse data. Seizing upon the visit of the cruiser *Indianapolis* to Russia, the DNI asked her intelligence officer to visit Leningrad and gain an impression of the Soviet government's stability, food supply, unemployment, and information on railroads and military facilities. Attempts to spread propaganda among the cruiser's crew while in the Communist harbor interested the director as well. In a related action, Puleston determined to pull language officers out of Harbin, which he considered too remote for an adequate training program, and after rejecting Tallinn in Estonia and Bucharest as alternate sites, he relocated Lieutenant Kemp Tolley in Riga, Latvia, in 1935. "Riga, especially due to the fact that the preponderance of the population is Russian or Russian speaking, and the social life there is Russian in character, as well as the fact that it is the focal point for intelligence on the U.S.S.R., Poland and Central Europe," he reflected, "makes it the most desirable of the available places for Russian language instruction."[7]

Clearly Puleston hoped the language officers in Riga would collect information about the Soviet Union and vicinity. At least junior lieutenants Harry Edward Seidel Jr., Samuel B. Frankel, and George F. Schultz, who began the two year language course in Latvia in 1936, considered such undertakings nearly as important as the departmental directive to translate the Soviet Navy's sailor's manual. Their espionage brought a State Department complaint, however, that the naval officers complicated the delicate process of normalization of Soviet-American diplomatic relations. Already the Russians had accused U.S. legation staffers of spying across the border, Minister Arthur Bliss Lane informed Washington. "Our efforts to show that the contrary is the case are not enhanced by independent investigating activities on the part of these young officers, the discretion of at least one of whom is seriously open to question," Lane insisted. Such complaints unhappily forced Puleston's office to order the trio to stop "your extraneous activities of an 'intelligence' nature," and to confine all energies to the study of Russian.[8]

The State Department interfered in other Puleston plans to collect data and secure information, especially by rigidly interpreting the Neutrality Act of 1935, which had passed hastily through the isolationist U.S. Congress on the eve of the Italo-Ethiopian War. The act prohibited export of arms and munitions to belligerents and forbade American citizens to travel on belligerent vessels. But like most such measures, the law of 1935 was ambiguous and State Department opinion sometimes differed from that of the navy. This was most evident in the case of the sale of weapons to foreign buyers. When the State Department issued an export license for the Douglas Aircraft Corporation DF Flying Boat to the Soviet Union, both military branches objected and claimed that the sale was illegal under the Neutrality Act. In response, the State Department contended that the transaction fell under the Aircraft Procurement Act of 1927. Finally FDR ordered the squabbling branches of government to establish a common policy in handling requests for the release for sale of defense material, but while the bureaucrats ironed out details, Puleston blocked the release of information. "Until such a decision is reached," he advised the department, "the Navy Department, through the courtesy of the State Department, can protect itself by refusing to release any military or naval developments to any foreign country."[9]

Puleston became more concerned about neutrality obstructions when he dispatched personnel overseas as war observers. Ever since its creation in 1882, ONI had sent naval officers to foreign battle fronts to collect information for the Navy Department, and Puleston considered current fighting in Ethiopia just another opportunity to study weapons and tactics, not an issue of neutrality. It was frustrating, then, to have the warring Italian government accept del Valle as the sole foreign observer on the East African front, only to have the legalistic State Department oppose it as a potential violation of American neutrality law. More disconcerting was the State Department discovery that ONI had secretly slipped aeronautical expert and assistant naval attaché in London, Lieutenant Commander Leslie Clark Stevens, down to Cairo with the Royal Air Force observation team. U.S. Minister Bert Fish complained to Washington, and the navy had to withdraw its man and apologize for the diplomatic oversight.[10]

Similar impediments surrounded plans to gather data from the Spanish Civil War zones, a rich field of technological developments. Backed by the lastest weaponry and money, and troops supplied by Mussolini and Hitler, General Franco led a revolt against the legal Republican government in Madrid, which was aided primarily by equipment and volunteers from Soviet Russia. The confrontation between the two bitter ideological and totalitarian opponents promised to lead to wider conflict, and Puleston wanted agents near the fighting to check the new tanks, dive bombers, artillery, and warships. He held del Valle in readiness for the same invitation from the Italians to accompany their forces into Spain that they had previously extended for Africa. At the same time ONI assigned aircraft expert Commander James M. Shoemaker as assistant naval attaché to Paris, Madrid, and Lisbon so that he would be available at a moment's notice to visit the war zone. Such an invitation arrived from Franco's forces. "I believe that Commander Shoemaker can obtain much valuable information from a visit of this nature," Ambassador Bullitt cabled from Paris, "but I realize that other considerations may be overriding and I should appreciate it if the [State] Department will telegraph me at once its views."[11]

As both Bullitt and ONI expected, Washington's response reflected the administration's views on neutrality and its fear of entanglement. "Commander Shoemaker should therefore take no action with regard to the invitation of the insurgent authorities," the State Department wired in January 1937. Undiscouraged, Bullitt, who operated from time to time as one of FDR's most confidential secret informants, urged Secretary of State Hull to allow Shoemaker to tour Spain as a private citizen in civilian dress. Bullitt knew that the officer and fellow assistant naval attaché Commander Theodore E. Chandler had slipped across the French border by motor car and had visited Valencia and Madrid, probably meeting secretly with insurgent officials. However, Hull's terse reply "No!" to Bullitt's suggestion that Shoemaker travel unofficially to Spain most likely ended further adventures.[12]

While ONI confronted obstacles from U.S. policies overseas between 1934 and 1937, troubles with isolationist and neutral conduct confronted Puleston's office back in the United States as well. Convinced that munitions makers, shipbuilders, and navalists conspired to entangle the U.S. in overseas conflicts, isolationist Senator Gerald P. Nye of North Dakota launched a senatorial investigation in 1934. Nye proposed to discredit proponents of a large navy, crusading for the regulation of the American shipbuilding industry, which hired unsavory lobbyists such as Shearer, and entreating Congress to establish taxes against war materials, which would put arms makers out of business. Thus the "agrarian liberal" from the isolationist Midwest and his chief investigator, Stephen B. Raushenbush, searched for damaging evidence of conspiracy everywhere, including in the U.S. Office of Naval Intelligence. Politely, Puleston informed the Nye Committee that he could not cooperate since ONI business was too confidential for public airing, but when the senator persisted, he launched his own counterinvestigation in an attempt to prove that an alliance existed between the Nye Committee and Communists.[13]

Puleston learned that isolationist senators and neutral diplomats were not the only obstacles confronting naval intelligence. Sadly, his own Navy Department approached the questions of security, secrecy, and counterespionage with an attitude ranging from cautious support to outright disdain. While Secretary Swanson had reaffirmed ONI's responsibility for security in the fleet, shore establishment, and defense plants, the department neither defined regulations clearly nor gave ONI power to enforce policy. For a time Puleston attempted to centralize and coordinate security from his Washington office, but effective programs depended entirely upon the good will or cooperation of commanding officers, naval inspectors, local police, district organizations, and civilian factory owners. In some cases the DNI received full cooperation, such as the tracking and trapping of the traitorous Thompson, but in the pursuit of a spy who stole secrets from the Naval Torpedo Station at Newport, the hostile commanding officer refused to cooperate with ONI's "amateur sleuthing."[14]

From ONI's perspective, the greatest hindrance within the department arose from decisions and recommendations made by the Judge Advocate General's office (JAG). In a series of opinions during Puleston's tour, the JAG blocked measures to strengthen naval intelligence, especially the counterespionage or B Section. The navy's legal branch advised ONI against lobbying for legislation leading to the registration and restriction of alien-owned fishing vessels, laws to bar public photography in and around naval bases, and it vetoed an attempt to secure power for ONI detectives to arrest suspects. And JAG rendered the decision that it was illegal under congressional appropriation acts for the State Department to pay for the maintenance of Hillenkoetter as a diplomatic courier.[15]

While differences in opinion and interpretation of policy might be understandable from other segments of the bureaucracy and department, Puleston could never quite reconcile the factions in his own naval intelligence service, some of which he created by vigorous recruitment and revitalization of district personnel. He reined in one enthusiastic DIO who issued police badges to naval investigators in violation of regulations, suggesting that identification cards were sufficient. In another case Ninth District Commandant Downes refused to cooperate with Puleston's efforts at centralization, objecting vigorously when the DNI asked him to close all zone intelligence offices except those in Chicago, Columbus, and Omaha, leaving the rest to Army investigators. "I fail to see why it should be considered that the Army has paramount interest in the interior areas of the country in this particular matter," the admiral asserted, and tossed about the names of some influential midwestern political and business figures who would cease to work as naval intelligence volunteers if these zones closed. Meanwhile, Third District intelligence officer Julian H. Collins warned that politics entered into the recruitment of reserve intelligence personnel in the New York area, asking Puleston to slow the expansion of the DIO in order to avoid all the political pressure to fill mobilization billets.[16]

Ironically, while expansion caused tensions, simultaneous shortages of personnel plagued Puleston as well. Despite additional research analysts, naval officers with intelligence experience, and aggressive district personnel, the ONI staff of twenty-two naval officers seemed barely adequate for routine business. Worse still, the relentless promotion and selection process threatened to deprive Puleston of top ONI planner Commander Frank Davis Pryor, who reached mandatory retirement age after being passed over for promotion—a problem the DNI confronted himself when passed over for flag rank for the last time in 1936. Nowhere was the personnel problem more serious than in Puleston's inability to recruit a language expert to translate and decipher Japanese messages and documents for ONI. By late 1936, staff officer Stapler admitted to DIO Commander Alfred Thomas Clay in San Francisco that ONI had failed to find a single expert proficient in Japanese, recommending that if the intelligence officer needed material translated he should consult Dr. Haworth, the octogenarian former translator believed living somewhere in the Bay area.[17]

As always, shortages reflected budgetary restraint, made more serious this time because promised funds had led Puleston to make extravagant budgetary projections of $800,000 for fiscal year 1936. Such a wild peacetime estimate received support neither in the department nor Congress, where a house subcommittee urged Puleston to save money by hiring retired officers rather than civilian analysts. In fact, ONI's budget for maintaining naval attachés and collecting information overseas fell from $121,000 in 1934 to $92,000 for 1935, forcing the termination of offices in Moscow and The Hague, and paring down clerical staffs in London, Paris, and Tokyo. The suddenly impoverished director lacked even loose change to purchase a new typewriter for one attaché, and gradually his dreams of expanding and sustaining a great naval intelligence organization capable of simultaneously fulfilling its strategic and security functions, both foreign and domestic, faded. "In effect the organization of the division is now very much skeletonized," he lamented. "In the foreign intelligence units one officer is assigned as many as twenty-two countries."[18]

An uncharacteristic note of pessimism appeared in Puleston's correspondence about ONI, reflecting both his disappointment with lack of support for ONI and perhaps his own personal chagrin at being passed over for flag rank. His good friend Admiral Yarnell feared some reaction. "I know what a blow it is to you and Marion," he consoled Puleston in January 1936, "but I also know that you both have too much good judgment and too sound a philosophy of life to let it embitter you." Maybe Yarnell was right. But after the selection board's decision, Puleston began to immerse himself more deeply in private research for his Mahan biography. And while not neglecting his intelligence duty, he started becoming more selective, narrowing his focus on domestic rather than international questions. Perhaps because strategy came so easily to Puleston, he let this side of his job slide in favor of the other; more likely, once he concentrated on the internal security job, it was only a matter of time before he became entangled in the American intelligence dilemma.[19]

Nevertheless, given the growing activities of political radicals and extremists in the United States during his tenure, the director's pursuit of the internal enemy was predictable. Political extremism reached epidemic proportions by the mid-1930s, feeding on the lingering depression, which defied all New Deal efforts to bring about complete economic and psychological recovery. Though still immensely popular, Roosevelt drew sharp criticism from both the left and right wings of the political spectrum for his failure to discover a solution to the nation's social and economic ills. Variously inspired by the European examples of Hitler, Mussolini, or Stalin, native demagogues and would-be dictators appeared everywhere with simple formulas for recovery, advocating totalitarian methods and spreading messages of racism, anti-Semitism, and hatred. William Dudley Pelley and his Nazi-mimicking Silver Shirts promoted violent attacks on Jews; radio preacher Charles E. Coughlin praised Fascism and slandered FDR; American Communist Earl Browder called for the overthrow of decadent capitalism; and Governor Huey Long simply closed Louisiana's borders to outsiders and established a vicious private police state. Desolately, Roosevelt wrote his friend Breckinridge Long, ambassador to Mussolini's Italy: "We, too, are going through a bad case of Huey Long and Father Coughlin influenza—the whole country aching in every bone."[20]

As long as these American extremists remained ideologically diverse and fragmented politically, they posed a pestiferous but minor threat to the democratic process. Potential danger existed, though. Journalist Raymond Gram Swing warned that extremists were forerunners of American Fascism, while liberal novelist Sinclair Lewis predicted in his best-seller *It Can't Happen Here* that the rise to power of an American dictator like Hitler could indeed happen in the United States. Swing noted another danger. If the U.S. government and those who wished to protect free democratic institutions resorted to nondemocratic methods to counteract extremism, they might destroy that very freedom and promote radical ideologies. Referring to Mussolini's black-shirted legions, Swing concluded that when patriotism "dons the Black Shirt," democracy was doomed.[21]

In a way, Swing's observation reflected the dilemma confronted by naval intelligence in the mid-thirties. Pledged to protect the laws and freedoms under the U.S. Constitution and at the same time to defend the nation against its enemies, the officers in Puleston's organization almost donned the black shirt in their program of domestic surveillance. Indiscriminately they accumulated data on a wide variety of individuals and organizations without regard to their potential as a real menace either to the United States or the naval establishment. As Puleston directed in 1934, ONI needed the latest information on any and all patriotic, pacifistic, subversive, radical, or suspect groups and individuals in order to "aid materially in building up the records maintained in the Office of Naval Intelligence." When such data filtered into the office from district intelligence, volunteer informants, the FBI, or other sources, Section B filed them in alphabetical order rather than by philosophical, ideological, geographic, or potential-threat categories. Thus, one bulging file contained a series of diverse and unrelated organizations—including the Blue Shirts, Bonus Marchers, Boy Scouts of Haiti, Carnegie Endowment for International Peace, Crispus Attucks Press Association, and the Ex-Serviceman's League.[22]

The makeshift nature of naval intelligence's filing system for domestic radicals, extremists, or political factions was to be expected. Outside of steps to gather data on Japanese and Communist agents in America, the office had not paid much attention to other types of alleged troublemakers. ONI had neither money, skill, nor interest in such matters and possessed no investigative doctrine or trained detective staff to deal with a large-scale observation of domestic radicals. Only the DIOs in New York, San Francisco, and to a lesser extent in Seattle and Chicago contained small investigative units. Consequently, when Puleston launched an all-out war against domestic radicals in 1934, he turned for assistance to reservists, volunteers, private detectives, vigilante groups, and ultra-patriots.

As early as 1932, naval intelligence in the Thirteenth Naval District had fallen under the spell of a super-patriotic vigilante group headed by a reserve lieutenant named Friedlander. Called the American Vigilantes, it organized navy and army reservists, local policemen, and patriotic reformers into an investigative team for the DIO. Though a private organization, the Vigilantes formed along official naval district intelligence mobilization plans and became inseparable from the regular operation. But its primary purpose was to suppress dissent. "The organization was originally formed for the specific purpose of breaking up the control the Communists had gained in the Unemployed Citizen's League," Friedlander explained, and now the Vigilantes would work for the navy to investigate the spread of Communism in the Seattle area. The following year another patriotic naval reserve lieutenant, Lloyd A. Kohler, volunteered to infiltrate for ONI the local Reforestation Camps in the Ninth Naval District, reportedly centers for Young Communist League propaganda among Negro youth. Acting DNI Joseph Vance Ogan hesitated, then refused to employ the volunteer. "While any information as to the objectives or underlying aims of the Radical element in this country is always of interest," Ogan admitted, "this office does not at present desire to request that officers of the Naval Reserve enroll for reforestation work." But then he added: "There is of course no objection to their doing so."[23]

Unwilling to discourage the eager reservist, Ogan nevertheless shared the attitude of earlier naval intelligence officers who doubted that ONI should dabble in such non-naval matters. Niblack had told the State Department in 1920 that ONI kept no such files, while DNIs Johnson and Harry Baldridge had dismissed as unimportant DIO reports about Communist agitation among U.S. sailors in Philadelphia and on the West Coast. Of course, Johnson had not discouraged Howell's burglary of Communist Party headquarters in New York City. As late as 1931 when American businessman Thomas D. Campbell, just returned from a trip to Soviet Russia, discussed the Communist threat with Acting Director William Baggaley, he found the intelligence officer indifferent. "It is evident that neither the Army nor the Navy Department is much concerned over the propaganda in this country yet," Campbell wrote a friend in April.[24]

This approach changed during Puleston's years as DNI. The director did not like Communists, Communist sympathizers, or fellow travelers of any description. Whether this aversion arose from his historical interpretation that creeping Slavism had replaced Teutonism as the world's greatest menace, or whether it stemmed from discussions with strongly anti-Communist friends such as Admiral Yarnell, Puleston's anti-Communism became an obsession between 1934 and 1937. Certainly, unsatisfactory relations with the obnoxious Russian naval attachés and the failure of his own people in Moscow to achieve anything of value added to his chagrin. But the most important influence lay in the director's cooperation with anti-Communist groups, especially the Board of the American Coalition of Patriotic Education, the Daughters of the American Revolution, and the Industrial Association of San Francisco.[25]

Most intimate relationships developed between ONI and an anti-Communist organization founded in 1934 by aging Pittsburgh investment banker and former naval reserve intelligence officer Horatio Garrott Dohrman. In April Dohrman had contacted the Washington office, expressing his concern for the growing wave of radicalism in the United States and proposing to revive a volunteer intelligence network formed during the First World War to counteract possible sabotage against naval property. ONI accepted his "generous and patriotic offer," promising to pay for postage on mail that enclosed data about radicals; in response, Dohrman asked friends in industry to collect fingerprints and photographs of potential troublemakers. Next he rented an obscure office with an unlisted telephone. "Everything in this office will be coded and the office code, in turn, governed by the master code," he confided to ONI.[26]

Apparently, the self-styled secret agent failed to cover up his operations, since a few weeks after they were organized FBI Director Hoover informed ONI that his agents had unearthed mysterious activities by a fellow named Dohrman. Hoover wondered if ONI had ever heard of him. The naval intelligence office ignored the FBI inquiries, however, considering the information now arriving from their new volunteer too valuable to share with the civilian investigative agency. "In addition to your reports of Communist activities in the vicinity of plants where naval work is in progress," Acting Director Stapler commended, "this office greatly appreciates such reports as the one you have enclosed giving the 'Educational Plan of the Waukegan Convention of Section 3 of the Communist Party'."[27]

Puleston encouraged further expansion of this private intelligence service, and the patriotic banker responded by enrolling in his organization sixty-two volunteers scattered throughout important industrial centers. Dohrman's group boasted a former national commander of the American Legion, a Catholic bishop, a midwestern governor, several police commissioners, prominent businessmen, several lawyers, and a few old World War I veterans. "Many of them were associated with me before and all are men of mature judgment, not at all inclined to go off at half-cock on any subject," he assured Puleston. They were inclined to suppress dissident opinions and labor strikes, though. "Locally, [I] have the Legion boys all up on their toes on the alert to scotch any unseemly and dangerous manifestations of radicalism," Dohrman told the DNI. At the same time, the patriotic volunteer personally infiltrated a meeting of the American League Against War and Fascism held at the Pittsburgh YMHA, where he jotted down names and license plate numbers for his "loose leaf ledger of the reds" and plotted the meeting on his "trouble map." Next, operating under cover as a nondescript Federal Housing Administration agent, Dohrman journeyed through western Pennsylvania spying on coal miners for signs of radicalism and labor unrest.[28]

Studying information supplied by the likes of Dohrman, Puleston decided that Communism permeated every aspect of American life, underlay labor strikes, backed civil rights gatherings and antiwar protest and motivated every liberal reform and political protest. In November 1934, Puleston advised Standley that no American remained safe from the Communist conspiracy, which bored into literature, movies, and stage plays. Even the school system was threatened according to the DNI, since Soviet agents from Mexico had allegedly infiltrated a Philadelphia educational convention "to interest teachers in the United States of Communistic teachings." A

Communist plot lay behind criticism of Roosevelt's New Deal and naval policies, Puleston insisted, and when anti-imperialist historian Charles Beard wrote the president to protest against a more aggressive administration naval policy, the DNI branded him as a dangerous radical. Similarly, when pacifists Sherwood Eddy, Frederick J. Libby, and Bishop Francis J. McConnell signed a letter protesting U.S. fleet maneuvers, Puleston added their names to a growing ONI list of domestic subversives. After Dorothy Detzer of the Women's International League for Peace and Freedom visited the White House with other peace workers to plead for an end to naval expansion, the busy DNI singled her out as one who promoted the same objectives as the Communists. And finally, the director labeled as radical American Civil Liberties Chairman Harry F. Ward and pacifists Robert Morse Lovett, J. B. Matthews, and Winifried Chappell. "It is safe to say that there was a militant 'united front' opposing the Fleet Maneuvers [of 1935]," Puleston informed the CNO, "and that it was wholly inspired by the Communist, radical-pacifist movement in the United States."[29]

Puleston turned next to Senator Nye's Special Committee Investigating the Munitions Industry after it released reports critical of naval expansion. Certain that Communists had infiltrated the Nye Committee, the DNI searched for evidence. Seemingly, committee investigator Raushenbush provided the link, because he advocated liberal causes, opposed the reserve officer training corps (ROTC) on college campuses, belonged to the ACLU, and numbered among his inner circle of friends socialist-pacifists Norman Thomas, Scott Nearing, and Kirby Page. Such information was enough to convince the DNI that Raushenbush was a Communist plant, and he asked Dohrman to collect damaging evidence for Puleston's use. Obediently, the volunteer photostated Raushenbush's confidential bank account and other personal materials. After sorting out the details, Puleston informed Assistant Secretary of the Navy Henry L. Roosevelt that Raushenbush directed a Communist conspiracy. "I might be so bold as to even suggest that the Nye investigation is Communist inspired and Pacifist operated and that the Munitions Investigation is merely a smoke screen under the cover of which the minds of the people of the United States may be poisoned against the National Defense, and that Mr. Raushenbush was purposely placed where he is by subversive activities," Puleston declared categorically.[30] (Underlined in original.)

Now searching relentlessly for Communists, the determined DNI focused next on revolutionary disturbances in Cuba. Based largely on data received from the Third Naval District and informants on the Caribbean island, Puleston claimed that Cuba had become the Communist nerve center in the Western Hemisphere, where Soviet agents arrived to disappear "among the students, among the colored people, the professional class, the workers and the armed forces." Recent bombings of American-owned properties were perpetrated by Communist agents, Puleston told the CNO, adding that once they stirred up a revolution in Cuba these same subversives would spread violence through Central America, the Caribbean, and the United States. According to one recent report in Puleston's office, a Soviet icebreaker passing through the Panama Canal had secretly landed additional agents to sabotage the canal itself.[31]

Puleston urged the Navy Department to present this information to the president and recommended support for supposedly anti-Communist Cuban strongman Fulgencio Batista. "The question arises if a time has not come when a more determined effort by the government should be made to combat the doctrines of those who are determined to destroy our present form of government," the DNI lectured Standley in late 1934. Apparently impressed by his forceful intelligence chief's opinions, the CNO responded immediately to this latest warning and ordered accelerated security measures around the Panama Canal Zone. However, the rest of the government was not as impressed, and the State Department dismissed his concern, with Undersecretary of State Sumner Welles assuring the DNI that disturbances in Cuba arose from internal unrest rather than from the work of imported foreign agents.[32]

Eventually Roosevelt followed the policy suggested by Puleston and moved closer to Batista in an effort to restore order and stability on the island, but in 1934 the president threaded a cautious course through all the political forces buffeting his administration; it would not do to further alienate increasingly disillusioned liberal elements in his Democrat party coalition by launching some anti-Communist witch hunt in Cuba, or any place else. Moreover, at this moment a recent ONI indiscretion troubled the president. In December, unaware of its contents, the sickly Swanson authorized the release of an ONI report on Communists in America to Congressman John W. McCormack's Special Committee on Un-American Activities. The naval intelligence document smeared many of FDR's isolationist and pacifistically inclined friends and supporters. Prepared by Commander Samuel A. Clement, the head of B-3 Section, ONI's domestic intelligence desk, this paper named as dangerous radicals over two hundred American organizations and many prominent individuals. Clement's list of "Communist-minded intellectuals" included Eddy, Libby, Detzer, Ward, Corliss Lamont, Jane Addams (who had just died), and many others, most at one time or another sympathetic to FDR and the New Deal. Further, the naval intelligence officer's conclusions were anything but professional "These are the 'fringe revolutionists' too lacking in intestinal fortitude to go all the way with Communism, but who stand by and urge the Communist to do his worse, and provide him with protection, sympathy and defense while he commits the overt act they had not had the courage to commit themselves," Clement pronounced almost hysterically.[33]

Release of such comments by a government office to the public would damage any chance Roosevelt might have of retaining liberal support for a troubled New Deal, and the president wished to avoid embarrassing revelations of this type. Consequently, Assistant Secretary Henry Roosevelt assured his boss that future statements to congressmen by naval officers would be cleared first with the secretary's office. The search for Communists would go ahead quietly, of course, and Puleston ordered DIOs to send in lists of local Reds. Inevitably word of ONI's continued antiradical operations reached ACLU Chairman Ward, one of Puleston's primary targets for surveillance. In March 1936, Ward asked FDR for a complete explanation of why the U.S. Navy pursued domestic surveillance measures against U.S. citizens. The president sent a characteristically pleasant but evasive reply. Ward wrote again, urging FDR to curb naval intelligence activities, prevent circulation of ONI information injurious to persons and organizations, and stop operations that created political prejudices and prevented freedom of speech.[34]

Despite Ward's plea, Roosevelt failed to restrain ONI's expanding domestic surveillance program; in fact, troubled by recent revelations of growing foreign espionage in the United States, the president increased counterespionage resources in September 1936 by instructing Hoover verbally to coordinate and enlarge the FBI's investigation of potential subversives and spies. Roosevelt urged Hoover as well to cooperate more closely with the intelligence arms of the Navy, War, and State Departments in a systematic accumulation of data on Fascists and Communists. The president may have discussed such operations with Puleston at the same time, since the DNI rushed to bring ONI in line with FDR's wider view of domestic surveillance, establishing close relations with Hoover's people and liaisons with other agencies and drawing up plans for expansion of the investigative staff from seventy-one in 1936 to over five hundred by 1941.[35]

By 1936 domestic surveillance and counterespionage had become an important part of Puleston's intelligence organization. Responding to growing radicalism and his own anti-Communist sentiments, the DNI made what had been a relatively minor aspect of ONI's mission the primary task of his office. By early 1937 he had convinced new CNO William D. Leahy of the importance of such work, and Leahy ordered all ships and stations to rush news of spies, subversives, and radicals to ONI at once. "As a result of this failure to submit reports," the CNO complained, "much time has been lost in the past in initiating appropriate measures of counter-espionage." Several months later ONI assured Leahy that his orders had brought fresh information into the office, although "many officers believe that this Division should concern itself only with naval matters, leaving political questions to other Departments of the Government."[36]

Indeed internal security questions had become so prominent during Puleston's tenure that the War Plans Division of the CNO's office worried that ONI had let down its vigilance of developments overseas and had begun to neglect larger strategic questions attached to its war planning mission. Hastily, Puleston assured the WPD that such was not the case. "It is not contemplated to neglect the activities in the Far East," he insisted. "I would like to state that all the activities of this Office are planned with a view to covering the Far East as effectively as possible."[37]

Despite his assurances, however, Puleston's office devoted an extraordinary amount of time and energy to domestic subversives and radicals. He knew that ONI had neither funds nor personnel to pursue extensive strategic and security operations simultaneously. Obstacles placed in the way of overseas observations and collection of data by his own neutral and isolationist government reinforced the emphasis on investigation of the internal enemy. Unfortunately, the DNI possessed neither professional nor philosophical judgment to cope with larger political and ideological issues, and viewed all opposition or unrest in the United States as somehow inspired by Communists. For the navy's intelligence chief, legitimate protest—especially if directed against naval construction and expansion—was subversion, not a constitutional right. Gradually, pursuit of radicals and spies merged into an obsessive crusade. Instead of focusing on legitimate threats to the naval establishment, Puleston wandered off in pursuit of real or imaginary enemies. As mentioned before, ACLU Chairman Ward, for one, considered ONI's violations of civil liberties serious enough to complain to the president.

CHAPTER NINE

STRATEGIC STIRRINGS

Shortly after Puleston left ONI and retired from the service in April 1937, his old friend Admiral Yarnell wrote a personal estimate of the world situation to the former DNI from his Asiatic Fleet command. "Conditions are shaping up rapidly where Japan, Italy, and Germany form one block and England, France, and the United States form another," he advised Puleston. "We may not know it or we may not like it, but the time is coming very soon when the United States must take a definite stand with other countries having forms of government similar to our own if we wish to continue as democracies."[1]

Unfortunately, at no time during his tour as head of ONI had Puleston seen the issue this clearly, but then perhaps no one else in the U.S. government expected such a rapid collapse of world order in the face of Japanese, Italian, and German militarism. Following the Japanese invasion of China in July 1937, the Far East confronted a crisis that promised to spill into Southeast Asia, the Pacific Ocean, and Russian Asia. At the same time, in Europe Nazi leaders demanded that all German-speaking peoples come under the protection of Adolph Hitler's Third Reich, forecasting the Austrian Anschluss and demands on the Czech Sudetenland. More dangerous still, in November 1937 Italy joined Germany and Japan in an anti-Comintern Pact, thus showing the world that Rome, Berlin, and Tokyo shared mutual interests.

Although international developments in the days since Puleston left ONI had brought the dangers to U.S. policy into clearer perspective, a careful study of intelligence signals during his tenure would have given him grounds to estimate possible future situations more forcefully. After all, Manchuria, Ethiopia, German remilitarization of the Rhineland in 1935, and the bloody Spanish Civil War provided adequate danger signals. It was the intelligence director's business to attempt an informed prediction of future trends and to present any number of possible situations so that war planners could draw up countermeasures and prepare for different even-

STRATEGIC STIRRINGS   87

tualities. Indeed, between 1931 and 1933 a far less formidable director with fewer sources of data had performed this function admirably, outlining potential trouble spots and projecting time tables for possible conflict. In his estimate for the CNO in 1933, Ellis had predicted that a Far Eastern war would occur in 1936 and would lead to a potential Japanese surprise attack on U.S. forces. At the time, Ellis had warned Standley of Mahan's dictum against dividing the fleet. "The movement of the Fleet, or any large portion of it, to the Atlantic," the DNI had concluded, "might afford the Japanese the opportunity they are seeking—a sudden blow that would place us at an initial disadvantage."[2]

Not once between 1934 and 1937 had the more gifted Puleston prepared such a forceful evaluation. Perhaps overwhelmed by domestic radicalism and the worsening intelligence dilemma, the strategically inclined director had taken these questions for granted. "There was very little information concerning the [possibility of] war in Asia" and "the Japanese occupation of Shanghai in 1932," one intelligence officer concluded about Puleston's years as DNI. Moreover, Puleston had stimulated little concern for an invasion of China proper by the Japanese from their puppet state of Manchukuo. Shortly before the actual outbreak of fighting, the director had assured War Plans that Japan would avoid armed intervention and had advised the naval attaché office in Peking that information in ONI indicated a more conciliatory Japanese policy toward China. "It is believed that the influences for peace outweigh those for war at least at any time in the predictable future," Puleston explained to the CNO on 29 December 1936.[3]

Nor was his estimation of the potential threats to peace from Fascist Italy any more realistic. Perhaps influenced by its anti-Communist tone, the director sympathized with this Fascist government. ONI doctrine accumulated since early 1922 when Mussolini had grabbed power, reinforced the impression that Fascist leadership provided stability and prosperity and prevented radicalism. Mussolini should be praised for "keeping his feet on the ground," naval attaché Hasbrouck had observed, while McNair had continued the favorable view, noting the Fascist's "moral and spiritual preparation of the men and officers of the Italian Navy." It was del Valle's work that colored Puleston's attitude. Allowed to berth with the elite 4th Black Shirt Division on the Italian transport *Saturnia*, del Valle became friendly with ranking Fascist officers on their way to fight the Ethiopians. Later, while accompanying General Graziani's forces in East Africa, the U.S. Marine Corps observer won a prestigious Italian combat medal for courage at the battle front. Not surprisingly, del Valle sympathized with Italian policies. Mussolini "got a bad press here," he insisted. "I can't sing his praises loud enough [for] the way he supported his troops in Africa," del Valle commented. Eventually del Valle's pro-Fascist and anti-Roosevelt statements caused considerable trouble and in 1941 ironically led to an ONI investigation of his loyalty; in March 1937, however, the DNI considered the marine a model intelligence officer, preparing an unusually warm and favorable report for the department about his work in East Africa.[4]

Another misestimation occurred in Puleston's almost nonchalant evaluation of Hitler and Nazi Germany in the mid-1930s. His directorship coincided with Hitler's consolidation of power, purge of opponents, open rearmament in violation of the Versailles settlement, remilitarization of the Rhineland, and extensive testing of powerful new weapons in Spain. Each step suggested increased threats to peace, and U.S. Ambassador William E. Dodd warned consistently of the Nazi leader's dangerous mentality that posed a threat to European civilization and Western democracy. Yet naval intelligence seemed unconcerned, and special assistant naval attaché James A. Furer found Hitler a "good-natured" leader. This scholarly Construction Corps officer and author later of an administrative naval history admitted that the German dictator had curbed some individual freedoms to preserve order but posed no great threat to Europe. Reflecting this analysis, Puleston made the sorry statement in late 1936 that: "The indications are that [Germany's] relative strength will never be great enough to encourage her to initiate hostilities without powerful allies."[5]

Failure to monitor and estimate affairs in Europe's third dictatorship, Soviet Russia, was hardly Puleston's fault, however. A combination of diplomatic tangles, budgetary shortcomings, and naval bureaucratic obstacles rather than the DNI's inaction influenced ONI's poor intelligence output about Russian aims and policies. In early 1935, Puleston closed the expensive and totally ineffective naval attaché office in Moscow, recalled the unproductive Nimmer and his staff, and determined to rely on the three language officers in Latvia for information about Soviet Russia. But the Riga listening post faded in importance when the State Department objected to the language students and tried to bottle them up. When Puleston turned over his office to new DNI Rear Admiral Ralston Holmes on 1 May 1937, the controversy had lapsed into name-calling and exchanges of sarcastic memoranda between officials of the two departments. "I do not believe that the Navy Department intended, nor that the Department of State itself would countenance, reports being made by Navy officers assigned abroad solely for language study to the Office of Naval Intelligence, the contents of which are allegedly so confidential that they may not be made known to the chief of mission who has been given the supervision and direction of their activities while on such duty," the senior diplomatic official in Riga cabled Washington. On their part, language officers Schultz, Frankel, and Seidel accused the minister of double-crossing them.[6]

While the inadequate intelligence legacy left by Puleston in regard to Russia could be explained in terms of larger policy, other strategic limitations handed over to Holmes in 1937 resulted more directly from Puleston's neglect of such duty in favor of domestic intelligence, spy hunting, and antiradical crusading. Puleston's poor evaluation of European dictatorships resulted in incomplete monographs on Germany, Italy, and other European countries; they were thus of limited value to departmental war planners. Moreover, the director failed to compile satisfactory strategic information packets about the Mediterranean, North African, or Iberian regions. Even the DNI belatedly recognized this glaring oversight. A few weeks before retiring, Puleston cabled his naval attaché in Lisbon, complaining that "the available information concerning Portuguese colonies is very meager; and as they may have an important role in the future, any information concerning them will be greatly appreciated."[7]

Remarkably, ONI's Japanese monograph suffered as well during these years despite sporadic efforts to provide unique new sources of information, such as the coast-watcher system and Worton's secret mission. The basic strategic information available to the War Plans Division in their constant updating of War Plan ORANGE remained the traditional lists of ships, sailing directions, some geography, and estimates of forces. When one young naval officer slated for duty as an assistant naval attaché in Tokyo stopped at ONI to study the monograph, he discovered many gaps in the basic data about the islands and people. The files displayed no familiarity with recent studies on Japan carried on at Harvard, Yale, and the Cornell Center for Studies in the Far East, or with the writings of sociologist Ruth Benedict on Japanese life and society. "I could have done as well, reading books on Japan and Japanese industry that I was aware of and had in my own library," the intelligence officer recalled.[8]

The disappointing strategic legacy left by Puleston seemed to infect other areas, even those fields where the DNI had labored diligently to upgrade the quality of personnel and organization, such as the district offices. Limited funds, lack of departmental support, and antagonism at the local district level contributed to the weaknesses, but the terrible morale among some DIOs and the poor preparation of district war plans in 1937 arose at least partly from Puleston's fascination with antiradicalism rather than naval matters. At least one district intelligence officer expressed disillusionment with the "red" question, which diverted time from naval business. Moreover, Puleston's concentration on improving continental naval districts where supposed radicals operated led to the neglect of such strategically vital districts as the Fifteenth (Canal Zone) and the Sixteenth (Philippine Islands), which while primarily the responsibility of military intelligence nevertheless required an ONI presence. And in the Sixteenth District, the commandant of the Cavite Navy Yard warned ONI in 1937 that the lack of district intelligence was "a cause for serious concern." The DIO's office in the Philippines had remained vacant for fourteen consecutive months, while sixteen of the nineteen reserve intelligence officers in the islands lived around Manila, making impossible full coverage of the other islands, where there were reports that a growing number of Oriental spies had penetrated U.S. Navy facilities. Continued the commandant, "This pertains particularly to foreign females affiliated in one way or another with navy enlisted personnel, and to civil employees at Cavite."[9]

Thus, on 1 May 1937 incoming DNI Ralston Holmes inherited more than the usual amount of troubles. The dignified, somewhat aloof officer required time to study his new assignment, familiarize himself with current intelligence, and recommend steps to rectify problems left by his zealous, popular predecessor. Under the best of circumstances, any incoming director needed months to adjust to this difficult and often strange job, and most naval officers never mastered the intelligence business before completing their tour and returning to sea duty. The urgent world situation in the spring of 1937, though, allowed Holmes no indoctrination period before plunging headlong into his work and no time to either review Puleston's organization or to recommend reforms.

Just six weeks after Holmes settled into his billet, the Far Eastern war that Puleston had considered unlikely exploded when Japanese troops crossed the legendary Marco Polo Bridge and moved south from Manchuria into China proper. Soon fighting spread down the coast to Shanghai and along China's great rivers into the interior. Japan could not hide its massive air, land, and sea operations from the prying eyes of inquisitive U.S. naval intelligence observers, and ONI strained every resource in an attempt to exploit all opportunities to examine heretofore closely guarded secrets. Regimental intelligence officers from the 4th Marines in Shanghai pressed close to the bitter Sino-Japanese fighting that raged around the vital port city. Intelligence specialist Major Ronald Aubry Boone climbed an exposed tower near the Japanese consulate to watch an attack on Chinese positions, while his Marine Corps colleagues supplied ONI with detailed tactical maps of troop movements, positions, and lines of advance, as well as weekly summaries of the military situation.[10]

Other naval intelligence officers followed the fighting. Assistant naval attaché Captain James M. McHugh, USMC, making use of "most intimate relations with the Generalissimo and his wife" and with Chiang's Kuomintang officials, accompanied Chinese forces into combat. In this manner, McHugh was able to scavenge Japanese casualties and wreckage for information and secure Chinese cooperation in locating downed Japanese aircraft. This Marine Corps officer not only recovered bomb fragments and aircraft parts but also a top-secret radio code book from the body of a dead pilot discovered in a remote region by McHugh's Chinese friends. At the same time, Lieutenant Tolley recovered the tail fin and one brace from a large Japanese bomb dropped near Shiukuan, while another intelligence officer examined a nearly undamaged Zero pursuit plane downed near

Chungking, and Asiatic Fleet intelligence officer Henri Smith-Hutton collected empty Japanese shell casings from the Shanghai battlefield. As ONI's Far Eastern desk head, McCollum claimed an entire shipload of war junk from the Far East arrived during the first year of fighting.[11]

The opportunities for collecting military information about Japan appeared unlimited, and Holmes clamored for more. "It has been reported by hearsay that the Japanese army employs extremely effective means of prophylactic treatment for prevention of venereal disease and for treatment after infection," he cabled the naval attaché in Peking, requesting samples. Whether or not the attaché sent this information, intelligence personnel forwarded a complete set of photographs documenting incredible atrocities made by Japanese soldiers against the Chinese, especially women. More useful were reports containing transcripts of interviews held by Boone with commercial attachés, local steamship officers, the Chinese Minister of the Treasury, T. V. Soong, and the British air attaché. One lengthy report recounted his conversation with wandering New York Times reporter Hallet Abend, a most seasoned observer of the "North China Incident."[12]

In addition to monitoring Japanese operations, several naval intelligence officers became China watchers. McHugh continued to work closely with Nationalist officials and became an avid student of Chinese history, language, and culture. Captain Evans Carlson and Major Edward Hagen of the Marine Corps "have been particularly fortunate in their circle of Chinese friends," naval attaché Harold Bemis wrote from Tokyo in late 1937, and he hoped they could introduce his volunteer intelligence agent Professor Hindmarsh of Harvard to some important Chinese contacts. Carlson toured the front with naval attaché Harvey Overesch, marveling at the courage of Chinese infantrymen in the face of relentless attacks by better armed and equipped Japanese units. He learned that the Communist Chinese 8th Route Army, in northern China after fleeing the Kuomintang purge of Chinese Communists a decade earlier, was an even more highly motivated and disciplined force than the courageous troops at Shanghai. Carlson gained Overesch's permission to visit the renowned Communist warriors, and between December 1937 and February 1938 the Marine Corps observer accompanied elements of the 8th Route Army and met their leaders, including Mao Tse-tung.[13]

Carlson's trip and subsequent observations caused a stir then and created controversy later. He compiled for ONI a "Report on Military Activities in the Northwest of China with Especial Regard to the Organization and Tactics of the Chinese Eighth Route Army (Ex-Communist)" and then published his views in the book Twin Stars of China. Both studies called Mao a "distinguished liberal" and compared his soldiers to U.S. Revolutionary War minutemen. Carlson's impressions contrasted sharply with ONI doctrine, which saw Chinese Communist "bandits" as nothing more than an extension of Russian Communism. Adding to the confusion, other reports from China portrayed the pro-American Nationalist leader Chiang as a lazy, corrupt, and cowardly warlord incapable of defeating Japan. Carlson implied that American policy ought to change and support Mao rather than Chiang, a controversial opinion in an administration committed to supporting the Nationalist government.[14]

The responsibility for sorting out, synthesizing, and disseminating war reports from Carlson, McHugh, Boone, and the others fell to the three officers, three assistant naval research analysts, and one clerk—ONI's entire Far Eastern section. In addition to battlefront material, the intelligence desk accumulated newspaper clippings about the war and information from the War and State Departments. All were presented in abbreviated form to the DNI and CNO in weekly summaries that focused on military activity, location of forces, and a smattering of political developments. Though compiled hastily and lacking scholarly insights, at least these summaries provided strategic material about the Far East. Unfortunately, the data were not always used. Several intelligence officers argued that no one in the Bureau of Ordnance ever examined reports on Japanese guns, bombs, and aircraft, and other technical bureaus remained ignorant even of the capabilities of the Zero fighter. However, cryptanalyst

The USS *Panay* operated as a "spy ship" on the Yangtze River in the 1930s, which undoubtedly contributed to the vicious Japanese air strike and the sinking of this "neutral" naval vessel in 1937.

Safford in the ONC employed code books recovered by McHugh to help crack some of Japan's more difficult codes.[15]

The U.S. Navy's aggressive pursuit of information during the first months of the Sino-Japanese War contributed possibly to a major diplomatic incident. Crammed with intelligence material, including a secret Japanese bombsight, a code book, technical pamphlets, and signal equipment, the U.S. gunboat *Panay* lay at anchor in the Yangtze River some twenty-seven miles above Nanking observing Japanese operations when at 1330 hours on 12 December 1937, three waves of Japanese warplanes attacked her. For years the *Panay* had gathered intelligence in China and had become the navy's most successful spy ship. But whether or not the Japanese knew that the tiny gunboat housed valuable information, on a bright clear day they repeatedly bombed and strafed a neutral ship with a huge U.S. flag displayed prominently across the deck canopy. Moreover, just before the abandoned *Panay* slipped to the bottom of the muddy Chinese river, two Japanese boarding parties scoured the entire vessel from stem to stern and may have discovered secret material not cast overboard. Indeed, the *Panay*'s loss forced an urgent ONI conference on measures to safeguard naval codes and secrets, while a confidential report made later in 1943 to Undersecretary of the Navy Forrestal admitted that the *Panay*'s officers had not destroyed her secret papers.[16]

Certainly, ONI suspected that the Japanese had attacked the ship to block its intelligence work, and persistent requests by the Japanese for permission to raise and salvage the hulk reinforced this impression. Worried that such an operation would reveal the extent of U.S. intelligence-gathering against Japan, since divers might find locked boxes thrown overboard, ONI recommended against such a course. Holmes masked the reason for opposition. "It is not beyond the bounds of possibility that if the PANAY were raised by the Japanese and towed down the Yangtze River to Shanghai for scrapping," the DNI warned, "a considerable percentage of the illiterate Chinese population of that area would be allowed to understand that this American naval vessel had been captured by the Japanese and was now being used by them as they saw fit." Just in case, though, the navy hired some local divers to recover several locked trunks, but the divers discovered that the turbulent river had carried away any evidence and that the *Panay*'s hull had cracked so severely that salvage would be impossible. In any case, Secretary of State Hull denied Japanese requests to recover the American gunboat.[17]

Naturally, the sinking of the first U.S. warship by air attack caused consternation among members of the Roosevelt administration. Secretary Swanson, for one, recommended a firm U.S. response. But prompt Japanese apologies and an isolationist American attitude that had forced FDR to pull back from his tough antiaggression Quarantine Speech in

October temporarily defused Japanese-American tensions and delayed war for another four years. Nevertheless, the *Panay* incident marked a turning point in U.S. naval preparations, even if as historian Dorothy Borg argued it created no shift in fundamental U.S. policies. FDR decided to support a 20 percent increase in naval shipbuilding and construction of naval bases in the Pacific. As a result, the Naval Act of 17 May 1938 authorized four new battleships and an aircraft carrier and created a new board under former DNI Hepburn to study naval base locations.[18]

While its primary focus was on the Far Eastern crisis, the FDR government, because of the Nazi's amalgamation of Austria and demands for the Czech Sudetenland, began to watch European affairs more closely as well. The president and his closest advisors, especially old friend and current CNO Leahy, initiated a major reappraisal of U.S. military and naval strategies. Various boards and committees gathered to study hemispheric security, base development, war plans revision, naval and aircraft building programs, and Anglo-American cooperation. Recommendations were tentative, and Roosevelt reined in any overly enthusiastic advocate of joint Anglo-American planning, defense measures for Latin America, or grandiose base development schemes, but the first steps were taken in these directions in 1938. Moreover, study of the ORANGE War Plan against Japan indicated a growing obsolescence that required extensive recasting to include planning against a combination of powers, an exercise code-named RAINBOW.[19]

The activity in the Navy Department in the wake of the *Panay* incident and the Nazi demands on Central Europe forced Holmes in one year to undertake more strategic adjustments in ONI than Puleston had in the previous three. Firm leadership by Leahy, the most effective CNO in the interwar era, helped, but in fact, in his own quiet fashion Holmes relished the opportunity to expand naval intelligence. A seasoned naval attaché with experience in both Europe and as a member of the naval mission to Brazil in the 1920s, he understood the larger strategic responsibilities of his office and at the same time displayed an unusual grasp of the potential dilemma confronting naval intelligence when it attempted to pursue both strategy and security. In July 1937 Holmes, assisted by retired intelligence officer Commander F. D. Pryor, prepared for Leahy one of the clearest statements of the U.S. Navy's intelligence dilemma ever attempted by any DNI. The confidential memorandum of 16 July read:

> Many officers believe that this Division should concern itself only with naval matters, leaving political questions to other Departments of the Government. This is theoretically correct, but our Government has no central intelligence service to serve as a clearing house to insure that pertinent information reaches all interested agencies. While liaison with other Departments is constantly improving, the situation does not yet warrant our sitting back and

waiting for someone to give us information that is not strictly naval. In case of tension, knowledge of conditions on the part of the Navy Department may indicate possibilities or probabilities, which, in turn, will indicate steps to be taken by the Navy that otherwise might be taken too late.

In the field of Domestic Security, internal unrest and increasing espionage activities in the United States are throwing an increasing load on the Division whose aim is to have information that will prevent or minimize disaffection of personnel in the Navy or working on naval projects, as well as information that will tend to the prevention of sabotage in times of tension or hostilities.

Suspension of activities does not mean a mere maintenance of the status quo. It means retrogression because many points of contact and channels of information established through long and careful effort will completely disappear, necessitating a slow and arduous rebuilding when the suspension of activities is lifted. Indeed, any item of information may open a new field requiring investigation and study. By its very nature an intelligence service must expand to be efficient.[20]

Both Holmes and Leahy wanted ONI to expand in order to counteract threats to the United States from foreign spies at home and aggressor nations abroad, but only if the pursuit of fundamental security or strategic policy required involvement in non-naval matters should ONI wander into peripheral areas. In order to avoid temptation, Holmes sought at once to steer ONI away from Puleston's ultra-patriotic, antiradical friends. Consequently, when Mortimer Kastner, past national vice commander of the Army and Navy Union of Milwaukee, offered his files on subversives to the DIO in the Ninth Naval District, Holmes's assistant director warned against accepting them, cautioning about the legal complications that might arise. In a similar case, when the American Protective League, World War I's most extensive and unprincipled private spy agency, reappeared in 1937 and recruited new members, the DNI warned reserve intelligence officers not to join. "It is not clear at this stage whether or not the American Protective League will carry out its original objectives or will deteriorate into a mere vigilante organization," Holmes advised one district commandant in December 1937.[21]

In early 1938, Holmes took an important step in redirecting ONI's energies toward basic naval security and war planning by establishing a Planning and Training Section, referred to in the naval organization chart as Op-16-X, with Pryor, who had headed an informal planning section since 1932, in charge. The new section studied weaknesses in the war mobilization plan for naval intelligence, advised the director on steps to improve the district network, and outlined measures to provide security for naval property. Work began on training manuals for censorship, propaganda, and counterespionage. Lieutenant Commander Charles J. Gass, USNR, ONI's World War I commerce and travel control expert, revised the manual of instruction for this function while other officers prepared estimates for recruitment of reserve and retired personnel for the Washington office, the DIOs, and the proposed Severn and Potomac River Naval Commands. And Commander Hamilton Bryan visited several districts, bringing Holmes's message that the local organizations needed to be coordinated more closely with ONI.[22]

Holmes's office began to consider the definition of ONI's investigative function, perhaps the most difficult aspect of naval intelligence. As a result, the office started to prepare an investigator's training manual and developed four distinct categories of naval detectives—including special agents, agents, investigators, and special employees. "Women may be employed in this classification, but the use of women operatives should be reduced to a minimum," ONI decided. Only the DNI held authority to appoint special agents.[23]

All the while, Leahy's office lent encouragement and support, and in February 1938 Assistant CNO J. O. Richardson ordered the sometimes recalcitrant DIOs to cooperate fully with ONI in developing district intelligence plans, and he also urged the Coast Guard to consult with ONI. On his part Leahy advised all ships and stations that the DNI held cognizance over security and classified matter, disclosures of naval information, and the release of photographs and publicity, listing specific data which the Navy Department considered classified and which ONI needed to review. Leahy specified that any information on shipboard airconditioning, damage control, radios, catapults, compass design, and smoke-screen tactics must be cleared with ONI. At the same time, the energetic CNO made certain that an ONI officer sat on the board that was revising the department's Latin American policies, advisory missions, and the release of technical data. Furthermore, Leahy directed his War Plans Division to consult ONI files for information on the industrial mobilization and war-making potentials of Germany, Italy, Japan, Great Britain, and France.[24]

Leahy's tutelage strengthened ONI's position in the naval hierarchy and aided in its expansion. At the same time, though, his guidance promised to subordinate the office to the CNO's war-planning machinery directly under Leahy and to curb the independent spirit fostered during the previous decade of strong DNIs and mediocre CNOs. Yet if Holmes recognized his boss's effort to submerge the office in the bureaucratic process, he never mentioned the fact. The current DNI was not one to question authority. Moreover, too many urgent duties precluded much thought about the potential loss of independence or prestige that troubled future directors. In addition to coordinating intelligence gathering from the Far Eastern war zone, Holmes ordered increased surveillance of Italian and German naval operations in the Mediterranean, Japanese tuna-boat movements along the Pacific coast of Mexico, tanker traffic in mid-Pacific, and Fascist infiltration of Latin America. At the same time, he reviewed continually the reliability of strategic data already in ONI files. Poor material on the Japanese mandated islands bothered Holmes especially, and in December 1937 he cabled former naval attaché in Rome Macgillivray Milne about the intelligence reports he had sent in 1933 concerning the presence of fortifications on the Pacific mandates. "I must tell you that the reports referred to are the only ones in our office," Holmes insisted, "stating that guns are actually installed in the Mandate Islands and that we have other reports of approximately the same date from persons who have visited or who were actually living in the islands at that time stating that no fortifications of any sort existed there." Holmes suspected that Milne's information had come from a deranged mercenary Hungarian informer named Pablo Laslo, now living in Latin America.[25]

Whenever he had a quiet moment in the hectic intelligence routine, Holmes worked on the inevitable budget estimates for the following year (1940). Unlike Puleston, who dreamed of $800,000 appropriations and scores of new personnel, Holmes constructed a more conservative $375,000 package and asked for two additional officers and two clerks to assist in a gradual and orderly expansion of ONI. Nevertheless, even a moderate 20 percent increase in funds and personnel required full justification, and the director explained his request to Leahy in terms of expanding counterespionage and security measures against the Japanese, mentioning Japan by name specifically for the first time in such budgetary estimates. Much of the additional money would contribute to the gathering overseas of strategic information through expansion of the attaché system, Holmes observed.[26]

For Holmes, this system, ONI's earliest source of information from abroad, was still the heart of the navy's intelligence program. Puleston had let the naval attaché network decline, however, partly for personal reasons and partly because promised funds for expansion never materialized as FDR struggled with the lingering depression. Holmes rebuilt the system. First responding to problems confronted by his naval attaché in Berlin, Commander Albert Ernest Schrader, in gaining access to the autonomous Air Ministry, Holmes and his counterpart in the Military Intelligence Division had the designations of all senior attachés changed to include a separate title for air. Thus, Holmes's people officially became naval attachés and naval attachés for air. More importantly, in 1938 the DNI pressed the department for attaché posts in the West Indies and Mexico City and the reopening of offices at The Hague and in Moscow. He considered the latter most urgent. "The reason being that we are in the dark concerning the Naval Building program of Russia, and her Naval Plans," Holmes told Leahy, and "we are also interested in Russia as the seat of communism." He estimated the cost of reopening the office, $7,500, well worth the investment: "as Russia is a connecting link between the Far East situation and European affairs much valuable information could be obtained by this office." The Hague office opened without incident, but the State Department objected for over a year to the Moscow attachéship. Additionally, placing an officer in Mexico City met with a slight delay, since former navy secretary and current ambassador to Mexico, Josephus Daniels, "preferred to be his own Naval Attaché."[27]

Despite minor setbacks, the naval attaché network prospered under Holmes. The director found extra funds to increase allotments, maintenance, and operating expenses, including $300 for the critical Berlin post. Holmes equipped his naval attachés with a new cipher machine and a box of code wheels. This 50-pound machine was driven by an electric motor. "The machine should be given as high security as is practicable," he explained. "The advantages of the cipher machine over the systems now held by the Attaché are its high speed of operation and greater security."[28]

Holmes labored to clear the way for his attachés by improving liaison and smoothing often strained relations with the State Department. He met with Assistant Secretary of State George Messersmith to discuss the assignment of naval attachés and other questions of mutual interest ranging over the sharing of codes, couriers, and information on the arrival and travel within the United States of German, Italian, and Japanese citizens. Messersmith reported Holmes's views to Hull. "He indicated that the facilities at the disposal of O.N.I. were relatively limited but that to the degree that it was possible for O.N.I. to cooperate in aiding this Department to follow the activities of certain persons it was very desirous to be helpful." Personal contact and the exchange of views allowed the DNI to explain why ONI wanted attachés at specific locations and in turn permitted the State Department to voice "frankly" opposition to a naval attaché in Moscow. "He will be under constant espionage and those who would have contact with him we have reason to believe from experience would be subjected to all sorts of dangers," Messersmith insisted.[29]

The naval attachés responded both to Holmes's support and the increased tempo of international tension by doubling their output of intelligence reports over the previous year with 1,607 from Western Europe, 1,144 from London, and even 506 from Berlin where Nazi officials obstructed overt accumulation of data by the American attaché. Attachés became more enthusiastic in initiating projects. Cogswell and his assistant Shoemaker in Paris proposed an inspection trip deep into Russia to study the air industry, but Holmes had to stop this project. "The difficulties which would be encountered in making arrangements for such a trip are very great and even if successful it would probably be fruitless because the internal situation in Russia has changed decidedly since Commander Shoemaker left Washington in 1936," Holmes cabled Cogswell. "Due to a substantial growth in the 'spy' mania in Russia" such a trip would fail.[30]

Attaché reports were used. ONI prepared twenty-four volumes of monographic data on the British dominions and colonies, bound seventy-seven important documents from the London attaché in chronological order and sent them over to the White House for Roosevelt's personal examination. Similar volumes from naval attachés in Paris and Brussels followed. Meanwhile, Holmes's office published twenty-nine strategic information bulletins for the department, including a study of air operations during the Spanish Civil War and an examination of the restoration of German military might.[31]

In his first months as intelligence director, Holmes had made some strategic stirrings. Influenced by the Sino-Japanese War, Nazi expansion into Austria, and Leahy's tutelage, the DNI strengthened the naval attaché system and increased the number and quality of ONI publications. Rather than concentrate only on domestic radicals, Holmes looked overseas as well for threats to American security, and began to focus on Latin American attachéships. Just in time, ONI realized that the greatest menace to the United States came not from internal enemies but from foreign aggressors. As naval attaché Monroe Kelly noted from The Hague in December 1938, German and Italian policies increased the danger of war every day. "I am sorry to relate but the situation in Europe now is anything but encouraging."[32]

HEMISPHERIC SECURITY

As European and Asian conditions deteriorated during the late 1930s, U.S. policy makers looked more closely at their relations with Latin America and to hemispheric security against aggression. Ever since 1823, when in an obscure part of his presidential message James Monroe had warned Europeans to stay out of the Western Hemisphere, the idea of U.S. protection over Latin America had developed into doctrine. It was an ambivalent policy, mixing Pan-Americanism with gunboat diplomacy and military occupation, and blending friendship with exploitation. Whether "Big Stick" or "Missionary" diplomacy, to Latin Americans U.S. policies meant intervention in their affairs and bred a legacy of mistrust toward the more wealthy and powerful North Americans.

In the years after the First World War, the United States government gradually began to dispel the worst fears through an attempt to become a better neighbor. Thus, Calvin Coolidge dispatched the immensely popular transatlantic soloist Charles Lindbergh on a friendly visit south of the border in 1927, while several years later Herbert Hoover visited Latin America on a tour designed to promote commercial ties and comity. But it was the internationalist Roosevelt who with characteristic vigor pushed something called the Good Neighbor Policy toward Latin America. FDR believed that prosperity, stability, and political independence throughout the Western Hemisphere strengthened U.S. economic and strategic interests. To this end, he pressed for the removal of all troops from the region, supported self-denying clauses against intervention, and advocated mutual cooperation. Not satisfied to simply proclaim this good neighborliness, Roosevelt brought his message personally to much of Latin America with all the force of his considerable charm.[1]

From time to time during the first century of U.S.-Latin American relations, the U.S. Navy had become an important instrument of policy, whether through the landing of troops in some Caribbean country, rushing cruisers to Brazil during disturbances, surveying a Central American canal route, or carting a president about on good will tours. For its part, the navy's intelligence office exemplified the dichotomy that symbolized the entire U.S. naval and diplomatic thrust into Latin America. Ever since 1882, ONI agents had prowled Latin America observing local wars, surveying canal routes, looking for advanced base sites, and watching out for European or Asian intrusions in the Western Hemisphere. Under the William H. Taft administration (1908–12), the office had operated as a sales agency for U.S. weapons and manufactured goods, while during early phases of World War I, naval intelligence informants and officers surged through Latin America looking for violations of the Monroe Doctrine by friend and foe. After U.S. entry into the war, ONI personnel interfered in local internal politics, pitting one pro-American faction in Mexico against another, and reportedly trading special favors in return for oil concessions.[2]

With the cessation of hostilities in Europe, ONI's interest in Latin America increased. Expecting involvement in this region now troubled by wide-scale postwar unrest, DNI Welles expressed concern that his Latin American expert and former naval attaché to Havana, Carlos Cusachs, faced demobilization along with the rest of the intelligence reserve force. "He is far too valuable a man for O.N.I. to permit him to go back to teaching languages," Welles wrote, "and should be kept in the office of O.N.I. where he can be sent to Cuba or Mexico, or any Spanish or French-speaking country on special missions." No sooner had Welles left, than the predicted troubles in revolutionary Mexico threatened to lead to a naval intervention similar to the occupation of Vera Cruz in 1914.[3]

The navy mobilized its intelligence resources. Intelligence expert Ellis scouted conditions around the Tampico oil fields, while informants watched the U.S.-Mexican border for signs of illegal arms shipments. In March 1920 CNO Coontz issued a general order for all naval forces in the area to rush information about Mexico to ONI, and by September, DNI A. T. Long sent ONI's Mexican package to commanding officers of the U.S. Atlantic Fleet. ONI publications included two bound booklets on the Tampico-Tuxpan region, strategic data on all major ports, and estimates of the military, economic, and political situation—twenty-one documents in all. At the same time, the department used the information to update War Plan GREEN for Mexico. Although conflict was avoided in 1920, the plan remained active throughout the decade, and ONI agents penetrated Mexico periodically to send information back for a "most secret" file on the Tampico and Tuxpan oil regions.[4]

After Mexican affairs quieted, troubles in Nicaragua during the twenties led to U.S. naval intervention. By February 1927, 2,000 marines landed in the revolution-torn country and battled nationalist rebel Augusto C. Sandino in an attempt to provide law and order and prop up a pro-American regime. The Navy Department expected ONI to provide data to the

Special Service Squadron supporting intervention. When naval intelligence learned that reporter Charles Gale Harris of the radical *New York Graphic* intended to interview Sandino and write sympathetic essays, DNI Johnson urged Squadron Commander David Foote Sellers to block the visit. At the same instant, the intelligence office forwarded data to Sellers about efforts to run guns from Mexico and the United States to the Sandinistas. "I am very glad to hear that the Department is active in trying to prevent gun running to Honduras and Nicaragua," Sellers wrote Johnson in 1928, "and recent events in Nicaragua would seem to indicate that very little, if any, ammunition or munitions of war of any description are getting into Nicaragua."[5]

In addition to disseminating information, ONI exerted some influence on the administering of Nicaraguan elections by the United States. Working in conjunction with Sellers, Johnson convinced Navy and State Department officials that the U.S. Army, which had monitored a previous election, had no business running the election of 1930, since the navy had restored law and order. The naval officers criticized the work of U.S. military attaché Major Fred T. Cruse. "I am concerned, the sooner he goes the better," Sellers cabled Johnson in late 1928, "because he has never furnished me with anything but incorrect, inaccurate and misleading information." In response, the U.S. government dispatched the DNI, himself, to supervise new Nicaraguan elections.[6]

Participation in Mexican and Nicaraguan affairs comprised the type of intervention familiar to ONI; however, the postwar era also introduced a new function. As early as 1906 Brazil had discussed a U.S. naval mission to Rio de Janeiro, and a few years later naval attaché Philip Williams had helped found a Brazilian naval war college. Then in 1918, Admiral Carl Theodore Vogelgesang had headed an informal U.S. Navy mission to Brazil, which led to a formal mission after the fighting in Europe ended. At the same time, in May 1920 Peruvian officials expressed to Niblack their desire to have a similar program and to purchase warships in the United States. Though these overtures coincided with American postwar indifference to foreign affairs, in this case Congress, perhaps concerned about European interest in establishing military missions in Latin America, passed legislation authorizing naval officers to receive compensation from Latin American governments while serving in their countries on naval missions.[7]

Overall, the Navy Department voiced slight enthusiasm for supporting naval missions to Latin America. Confronted by cutbacks in funds and personnel, the navy wondered where it might find the resources to man the proposed missions. Acting Chief of the Bureau of Navigation Williams, once an informal advisor to the Brazilian navy, offered a solution. "My slight experience in this matter leads me to believe that there is rarely enough to do in the post of Naval Attaché to a South American country to keep an officer contented with that post alone," Williams told Coontz in June 1920, concluding that in his spare time the attaché could administer the naval mission as well. However, Coontz's Plans Division doubted that the intelligence office could deal simultaneously with secret matters and educational missions. A conflict of interests would be unavoidable. Nevertheless, the war planners admitted that since the department lacked any doctrine on the subject, ONI ought to direct both of these contradictory services; in response, the CNO recommended organizing a section for naval missions within the intelligence office.[8]

Thus, bureaucratic bafflement rather than careful planning placed responsibility for the administration of naval missions overseas in the intelligence bureau, just in time to send a four-man mission headed by Commander Frank B. Freyer to Peru in September 1920. Once in Lima, the North American officers founded a Peruvian naval academy, trained personnel of the six-ship battle fleet, and acted as liaison for the purchase of four submarines from Electric Boat of New London, Connecticut, and several Douglas flying boats. Meanwhile, in November 1922 the U.S. Navy sent a second mission to Latin America to modernize the Brazilian Navy. This undertaking was far more ambitious than the Peruvian affair and comprised sixteen naval officers and nineteen chief petty officers. Each mission member was briefed by ONI, and as gunnery officer Felix Leslie Johnson recalled: "I had six weeks in Washington in ONI, being told what Brazil was all about, what their navy was like, what it needed, what we could give and sell them, and going to Berlitz School trying to learn Portuguese."[9]

Both Brazil and the United States considered the increased contacts beneficial—Brazil because of its rivalry with Argentina and because it was a Portuguese-speaking anomaly in a Spanish-speaking world, and the United States because of Brazil's strategic location for the defense of the Western Hemisphere and because of concern about the substantial Japanese, German, and Italian minorities residing in that South American country. Underscoring the latter concern, naval attaché Howell in Rio de Janeiro warned in 1924 that unless a U.S. naval mission pushed American weapons, Brazil would buy from Europeans. "The Italian Ambassador has visited the Minister [of Marine] three or four times recently," Howell cabled the DNI, "and has informed the Minister that Italy is prepared to treat very favorably with the Brazilian Government on the subject of immigration and commerce should preference be given to the purchase of new submarines from Italy."[10]

The Peruvian and Brazilian enterprises remained ONI's only formal naval missions during the 1920s, but individual intelligence officers operated in other Latin American areas. For a short time in late 1923, Lieutenant Commander Cortlandt C. Baughman served as legal adviser to the Cuban government until the Navy Department sent him to sea. In Santiago the following year naval attaché Reuben Lindsay Walker promoted U.S. manufactures among Chilean naval officials, and ONI forwarded Commander Walker's reports directly to leading U.S. firms—including Bethlehem Steel, Newport News Shipbuilding and Dry Dock, New York Shipbuilding (Camden, New Jersey), Electric Boat, and William Cramps & Sons. At the same time in Mexico, Ambassador Dwight Morrow reported that Lieutenant Commander Donald W. Hamilton, the naval attaché in Mexico City, had performed similar liaison work with local administrators.[11]

Surprisingly, these efforts to advance American economic interests in Latin America were not always welcomed by U.S. businessmen. Naval attaché Andrew Samuel Hickey in Buenos Aires indicated that the Argentine government would probably purchase weapons from Italy and Great Britain because some U.S. merchants had slandered an Argentine contractor. "If the American businessmen feel that it is worth $32,000,000 gold dollars to call a man a 'wop,' then I am afraid it is a rather expensive expression," Hickey wired ONI in 1926.[12]

While ONI representatives in the field flirted with remnants of gunboat diplomacy or hinted at a better neighbor policy, back in Washington the Navy Department merely tolerated their work. Plagued by larger problems, such as defending both oceans with a shrinking fleet and maintaining adequate personnel, bases, and battleships in the face of naval limitation agreements, the navy displayed only a token interest in naval missions to Latin America. In fact, the State Department in the twenties hoped that the navy would do more, such as assigning an attaché to Central America. According to Montgomery Schuyler of the Division of Latin American Affairs, the naval officer might provide valuable information to the naval patrols sent into the region to suppress local disturbances and at the same time collect data on ports and shipping. "These duties at present are performed by the already overworked consular officers who have neither the time nor the technical knowledge for travel and observation of such matters," Schuyler contended. At least one intelligence director agreed, but instead of opening a new office for Central America, ONI had to close the important Brazilian office in order to save the $5,000 annual maintenance costs.[13]

The economic depression that settled over the Western Hemisphere in late 1929 threatened even more cutbacks in ONI's Latin American presence. Yet just at the moment reductions were to be made, depression-induced instability and unrest called for more surveillance of potential trouble spots such as that required by War Plan TAN, outlining measures

for U.S. intervention in Cuba during anti-American disturbances. Working on this plan, ONI updated information for its Cuban monograph and
provided details for an intelligence network in Cuba, which would be
composed of fifteen naval reserve officers located at Guantánamo and
Havana. Acting DNI Baggaley looked for alternative data sources as well.
"We have recently been endeavoring to establish a line of communication
with prominent Americans living in Cuba—so as to obtain up to date data as
to what is going on," he explained in 1931. "From all indications it appears
that we may be involved in the not distant future." Several months later he
dispatched a reserve intelligence officer on an undercover trip through the
interior of the Caribbean island to study political conditions.[14]

Deepening depression and unrest accelerated ONI activity. In 1929 the
navy assigned an attaché to Central America, headquartered in Tegucigalpa. A Marine Corps aviator, the attaché flew throughout the region in an
unarmed, open-cockpit biplane, searching for "communist bandits," political unrest, and evidence of anti-American sentiment. Major Harold S.
Fassett, who held the post in 1931, apparently discovered evidence of
Communist activity, since he maintained a thick "Red File." Meanwhile,
the naval missions increased their observation of radicals elsewhere in Latin
America. Throughout most of the 1920s, mission personnel had observed
an informal proscription against mixing their educational and intelligence
duties, but the current economic, social, and political crises demanded
extreme measures. In most cases, officers in the naval missions were the
only trained professional government observers present. Thus in 1932, the
head of the Peruvian naval mission, William O. Spears, forwarded a report
to ONI packed with data on ship movements, political intrigue, and evidence of the rapid growth of Communism in South America. Moreover,
apparently Spears intruded blatantly in internal Peruvian politics, because
the Commandant of the Fifteenth Naval District, Rear Admiral Noble E.
Irwin praised him in 1932 for becoming "the real 'Power behind the
Throne'."[15]

The most direct expression of ONI's new aggressiveness in depression-
torn Latin America appeared in the Dominican Republic. In 1930 Major
Thomas Eugene Watson, USMC, arrived in the impoverished and troubled
Caribbean country to direct emergency relief work and administer food
doles in the wake of a devastating hurricane. Staying on as naval attaché,
Watson began training the Dominican constabulary for local strongman
Rafael Trujillo, and soon moved into the presidential residence next to the
national palace. Then Senator William H. King of Utah, a leading isolationist, learned about the arrangement and in June 1931 demanded an
explanation from the State Department. In response, the diplomatic branch
admitted that Major Watson occupied an office in the presidential palace

but claimed his work had stabilized the political condition in the Dominican Republic. Nevertheless, Washington closed the office in San Domingo City on 24 July 1931.[16]

Roosevelt's election in 1932 breathed fresh air into U.S. policies in Latin America, where the president promised to act like a good neighbor. Intent upon projecting this image, FDR hastened to withdraw forces from Central America and to ensure Latin Americans that the United States would not intervene in their internal affairs. Consequently, the administration found no further reason to maintain the naval attaché in Central America. "Now that the marines are out of Nicaragua and the frontier situation between Honduras and Nicaragua has quieted down," one State Department official advised, "I see no reason why Major Fassett should continue in Tegucigalpa." After an unsuccessful attempt in 1933 to relocate Fassett in Managua, ONI pulled its man out of Honduras. Similarly, the State Department urged ONI to relax its operations in Cuba, and when in 1934 Puleston warned that the island harbored Communist agitators, Assistant Secretary of State Welles assured him quietly that it was "purely a domestic concern of the Cuban Govt."[17]

Such restraint was short-lived. German rearmament, Italian aggression in East Africa, and Japanese stirrings in China sent shock waves into the Western Hemisphere. As Ambassador Fred Morris Dearing in Peru explained to his personal friend FDR in early 1936, Communist, Fascist, and Japanese agents had infiltrated throughout Latin America. The Japanese were most active in Peru, he warned, pushing trade and reconnoitering local waters with their submarines and tenders. "Our Naval Attaché is following it closely," he assured the president. At the same time, Puleston insisted that Communist, Fascist, and Nazi agents flooded Latin America while the head of the Latin American desk, Lieutenant Colonel Maurice Gardner Holmes, USMC, noted that the Germans had military missions in Argentina, Colombia, and El Salvador, and that Italy supported similar enterprises in Bolivia and Ecuador. Holmes's successor, Colonel Robert Blake, USMC, admitted that while some of the fears of Nazi secret bases were so much "hot air" stirred up by the *New York Times*, nevertheless even he believed that the situation required two new agents in the Caribbean zone to investigate rumored German activity.[18]

ONI strengthened its Latin American desk in Washington and its attaché network south of the U.S. border between 1937 and 1938, partly in response to a departmental study in December 1936 on how to confront a "challenge to the Monroe Doctrine in Eastern South America by a European Dictatorship." Traditionally manned by a Marine Corps officer, the Latin American unit had taken a back seat in the interwar years to Far Eastern and Western European desks. But in the late thirties, two exceptionally capable Spanish-speaking intelligence officers, M. G. Holmes and

Colonel Blake, directed Latin American affairs in ONI. University of California graduate Blake had visited every major Latin American port, most recently as Admiral Husband Kimmel's interpreter when his heavy cruiser squadron made a good-will swing around the region. Blake's memoranda for the DNI offered in-depth social, political, and strategic analyses of conditions in the "other American Republics" and offered appraisals of naval policies for Latin America. In one paper, Blake explained how the U.S. must exploit Brazilian animosity toward Argentina and Peruvian rivalry with her neighbors to tie both more firmly to U.S. interests and policies, thus securing outposts for the navy on both coasts of South America. Furthermore, he urged the development of a Central American Union to offset socialistic Mexico.[19]

The distribution of naval attachés and advisors reflected the thinking in ONI's Latin American section. In March 1937 Holmes advised the Navy Department to divide the Central American attachéship into two posts— one to cover Panama, Colombia, Venezuela, and Ecuador, the other stationed in Guatemala City to monitor affairs in the rest of Central America. Several months later ONI opened an office in Guatemala with Marine Corps aviator Captain Frank H. Lamson-Scribner as naval attaché and supplied him with a single-engined, silver and yellow Gruman J-2F-1 amphibian plane. The next year Blake pressed for another attaché and observation plane for Mexico, especially to watch the Pacific coastal region for signs of Japanese infiltration. Though Ambassador Daniels opposed this, his former assistant and current boss, FDR, personally favored the appointment; consequently, on 11 August 1938 naval aviator Commander Wallace Myron Dillon and his Vought SBU-16 scout-bomber, with "NAVAL ATTACHE, AMERICAN EMBASSY, MEXICO CITY" painted neatly on each side of the fuselage, landed in Mexico.[20]

The addition of new attaché posts contrasted markedly with the earlier U.S. position. Opposed five years before to such work, Secretary Hull now endorsed the expansion of military and naval intelligence missions in Latin America, and ordered the people in his recently reorganized Latin American Division to consult with the other departments in a common policy. In March 1938 Hull wrote Swanson about his desire for the dispatch of more naval attachés. "Our military and naval attachés have made a very valuable contribution to our relations with the other American Republics," Hull observed, "and I hope that cooperation among the three Departments in this respect may be continued and increased."[21]

Concurrently, the administration and the Navy Department were in favor of expanding the naval mission system. Recently the CNO and ONI had redefined the system and its purpose. "A naval mission should not preclude an attaché; both aid and complement one another," the CNO's report for 1935 explained. "If we do not have missions, other countries will;

they enhance prestige and add political and economic ties." In rapid succession in 1937 naval missions were established in Argentina, Ecuador, and Colombia, while existing arrangements with Peru and Brazil were expanded. Increased naval and military aid to Brazil caused some difficult moments for FDR, however. Argentina protested vigorously against the sale of three overage U.S. destroyers to Brazil, while U.S. congressmen opposed efforts to sell new 5-inch twin-gun turret mounts to the Brazilian navy. Reportedly the president told one intelligence officer that the sale of this new weapon, in violation of the Neutrality Act of 1936 and without specific congressional authorization, would put him in jail, but withholding the weapons would drive Brazil toward purchases in Europe.[22]

For over two years ONI attempted to coordinate the sale of some *Mahan*-class destroyers to Brazil, especially through senior mission member Captain Charles C. Gill, but obstacles persisted at both ends. The Brazilian government seemed short of funds, and officials uncertain about their specific needs. In Washington, congressional and legal tangles plagued the Brazilian destroyer deal, and even different offices of the Navy Department disagreed on the arrangements. The JAG opposed the sale, while the Bureau of Ordnance agitated to rush the latest guns to Brazil. As a compromise, the CNO ordered the sale of an outdated fire control system to delay the question momentarily and prevent Brazil from turning elsewhere for help. Necessary legislation to conclude the deal failed, but in 1939 the Roosevelt administration secretly shipped the weapons to Brazil anyway as an emergency measure to bolster hemispheric defense against external threats.[23]

Although it would not be until the summer of 1939 that FDR would apply to Latin America his wider interpretation of executive authority, by late 1938 the machinery for expanded diplomatic and military collaboration had been established. The State Department had its Standing Liaison Committee for Hemispheric Defense, the Justice Department had agents in Rio de Janeiro to organize a Brazilian secret service, and the army had six military attachés and two army missions. But although soon overshadowed by an FBI network in South America, in 1938 it was the navy operating through ONI that expanded most aggressively. ONI directed five naval missions, twenty-two language officers, and twenty-seven officers and thirty enlisted and civilian personnel working in naval attaché offices in every major Latin American capital. Two intelligence officers on board a private yacht cruised the waters off the Yucatan Peninsula in search of suspicious craft. The Latin American network had become such a critical part of ONI operations that when in December 1938 one attaché lost interest in his job after being passed over for promotion, the intelligence office yanked him out at once.[24]

Whether through direct intervention or more subtle intrusions, ONI officers formed a Latin American doctrine in the two decades following the First World War. According to M. G. Holmes in 1937, naval intelligence was in Latin America to prevent revolution, develop indebtedness for military assistance, and promote U.S. institutions. Blake expressed ONI's role more clearly: an obligation to counter anti-American propaganda and activities and to prevent the loss of the dominant U.S. position in the Western Hemisphere. In conclusion, Blake argued that U.S. naval attachés to Latin America were used in "discreetly advising, whenever requested, on naval and military matters, thus keeping alive our direct influence on the military forces of these countries."[25]

Keeping a predominant U.S. influence in Latin America became more urgent still in the closing months of the decade, as the growing threat of world war promised to increase the strategic value of the region to U.S. national security. With world conflict and agonizing U.S. neutrality, the defense of the Western Hemisphere would entangle the navy's intelligence organization in new and conflicting missions, dragging it further into the ongoing naval intelligence dilemma.

PART TWO

NEUTRALITY AND WAR
1939–1945

CHAPTER ELEVEN

DOMESTIC SECURITY

In a stirring message to both houses of Congress on 4 January 1939, President Roosevelt called upon the assembled legislators to assist in strengthening the nation's defenses to preserve American democracy and freedom against the rising threats from foreign dictators. Response to this State of the Union address followed predictable partisan lines, however, with isolationist Republicans, such as Senator William Borah of Idaho, bristling at the mention of increased war preparations. This isolationist reaction underscored the frustrating and dangerous situation confronting Roosevelt in early 1939. On the one hand, he recognized that he could not push military preparedness too quickly, especially if he decided to run for an unprecedented third presidential term in 1940. On the other hand, as commander in chief, pledged to defend the nation, he worried about warnings from his military advisors that current war planning against a coalition of enemies indicated that the United States could barely defend herself on one ocean against one enemy, never mind simultaneously battle two or even three enemies attacking from opposite coasts.

The situation grew more perilous still. In March, Hitler absorbed the remainder of Czechoslovakia in violation of his Munich pledge to British Prime Minister Neville Chamberlain that the Sudetenland would be his last demand. Then, no sooner had the shock of Czechoslovakia passed than in April Mussolini disabused any hope that Roosevelt might have held of dividing the European dictators by marching his Fascist troops into helpless Albania and by threatening Greece with invasion. Not to be overshadowed, Hitler began to issue demands for the Polish corridor and the strategic port city of Danzig, suggesting that invasion of Poland was next.

Back in Washington an agitated but still cautious FDR asked Congress to amend the Neutrality Act of 1937 to allow direct shipment of arms to Britain and France, and he discussed measures to curb the sale of strategic material to dictator states with Secretary of the Treasury Henry J. Morgenthau. Also the president urged speedy congressional action on appropriations bills for more war planes and ships, to overhaul aging battleships, and to expand and strengthen a number of overseas bases such as Guam. And finally, Roosevelt encouraged the rapid completion of the RAINBOW war plans and a mobilization schedule in the event of a national emergency.

The developments in Central and Eastern Europe in the spring of 1939 provided some leverage to secure passage of these defense measures, but were not enough to obtain a revision of the neutrality law. The ability to supply war goods rapidly to European democracies became entwined in lengthy legalistic debates, frustrating delays, and obstructionism organized in Washington by Borah and in the nation by air hero Charles Lindbergh, who had returned from a tour of Luftwaffe facilities in Germany with the conviction that it would be futile for the United States to resist awesome Nazi air power. The popular American transatlantic soloist's position was particularly disconcerting. "Not for one moment do I doubt his honesty and patriotism," Assistant DNI Captain Jules James wrote a friend, "but I do *not* believe that he is a big man with a big, comprehensive view of the international situation."[1]

Confronted with such opposition, Roosevelt determined to expand his executive authority in order to defend American interests by aiding in many quiet and extralegal ways those who resisted aggression. Consequently, in the months ahead he organized naval patrols in an unneutral manner to warn British ships about lurking German submarines, approved secret Anglo-American military and naval staff conversations, and most importantly encouraged many secret operations against potential foreign enemies both at home and abroad. If some of these measures stretched his constitutional prerogative, FDR believed that international crisis and danger to U.S. interests required such risks. "Roosevelt never overlooked the fact that his actions might lead to his immediate or eventual impeachment," New Dealer Robert Sherwood contended.[2]

Clandestine preparedness increased the employment in the White House of both official and unofficial intelligence resources. Ever since the First World War when as Assistant Secretary of the Navy he had selected reserve officers personally for ONI, FDR had displayed a fascination with spies and spying. In private, he devoured spy novels and literature on espionage, and as president encouraged diplomats such as William Bullitt to bypass regular, overly legalistic State Department channels and send confidential information directly to him. Also he employed private secret agents such as wealthy New York neighbor Vincent Astor and Washington journalist John Franklin Carter. Meanwhile, the president strengthened official security and information services, allowing zealous FBI director Hoover to expand operations outside the United States and into Latin America. From time to time after regular business hours, Roosevelt invited naval and military intelligence directors to drop over to the White House

FDR enthusiastically greets Astor, his personal naval secret agent. (Courtesy UPI INS)

to brief him and military aide General Edwin M. "Pa" Watson. At these conferences, Roosevelt advised and recommended intelligence measures, and most importantly urged coordination of intelligence. Such meetings culminated on 26 June 1939 in a presidential memorandum directing FBI, MID, and ONI to define and delimit their fields of investigation, avoid overlapping work, and accelerate the exchange of information. He gave the three agencies sweeping authority. "No investigations should be conducted by an investigative agency of the Government into matters involving actually or potentially any espionage, counter-espionage, or sabotage, except by the three agencies mentioned above," the president instructed.[3]

At this critical moment when Roosevelt began to rationalize American intelligence policy, the Navy Department made another of its routine bureaucratic shuffles at the top, removing Ralston Holmes, perhaps the only director in the interwar years to understand the naval intelligence dilemma. Learning of his impending detachment, Holmes tried to complete his outline for a wartime naval intelligence service that would contain over 600 additional personnel under an estimated budget of nearly $400,000; he urged DIOs to rush by airmail special delivery rough drafts of their organizational plans even if written only in pencil. But despite his last minute

DNI Walter Stratton Anderson directed ONI during the most agonizing months of neutrality between 1939–1940.

efforts, Holmes handed over an incomplete expansion plan to his replacement, Rear Admiral Walter Stratton Anderson, an officer who Chief of the Bureau of Navigation James O. Richardson insisted lacked the respect and confidence of fellow officers and had received the intelligence billet only after being passed over in favor of an officer lower on the promotion list for the prestigious Bureau of Navigation post.[4]

Criticism of Anderson aside, the new DNI possessed intelligence experience including service as naval attaché in London between 1934–37, during which time he had gathered data from Gibraltar, Malta, Alexandria, and Haifa as well as from the London circuit. Moreover, Anderson displayed some of the administrative skills necessary to cut through bureaucratic snarls likely to accompany expansion of ONI. As his Latin American section head Blake concluded: "Admiral Anderson liked short letters."[5]

Administrative acumen and experience in collecting overt information hardly prepared Anderson for what he confronted in the troubled summer of 1939, however. Departmental planners demanded data from his office for the new RAINBOW plans, the president expected tighter security measures, the General Board called for an expanded naval espionage system, and ONI itself needed a steadying hand to guide the expected increase in personnel, services, and operations. More importantly, the naval intelligence dilemma had never been quite so prevalent, since during the previous months Holmes and Leahy had plunged ONI into the dark world of spies, surveillance, and secret operations. Anderson learned just how deeply several days after assuming the directorship when counterespionage chief Captain Elliott Bodley Nixon explained how for the past year naval intelligence had aided the FBI and other police agencies in uncovering, capturing, and convicting notorious Nazi secret agents Gunther Gustave Rumrich, Otto Hermann Voss, Erich Glaser, and Johanna Hofmann, members of a spy ring that had stolen some of the nation's top defense secrets, including the Norden Bombsight. ONI had contributed as well, Nixon revealed, to the capture of Soviet espionage agents Hafis Salich and Mikhail N. Gorin. Though touching on naval interests, these operations had gone far afield from the naval establishment and into wide-scale snooping, wiretapping, and mail openings.[6]

Even in most tranquil times, this dilemma had puzzled and humbled new DNIs, who as naval officers pledged to defend the law and serve the navy, discovered that they headed an agency that drifted beyond the law and naval interests. Surprisingly, Anderson recognized the problem. "Literally, we were all in disobedience to the law," he admitted candidly. But he could do nothing to avoid it since the only guidance he received in the department during the first phase of his directorship came from Holmes, who was already involved in the naval intelligence predicament. With both Secretary Swanson and Assistant Secretary Charles Edison ill, top civilian leadership was nearly nonexistent. In fact, Swanson died a few weeks after Anderson entered ONI, and a nearly deaf Edison assumed the title of Secretary *ad interim* while FDR sounded out Republican newspaperman Frank Knox for the post in his proposed bipartisan cabinet.[7]

In the meantime, Anderson's immediate naval superior, Leahy, stood a few weeks away from mandatory retirement and in August was replaced as CNO by Admiral Harold Raynsford Stark. Anderson might expect direction from this officer, who years before as a member of Admiral Sims's war-planning section in London during World War I had displayed ability in war planning and strategy. But "Betty" Stark lacked the dynamism and ability of Leahy, found the wide-ranging responsibilities of his office taxing, and focused on close liaison with his War Plans Division rather than with ONI for information and analysis.

Searching for guidance, Anderson received inspiration in the intelligence business from FDR. Several days after taking charge of naval intelligence, the admiral read Roosevelt's directive for pooling intelligence resources. This directive profoundly influenced the character of Anderson's directorship between June 1939 and December 1940 and drew ONI further still into the intelligence dilemma. In response to the president's desires, Anderson consulted as many as three times weekly with FDR and once a week sat in conference with MID Director General

Sherman Miles, State Department intelligence liaison Adolf Berle, and J. Edgar Hoover. At these meetings Anderson fell under the spell of the FBI director, who was only too eager to tutor the novice intelligence director in the business of security.[8]

Hoover fascinated Anderson. "I conceived a very high and warm regard especially for J. Edgar Hoover," Anderson recalled. Such a high regard, in fact, that the naval intelligence director sided with the civilian rather than with his fellow officer Miles in an ongoing feud over intelligence policy in joint intelligence committee meetings. Cooperation went beyond the presidential directive; the DNI ordered his people to share their information and suspect lists fully and openly with FBI agents in the field. To assist the FBI in its surveillance of Japanese-Americans and Japanese visitors, Anderson lent language expert Arthur H. McCollum to Hoover. The FBI reciprocated, helping in plant security, fingerprinting, and the training of investigators. For this training, ONI personnel took a four-week FBI course featuring lectures by the bureau's top Communist-hunter Kenneth McIntire. Particularly useful were radio intercepts from FBI stations in Latin America sent over to Anderson by Hoover and news from the special FBI team dispatched to Quito to aid the naval attaché in an operation against Nazi agents in Ecuador. In an uncharacteristic moment of enthusiasm and praise, Hoover wrote Anderson about their collaboration. "Our relationship during the entire tenure of your assignment to the Office of Naval Intelligence has been an ideal one," he insisted, "and I feel that greater progress has been made in real coordination and cooperation of the Intelligence agencies during this period than at any time heretofore."[9]

Hoover's constant tutelage influenced Anderson's emphasis on domestic security, detective work, and the pursuit of America's internal enemies, eventually at the expense of strategic and naval questions. During his first months as DNI, he urged retired naval personnel to learn all they could about subversive elements in the United States, while selecting for active duty those who provided expertise in investigative work, police methods, safecracking, and other aspects of domestic surveillance. He troubled over his naval investigators' lack of legal authority to detain and arrest suspects. "The effective operation of naval intelligence in connection with espionage in the United States," the DNI informed the General Board in August 1939, "is handicapped by the fact that a Naval agent has no legal authority to make an arrest outside of strictly Naval jurisdiction no matter how vitally the Naval interest may be involved, nor how urgent it may be that the arrest be made." In the same vein, Anderson supported pending legislation to allow government agencies to wiretap, to register all alien-owned fishing boats operating from U.S. ports, and to restrict photography near any U.S. military facility.[10]

The urgent need for such measures increased in August as a sense of imminent crisis descended upon Washington. "The situation is still uncertain, but it is woeful," Secretary of the Interior Harold Ickes observed. "If war does not result, it will be a miracle." The expected conflict occurred sooner and with more fury than even the pessimistic Ickes suspected, when on 1 September sixty German divisions and over one thousand warplanes blitzed into neighboring Poland. Two days later Britain and France declared war, while Russia, ruthlessly exploiting the situation shortly thereafter, invaded eastern Poland. The long-expected Second World War had begun, ushering in history's most titanic military struggle, which resulted eventually in fifteen million combat and thirty-four million civilian deaths.[11]

For the United States, the commencement of fighting led to a neutrality declaration on 4 September and a proclamation of limited national emergency four days later. The latter empowered activation of 145,000 reserve and retired personnel for partial readiness. Though a tentative measure with voluntary enrollments, limited emergency was the first step toward providing the navy with enough manpower to flesh out ship crews and shore complements. It provided Anderson with the opportunity to attach twelve reserve and retired officers to ONI, including Commerce and Travel control veteran Gass and censorship expert Victor F. Blakeslee, and to take additional measures to provide security of secret material. As he wrote Captain Alan G. Kirk, the naval attaché in London, "I find this job quite interesting and very engrossing—particularly under present war conditions and in view of the fact that I want to do one or two constructive things along security lines."[12]

Despite his enthusiasm, though, Anderson discovered that the invasion of Poland and limited emergency had little immediate impact on the thirty officers and thirty-eight civilian employees in ONI. Almost leisurely, the office finished mobilization plans begun under Holmes and worked slowly on developing doctrine to govern delimitation of intelligence. Opposition to Anderson's conception of ONI's wider security obligations appeared within the office, most notably from Captain Carleton F. Bryant, who insisted that naval intelligence should have nothing to do with civilian operations. Moreover, promised funds arrived too slowly to undertake rapid expansion or wide-scale projects, prompting Anderson to contemplate momentarily the juggling of appropriations. "I believe that we can get away with it," Administrative Section head Captain George A. Rood advised, "but, on the other hand, we may have a rude awakening."[13]

In fact, there seemed no cause for taking unnecessary chances or rushing security measures. The collapse of Polish resistance in October led not to wider warfare but to a period referred to journalistically as the "Phony War," during which time France hid behind the massive Maginot Line,

Mussolini waited opportunely to jump into the fight, and Hitler consolidated his gains while planning future adventures. The Russian invasion of Finland in November disturbed the apparent calm only slightly, as this winter war seemed as remote as the frozen wastelands where the Finns battled the Soviet Army to a standstill.

U.S. policies in late 1939 and early 1940 reflected the atmosphere of the Phony War. FDR asked Congress again for neutrality law revision to permit cash-and-carry of war supplies to France and England, but at the same instant insisted that the United States would remain neutral and stay out of the fight. The president took advantage of the lull to dispatch Undersecretary of State Sumner Welles as his special envoy to belligerent capitals to discover if sentiment existed for a peace conference.

Visions of peace disappeared abruptly, however, in the spring of 1940, when in rapid succession Hitler's armies invaded Denmark, Norway, Holland, Belgium, and France. The irresistible force of modern German weaponry and tactics—combined with months of internal intrigue by Nazi sympathizers and subversives, known since the Spanish Civil War as Fifth Columnists—led by June to the startling collapse of organized resistance in Western Europe. Only an incredible rescue operation at Dunkirk saved Allied troops from total destruction, depositing them safety across the English Channel. Their preservation seemed temporary, though, as now Nazi forces massed on the French coast for an invasion of Britain, where a few Royal Air Force fighters were the only British defense against the mighty German war machine. Expecting total German victory, Mussolini chose this moment to enter the war, threatening the British position in the Mediterranean and North Africa.

The French collapse and the threatened invasion of the British Isles stirred the American public, not as FDR hoped to military preparedness, but to anti-alien hysteria. Seemingly nothing stood in the way of Axis agents sweeping across the Atlantic, inundating the Western Hemisphere and combining with sinister Fifth Columnists in Latin America, the Caribbean, and United States. Ultrapatriotic Texas Congressman Martin Dies and Senator Robert R. Reynolds of North Carolina urged Americans to hunt down their internal enemies, while Governor E. D. Rivers of Georgia declared war on all aliens. Such hysteria was contagious; Admiral Leahy insisted that the Fifth Column had infested Puerto Rico already, while Commander in Chief of the U.S. Fleet J. O. Richardson traveled to Washington under the cover of "Mr. Manley" to throw off the secret agents he believed would tail him. At the same time FDR, Berle, and Ickes worried about someone tapping their telephones and spying on them, although Ickes insisted that "to regard every alien as a possible enemy spy or saboteur is the height of asininity."[14]

Confronted by the atmosphere of tension and the fear of aliens, FDR issued another executive order for the FBI, MID, and ONI to coordinate further their battle against subversives, spies, and saboteurs. Designed to improve domestic intelligence and security, the delimitation agreement of June 1940 failed either to clarify doctrine or eliminate overlapping operations and incessant petty rivalries. Most DIOs expressed dismay at the ambiguous nature of the agreement, which left their responsibilities overly vague, asking Anderson for a definition of naval intelligence policy. But the DNI clouded the issue by instructing personnel to leave detective work to the FBI except in cases where the national defense required involvement. Thus, as he advised DIO Captain Roscoe MacFall in the Third District, "in specific and exceptional cases, when it is within the capacity of our service, we should accept information of potential national defense value if it is available to use and the sources refuse to make it available to F.B.I. directly."[15]

Basically, Anderson wanted the DIOs to handle cases without too much interference from other agencies, despite adherence to the delimitation agreement and apparent loyalty to Hoover. In fact, ONI's partnership with Hoover was limited by the naval interest "of which FBI should not have knowledge," and Anderson urged district intelligence people to develop their own investigations and prepare their own suspect lists and card files on Nazis, Fascists, Communists, Japanese, and "Miscellaneous" suspects. In preparing these files, naval investigators were encouraged to discover unpatriotic expressions and threats to naval property among navy yard and base employees by snooping and using paid and volunteer informants. Although Anderson insisted that "informers should be used only for strictly legitimate purposes to further the accomplishment of the mission of the Naval Intelligence Service," he unleashed inevitable excesses such as the pursuit of petty criminals, homosexuals, or supposedly dangerous subversives such as Albanians, Armenians, and the Jehovah's Witnesses. Of particular interest were Afro-American workers in navy yards and private factories doing naval contract work, who according to interception and decryption of coded Japanese wireless messages—a system known as MAGIC—were prime targets for Japanese Fifth Column activity in the United States. The aggressive pursuit of these and other suspects led, as one intelligence officer in the First Naval District observed, to "well meaning but prejudiced, ignorant, often hysterical informants."[16]

Even Anderson became disturbed by the direction of his informant network, warning one volunteer to turn all investigations over to the DIO. "The fundamental idea is to try to keep the control of these important matters within the hands of legally constituted agencies, assisted by information freely given from every possible source," he explained, "but not doing anything which might encourage the formation of vigilante groups that wouldn't have any legal authority and might do harm." Wishing to avoid embarrassment and to coordinate investigative personnel, the DNI brought Lieutenant Commander Coggins, veteran of the Thompson spy case, from the Eleventh Naval District to Washington to compile a coherent investigative training manual so that ONI personnel might learn to locate potentially dangerous individuals at plants and installations without following false leads and pursuing unrelated matters. Discovering a patchwork of training pamphlets, including one FBI publication that guaranteed to train an investigator in a few weeks, Coggins set to work to complete ONI's first professional training manual for naval investigators.[17]

At the same time, Anderson hired special investigator Rhea Whitley, a former FBI agent and counsel for the Dies Committee on Un-American activities, and a pair of FBI detectives named Joseph Cannon and James O'Leary. With Whitley, the DNI gained access to the congressional committee's extensive files on suspected internal enemies such as German-American Bund leader Fritz Kuhn and American Communist Party chief Earl Browder, but also acquired the ultrapatriotic Dies's particular selection of suspects, which included the more liberal members of FDR's New Deal administration. Anderson hired other professionals, but most marched through ONI in search of higher paying jobs. In order to retain Whitley, the DNI secured a boost in rank and pay but still lost his expert along with Cannon and O'Leary to a special police unit organized by the department in late 1940. "Their absence from duty for this protracted period very seriously interferes with the investigative work of this office," which included over 300 cases, Anderson complained bitterly.[18]

For various administrative and organizational reasons, replacements for Whitley and the others were delayed. When veteran Treasury Department sleuth, safecracker, and counterespionage expert Willis George applied to ONI, months passed before he was called to duty. Twice ONI lost his application papers and he had to reapply. "To this day I regard the fact that they ever got around to accepting me as something of a miracle," George recalled. Other skilled operatives were rejected because ONI could not trust them. Thus, when former intelligence officer Carlos V. Cusachs, naval attaché in Havana during World War I and once one of ONI's most valuable agents, applied for duty in 1939, Acting DNI Captain William R. Munroe vetoed the proposal. "There is an extensive record on Mr. Cusachs on file in the Division of Naval Intelligence which definitely establishes him as untrustworthy and entirely unsuitable for employment of this or any other nature with the Navy Department."[19]

Whether trustworthy or not, recently enrolled reserve intelligence officers provided no more assistance in combatting international agents than regular naval personnel in ONI. The Navy Department would not permit naval investigators on duty in the districts to chase a suspect who left the country nor allow an overseas officer to track foreign agents back into the United States. Such transfers were tied in routine red tape and bureaucratic rules and regulations. Thus Anderson needed agents who could travel at will in the course of investigations for ONI. To meet this requirement of countering international espionage and its Fifth Column worldwide, the DNI hired a civilian agent named Wallace B. Phillips to head a secret intelligence section directly under, and answerable solely to, the naval intelligence director. A former intelligence officer with the American Expeditionary Force in England and France during the last world war and since then head of the Pyrene rubber products company in London, Phillips had offered his services to Kirk in October 1939, but the naval attaché had warned Anderson then not to employ him because of his close affiliation with the British war effort and possibly with British intelligence. Ignoring Kirk, the DNI hired Phillips as his special civilian assistant, reportedly at a dollar-a-year salary and with unrestricted access to ONI secret funds and files.[20]

Whatever the propriety or legality of such an arrangement, Anderson used Phillips with the full knowledge of both Secretary of the Navy Frank Knox and FDR. Moreover, Phillips's attributes gave ONI a new dimension. The civilian secret agent boasted extensive personal and business ties on the European continent and in Britain, perhaps including Winston Churchill, and in New York City, especially Sir William Wiseman, coordinator of British espionage in the United States during World War I. Furthermore, in 1940 Phillips directed the American Red Cross drive to supply 350 ambulances and other medical supplies to the hard-pressed British, providing a perfect cover for regular travel back and forth between New York and London to oversee a network of more than 100 paid agents, some on an annual salary of $9,000 plus $10 per day expenses.[21]

Phillips worked for ONI until late 1941 when Colonel William Donovan, then Coordinator of Strategic Information, hired him as director of British operations. What Phillips accomplished for ONI in 1940 remains a mystery. ONI auditor Commander Paul Cassard informed the CNO that naval intelligence wished to keep secret the names and details of Phillips's secret intelligence section. However, ONI did maintain a record of his expense account, which by the late summer of 1941 included $34,500 for secret agents, $15,903 for investigations, and $10,000 direct cash payment to Phillips's bank account.[22]

Employment of Phillips as a civilian assistant underscored Anderson's struggle with the intelligence dilemma. Never before in peacetime had ONI become so entwined in the problem of reconciling the naval and intelligence interests. During the First World War Captain Roger Welles had pursued this course of domestic security, surveillance, and secret operations on a large scale, but after the war ONI limited such clandestine activities primarily to strategic and naval questions in relation to war planning against ORANGE. But when FDR opened the door in 1939 with his memorandum making ONI one of three agencies responsible for domestic security and intelligence, Anderson pushed ONI fully into the unstable world of secret operations. Unfortunately, while focusing on security aspects, naval intelligence's traditional information-gathering work was reduced to what he told his staff was a decidedly "secondary concern."[23]

CHAPTER TWELVE

NEUTRAL OBSERVERS

Most naval officers knew little and probably cared less about ONI's battle against domestic enemies. If they thought about naval intelligence at all, it was as a source of news about foreign naval developments and international conditions. Officers in the War Plans Division (WPD) of the Office of Chief of Naval Operations, on the General Board, or in technical bureaus wanted the latest data on the aerial war in Europe, submarine activity in the Atlantic, and the progress of fighting generally. The General Board, which in late 1940 had as members former DNIs Johnson, Ellis, and Holmes, was especially anxious to hear from all returning naval attachés and intelligence officers, while naval attachés just back from the war zone were interviewed personally by Secretary of the Navy Knox.[1]

Though concentrating on domestic security, Anderson's office routinely collected information about the war. Shortly after the Polish invasion, Anderson instructed all DIOs and naval attachés to rush combat information to his office, explaining that he had some additional funds for the purpose of collecting data on possible threats to the U.S. from belligerent forces, on the disposition of warring fleets and forces, and about the war plans and operations of the various combatants.[2]

Observing wars and accumulating details on weapons and battles was familiar work for ONI, and the staff plunged into this business with far more expertise than that displayed in security areas. Initial reports presented an ominous picture of the war as daily intelligence described attacks on Allied shipping by Nazi submarines in the Atlantic Ocean. Once again the spectre of unrestricted U-Boat warfare and violations of freedom of the seas appeared, threatening to repeat the situation two decades before that had dragged the United States into World War I. Inevitably, rumors arrived about German subs lurking just off the New Jersey, North Carolina, or Maine coasts, disembarking secret agents and making clandestine rendezvous. Between September and December 1939, Anderson's office processed and disseminated reports on everything from a mysterious undersea craft in the Florida Straits to a secret U-Boat base on some Caribbean island, from a Nazi fuel depot in the Galapagos Islands to a sinister sub tender off the Guatemalan shore. Alleged sightings became so numerous and information so uncertain that the DNI urged Admiral Stark to assign a minesweeper or some other small craft to cruise about the American Republics investigating rumors of foreign visitors to the Western Hemisphere.[3]

Activities of German surface raiders raised additional concern that U.S. naval intelligence provide details on the naval side of the war. In December, British cruisers off the Uruguayan coast cornered the notorious Nazi pocket battleship, the *Graf Spee*, fresh from destroying 50,000 tons of Allied merchant shipping. Outnumbered and damaged, the German raider slipped into the temporary refuge of neutral Montevideo harbor, but fearing capture Berlin ordered the prize warship scuttled. Anderson's staff buzzed with excitement as reports of the chase, battle, and final destruction reached their office. The British Empire desk assembled data in a confidential monograph on the Battle of the River Plate, which discussed the tactical aspects of the maritime encounter, and Anderson ordered naval attaché Captain William Denny Brereton, Jr., in Buenos Aires to slip over to Montevideo and purchase at junk prices a piece of armor plate salvaged from the powerful German warship.[4]

ONI tackled the *Graf Spee* exercise with an enthusiasm reminiscent of the office's formative days in the 1880s and 1890s when it had gathered all kinds of blueprints, armor plate samples, and technical data to build the New American steel and steam navy. Indeed, this exercise was strikingly similar to ONI's first real assignment in 1882, which was to scavenge the wreck of a Peruvian armored ram, the *Huascar*, damaged by some Chilean warships. Collecting samples and preparing monographs on tactical exercises were the traditional functions of ONI, easily understood by any U.S. naval intelligence officer. If duty remained this basic, there would be no intelligence dilemma, but unfortunately even the traditional type of assignments in Latin America during the early months of the Second World War indicated that naval intelligence would be far more complicated than the *Graf Spee* affair.

Responsibility for hemispheric defense and the acquisition of information from Latin America rested heavily on ONI. Throughout the interwar period, the office had administered the U.S. Navy's missions in Latin America, and during the early months of World War II the Navy Department reaffirmed ONI's authority over naval aid programs. Pressure to increase naval missions came from FDR and from several Latin American governments. Staff conversations with all republics except Argentina and Ecuador resulted in an accelerated exchange of information and new programs to train and equip Latin American navies. Closest relations developed as usual with Brazil, where head of the U.S. naval mission Admiral Auguste Beauregard urged a candid exchange of technology to "enhance the traditional friendship between the two countries and their navies." Anderson's office selected officers to man the new missions and negotiated contracts with Latin American officials, many of whom visited U.S. facilities and factories. Stark ordered a somewhat reluctant DNI to ease restric-

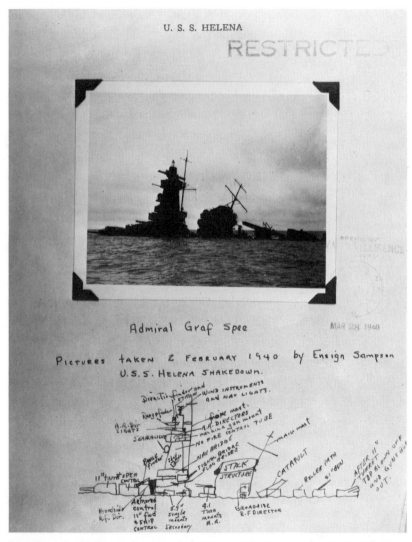

Page from an ONI scrapbook on the sinking of the German battleship *Graf Spee*, reminiscent of the sketches presented in the ONI Information Series in the late nineteenth century.

tions against these visitors so that they might see naval batteries, turrets, and engine rooms on the latest warships. "The object of this relaxation of existing security letter," the CNO explained, "is to further the national policies and the work of our Naval Missions."[5]

Maybe, but the release of information and the increase of aid to Latin America through the naval missions placed ONI in a most difficult position. The office's primary object was to collect data, while denying it to others, but at the same instant FDR's policy of hemispheric solidarity required an extension of confidential information to these people. Latin American chief Blake argued that the more liberal policy posed a grave danger to the navy, since reports crossing his desk revealed that many intimate contacts existed between Latin American officers and German and Italian visitors. Undoubtedly, Nazi and Fascist agents learned at once about any data given in confidence to those governments. Foreign Section head Captain Howard Douglas Bode, one of ONI's most careful officers, warned that all information in his unit pointed to constant inadvertent or intentional divulging of information by Latin American officials to a third party. Bode recommended an exchange of technical data only under exceptional circumstances.[6]

What troubled ONI most was growing evidence that an Axis Fifth Column had become entrenched in the entire area. "I am amused at your agent from Mexico City reporting no German propaganda in Mexico and no Fifth Columnists," Assistant DNI James chided a business friend. "This propaganda and Fifth Column are everywhere, including this country. One part of their Fifth Column activities is for foreigners, whom they may later control, to get charge of American business in Latin American countries." Similarly, reports from naval attachés throughout Latin America pointed to an increase in local German populations. In Bogotá, Captain John C. Munn, USMC, observed thousands of Colombians cheering the news of each Nazi victory in Europe. Meanwhile, U.S. radio interceptions showed extensive traffic between Germans in Cuba and Santo Domingo and a suspected Nazi secret police headquarters in Mexico City. "My reaction in general is that Germany will attempt to use Mexico as a base for her various nefarious schemes," one attaché wrote Anderson in November 1939, "just as in the last war."[7]

During the winter of 1939–40, the Fifth Column troubled ONI representatives in Europe as well. Reports from the Balkans, Scandinavia, and Western Europe warned that Hitler was employing the false quiet of the Phony War to undermine the morale in those regions in preparation for invasion and conquest. Restricted by Nazi officials from traveling around Germany, U.S. naval attaché Schrader wandered to nearby Copenhagen where he discovered German influence everywhere, including twenty-nine press attachés spreading propaganda and subversion in the Danish capital.

Schrader urged ONI to appoint a permanent naval attaché to Denmark before the inevitable spring invasion and absorption of Germany's tiny neighbor. Even in Britain, naval attaché Kirk found what he believed were Fifth Column symptoms among demoralized and defeatist Englishmen during the Phony War. "Inside England there is also an undercurrent of apathy and distaste for the whole war," he cabled Anderson.[8]

The abrupt end of the Phony War in the spring of 1940 forced U.S. observers in Europe to turn their attention from Fifth Columnists to the awesome advance westward of German armor and troops, who by 26 May had reached the English Channel. Kirk trembled at the speed with which the Nazis attacked and overran Dutch, Belgian, and Anglo-French defenders. "In some ways it is like the Harvard football team up against the Green Bay Packers," he wrote former all-American athlete Anderson, offering the DNI two-to-one odds that Nazi troopers would land in England before the autumn. Continuing his exercise in dark humor, Kirk reported how sturdy English farmers armed with fowling pieces stood guard to repulse an expected blitz by heavily armed German paratroopers. "Road signs are beginning to be painted out," he noted sarcastically, "so the Germans can't find their way too easily." After the Dunkirk evacuation, Kirk predicted a cross-channel invasion. "This Island is no more fortified or prepared to withstand an invasion in force than Long Island, New York," he concluded.[9]

Captain Alan Kirk served as naval attaché in wartime London 1939–1940, and then a troubled nine-month tour as DNI in 1941. (Courtesy Franklin D. Roosevelt Library)

Except for the occasional German bombing, which forced relocation of the U.S. Embassy to Headley Park outside London, at least Kirk escaped the war's fury that swept up his colleagues on the continent. In Norway, Lieutenant Commaner Ole Hagen, USNR, the naval attaché assigned to Stockholm and Oslo, evacuated American legation families by driving a Norwegian police car bedecked with tiny U.S. flags through a blinding snowstorm along roads clogged with Nazi troops and vehicles. In fact, Hagen's car slid off the road, and a German armored machine pulled the Americans out of a snow bank. At the same moment, Captain Gade, representing the navy in Belgium, lost contact with ONI for weeks as the fighting raged all around his office. Also cut off from Washington, naval attaché Captain Monroe Kelly risked Nazi wrath in Holland by protecting British interests in that occupied country and remained on station despite growing personal danger in order to monitor news about Japanese activities from the Dutch East Indies, which arrived back at The Hague. For several tense weeks ONI waited for some message from its agents. "There is no communication to or from either The Hague or Brussels," James troubled. "The Western Union and Postal state that they will take messages only at the sender's risk to be delivered when and if the ban is lifted. We have no radio communication at either place."[10]

By far the most important observation post in June 1940 lay in the French capital, where a few days before the collapse of organized resistance Commander Roscoe Hillenkoetter became the U.S. naval attaché. Hill-enkoetter possessed nearly a decade of intelligence experience, including courier service in Russia and Central Europe and frequent trips into Spain, both to observe the civil war and to help evacuate Americans and probably Spanish loyalists after the Barcelona government surrendered to Franco. Thus, when the Germans goose-stepped into Paris on 14 June, ONI had an able observer on hand to report on the occupation. Indeed, Hillenkoetter went into action at once, calling on the German commander, who over a glass of liberated French brandy boasted about Hitler's plans to invade Britain. Then, unable to decline an invitation to review Nazi troops, the neutral U.S. attaché stood at attention as the columns passed, but disappeared opportunely into the crowd before a German cameraman could record the event. Hillenkoetter remained in Paris gathering information about Nazi strength as long as possible, and when Ambassador Bullitt moved the entire staff to Vichy, capital of unoccupied France, the naval officer moved to this vital intelligence listening post, from which he dropped down to North Africa to spy on German activities. His reports from Vichy convinced Washington of the importance of a thorough intelligence network in this strategic region.[11]

Anderson attempted to cover North Africa, the Mediterranean, and Atlantic approaches more thoroughly, and at least as early as August 1940 asked the State Department for permission to place naval reservists as observers in the Canary Islands, Azores, Cape Verde, and Dakar, the last a natural point of departure from the African coast for any force sent to invade South America. The diplomatic branch refused to cooperate, however. As a consequence, ONI employed civilian shipping advisers as substitutes and sought to use a Civil Aeronautic Authority official, who had been invited by Vichy to develop an airport in Dakar, as a cover for a naval intelligence officer. At the last moment, though, Vichy refused a passport to the American aeronautical expert. ONI turned next to something called a food control officer for North Africa and a petroleum observer for Las Palmas in the Canary Islands. None of these ruses was entirely satisfactory, and it would not be until 1941 before a naval observer network connected Gambia, Senegal, Sierra Leone, Portuguese Guinea, Morocco, and the strategic Portuguese islands in the Atlantic Ocean.[12]

Problems in placing U.S. naval agents in Africa exemplified the general difficulty neutral observers had during the first months of world war. In belligerent European countries, naval attachés confronted severe restrictions as to movements and interviews. Captain Thomas Cassin Kinkaid in Rome never got close to an interview with Mussolini, and though he slipped down to Sicily with his wife and an assistant to collect strategic data while pretending to be on vacation, he became nearly useless as a source of valuable information. Schrader grew so unhappy with obstructions that he cabled ONI to restrict the movements of the German naval attaché to within seventy-five miles of Washington. Noting that the Gestapo kept him under constant surveillance, Schrader asked to have the FBI tail the German naval attaché, adding that he stayed alert for key code phrases "Remember Dewey" and "Chicago 1871," which would indicate a break in German-American relations, so that he could destroy secret papers before the Gestapo seized them. There were similar problems even in friendly nations, where U.S. attachés complained of obstacles placed in their way. This was true especially in Britain, where Naval Intelligence Director John H. Godfrey avoided talking to attaché Kirk about substantive matters.[13]

Thus, just as neutrality and limited national emergency led Anderson to turn to Phillips and irregular channels of information, so, too, restrictions on overt gathering of information forced the DNI to consider alternate sources of overseas news. Initially he favored using informants employed by private U.S. shipping companies or airlines to collect details about foreign warships, merchantmen, or submarine activity as well as about ports and commerce. But using civilians to spy on belligerents posed a potential danger to U.S. neutral policies. "The source and transmittal of such information," Anderson advised the General Board, "must be carefully guarded to avoid the suspicion of performance of unneutral service." Therefore he decided to develop a system of reserve naval officers placed at strategic spots around the world and administered under the innocuous title of "naval observers."[14]

The designation naval observer appeared at least as early as 1921 when Captain Weyman Beehler served as the American naval observer to the Allied Commission in Berlin. Such a title became necessary when as a result of U.S. failure to ratify the Treaty of Versailles, the navy could not send a formally accredited naval attaché to the Allied Commission, but wished to retain an observer. In 1935 Puleston revived the naval observer position in order to dispatch del Valle as the only neutral officer to accompany Italian forces into East Africa, and his success prompted the DNI to prepare an entire mobilization slate for naval observers to be activated during a world war. Three years later the title took on new importance when Holmes attempted to send a naval officer to Moscow, and Undersecretary Messersmith told him that Russia would never accept a formal naval attaché. "We know that any agent who goes to Moscow with the label of Military, Naval or Commercial Attaché will be definitely restricted and isolated from the outset," he contended. "He will be under constant espionage and those who would have contact with him we have reason to believe from experience would be subjected to all sorts of dangers." Perhaps the navy could slip in a naval observer instead.[15]

However, the use of naval observers had not become an established method of intelligence when the war broke out in 1939. But using precedents already established, Anderson adopted this means of monitoring affairs in belligerent or neutral nations, and working with sympathetic State Department officials Berle and Ray Atherton, outlined an observer network. The system would extend across the air and shipping lanes along strategic routes from Recife across the Atlantic to the Canaries and Azores and on to Freetown, around the tip of South Africa, and on to Colombo and the Indian subcontinent. From here, Anderson's naval observers would cover Singapore, Port Darwin, and Auckland. Meanwhile, in December 1940 Bode added a routine and doctrine for observers that directed them to acquire, study, and collate any information about the movement of maritime traffic in time of war, most particularly significant changes in the flow of commerce or direction of shipping that might indicate signs of hostile intent against the United States.[16]

The focus of the naval observer skein showed vividly ONI's growing concern with affairs in Asia and the Pacific Ocean, which in recent months had been subordinated by the European war and defense of the Western Hemisphere. While concentrating on the Atlantic phase, the office had monitored the China war as well. Like the army and navy war planners wrestling at the moment with a series of five RAINBOW plans, the intelligence office puzzled over their estimation of whether the Pacific or Atlantic Ocean strategy should assume top priority and precedence. Kirk, for one, insisted that the U.S. assemble the fleet in the Atlantic and Caribbean rather than the Pacific. "For us to take on a war in the Far East would be in my opinion, a most serious error," he warned Anderson from his London vantage point. "Our vital interests are far more concerned with the preservation of the Panama Canal and the Caribbean than with the Philippines or the Dutch East Indies." On the other hand, possessing a more complete picture, Assistant DNI James warned that "the time has arrived when the United States fleet in force should be at Singapore, in order to insure the continued separation of the Japanese fleet from the hostile fleets of Europe." James and most of his comrades in ONI insisted that Japan and the ORANGE War posed the gravest danger to the United States. "I trust that we will not lose sight of the fact that our part of the problem lies largely in the Pacific."[17]

Eventually, American strategic planners would opt for an offensive war in the Atlantic while holding a defensive perimeter in the Pacific, a strategy based on a combination of Anglo-American staff conversations, RAIN-BOW War Plan No. 5, and a paper drawn up by Stark known as Plan Dog. Nevertheless, as reflected by the top quality officers selected for Far Eastern duty during late 1939 and early 1940, Anderson's organization continued to emphasize the Pacific strategy. Commander Harvey Edward Overesch in Peking was simply a "tower of strength," while assistant naval attaché McHugh appeared better yet. "Major McHugh has been indefatigable in maintaining contacts with important people throughout the Chinese Government and in keeping his Department and this Mission informed of developments in a situation where high qualities of tact and patience have been demanded," Ambassador Nelson T. Johnson told Secretary of State Hull.[18]

From Chiang Kai-shek's mountainous capital in exile at Chungking, McHugh intrigued to coordinate Chinese, British, and American espionage and dropped down secretly to Hong Kong in the autumn of 1940 to discuss joint intelligence measures with the British. Undoubtedly reflecting his naval attaché's influence, Johnson asked the State Department to assign McHugh as assistant naval attaché to both China and Britain simultaneously so that he could come and go at will between Chungking and the British colonies of Hong Kong and Burma. Predictably, Washington rejected this unwieldy dual assistant attachéship, and mysteriously the Navy Department recalled McHugh for "service reasons."[19]

The State Department opposed as well ONI's suggestion to relocate the naval attaché's office in Shanghai, site of Japanese naval headquarters in China. Considering diplomatic rather than military needs, Assistant Secretary of State Breckenridge Long advised the Navy Department that such a move was inconsistent with the practice of attaching naval officers to foreign capitals only. In this case, though, obstructionism provided naval in-

Despite growing obstacles to the collection of information in Japan in 1940, ONI's agents Lieutenant Stephen Jurika, assistant naval attaché for air (top row fifth from left), assistant naval attaché and code expert Lieutenant Commander Arthur H. McCollum (top row extreme right), and Commander Henri H. Smith-Hutton, the naval attaché, (seated front row extreme right), provided considerable information about Japanese naval developments before Pearl Harbor.

telligence with an unexpected improvement in its China watch. Instead of relocating the attaché, ONI assigned to Shanghai one of the most able observers in the office's history, Major Gregon A. Williams, USMC. A short, stocky marine with intelligence experience in the Dominican Republic and in ONI headquarters, Williams worked an eighteen-hour day in China to develop networks of observer posts along the coast, informers in the interior, and spies on Japanese merchant ships. "He was an extremely intelligence-wise person who had many, many contacts in the Chinese community and foreign community," assistant naval attaché in Tokyo Stephen Jurika observed later. Williams's agents followed and mapped Japanese Army movements in Eastern China, counted the white boxes that contained cremated remains of Japanese soldiers killed in the China war, and transmitted by radio information to the U.S. Asiatic Fleet about Japanese ship movements. "He was really our operator over there," an admiring Jurika exclaimed.[20]

Williams was not alone. Fourth Marines regimental intelligence officers Majors James S. Monahan and Howard N. Stent, code expert Captain Alva Bryan Lasswell, and assistant regimental intelligence officer Lieutenant Donn C. Hart provided detailed maps of Chinese and Japanese battle positions, lines of advance, photographs of action, and weekly intelligence summaries from their China posts. Despite this successful accumulation of military data, though, these Marine Corps officers displayed somewhat less acumen in recording political events, especially the bitter struggle between Chiang's Kuomintang and Mao's Communist Chinese. Perhaps reflecting the impressions of Evans Carlson and earlier USMC observers that some-how Mao's people might be harnessed to fight the Japanese, Stent mini-mized the conflict between Chinese factions. "While reports of the Chung-king-Communist struggle are being widely circulated especially in the United States," Stent reported, "they are believed to be largely fabricated by American press reporters." But in fairness to Stent, few other American military or diplomatic observers in 1940 displayed any better understand-ing of the convoluted Chinese political situation.[21]

Special reports from naval personnel in China supplemented regular channels of intelligence. Lieutenant Commander Milton Edward Miles, soon to head the controversial Sino-American Cooperative Organization (SACO), wandered through southern China, compiling data for the navy, while Lieutenant Commander Hyman George Rickover, later pioneer of nuclear propulsion but in 1939 commanding officer of an old minesweeper in Chinese waters, forwarded an illustrated intelligence report on the Yunnan-Burma military highway. A few weeks later, Russian language expert, intelligence enthusiast, and constant visitor to Eurasian trouble spots Lieutenant Tolley sent the department his evaluation of current Chinese military and political conditions from his post on the Yangtze patrol. Tolley noted how the Chinese business community, increasingly tired of the fighting, leaned toward full collaboration with Japanese occupa-tion authorities.[22]

Unfortunately, information from Japan paled by comparison. Not only did the Japanese restrict operations by naval attaché Commander Henri Harold Smith-Hutton, but his assistant, Lieutenant Commander Donald McCallum, worried so much about the dangers of travel that he stayed put in the U.S. embassy office. "You could not sit in the embassy in Tokyo and expect to find out what was going on," fellow assistant attaché Jurika contended rather derisively. Nor, despite earlier efforts by Zacharias, had ONI developed an espionage net within Japan. Moreover, Ambassador Joseph C. Grew displayed little sympathy with intelligence operations that might anger his Japanese friends. According to Smith-Hutton, Grew ignored advice to employ more secure codes to transmit secret messages to Washington.[23]

There were sources to be sure. The Standard Oil Company and Na-tional City Bank of New York provided information from their representa-tives in Yokohama and Kobe about ship launchings, while naval reservists working for the American President Lines photographed naval construc-tion clandestinely from behind portholes, and off Kyushu clocked landing intervals of planes coming in on Japanese carriers during training exercises.

Information supplied by the daughter of an International Telephone and Telegraph Company executive proved of such value that naval intelligence enlisted her later as a political analyst. American and European newspapermen and assorted diplomatic officials helped, but despite these sources ONI information about Japan, Japanese naval and military planning, and tactical operations remained tantalizingly incomplete. "I think there were a great many sources," Jurika remembered, "but each one had his own or her own particular piece of a mosaic, and it took a group of us to try to put it in context."[24]

Back in ONI, Major John W. Thomason was concerned less with Jurika's mosaic than with the quality of the pieces. The articulate and iconoclastic marine, author of numerous short stories and head of the Latin American desk, felt that ONI misemployed all overseas personnel. He castigated naval attachés and observers for wasting their time and effort on political, economic, and other peripheral subjects suited better to State Department agents than to naval intelligence officers. Thomason claimed that most information collected during the first year of World War II by ONI personnel had no value whatsoever for naval commanders at sea or war planners in Washington. He urged teaching of the doctrine "that general intelligence is of slight practical value; that it must be collected, evaluated, and tabulated from a point of view; and that point of view is *practical application in war.*"[25]

Thomason's criticism, however valid, assumed a wartime status dominated by combat and operational intelligence. But in 1939 and 1940 the United States was not at war, even if ONI was. Neutral observers were subject to restrictions imposed by both belligerent nations and an isolationist U.S. foreign policy. They were to remain strictly impartial and were forbidden to accompany hostile forces into combat. Even if sympathetic to the Allied cause, naval observers had to be careful not to compromise their government's cautious neutrality nor do anything to draw public or congressional notice through unneutral acts. All the while, a legalistic State Department served as a watchdog to ensure compliance with neutrality policies, and foreign service personnel informed regularly on ONI agents for stretching the correct diplomatic and legal boundaries. Such was the case when the consul at Alexandria expressed shock and demanded an explanation after discovering that Lieutenant Commander John Newton Opie had arrived in Egyptian waters aboard a British man-of-war. At the same instant, U.S. Minister Hugh Grant in Bangkok complained to Secretary Hull about naval attaché Commander Armit Chester Thomas's refusal to reveal confidential matters to him, becoming more agitated when, under secret instruction from the Navy Department, Thomas disappeared from Siam and surfaced in Singapore where he discussed Pacific affairs with British officials.[26]

But while the diplomatic office tried to do its duty under neutrality, at times this conflicted with the naval intelligence mission to keep the U.S. Navy and government informed of the war's military and naval progress. Naval intelligence officers complained incessantly about their problems with diplomats, some of whom reportedly leaked details of the navy's intelligence operations to potential enemy countries. Ambassador Grew's careless use of codes was only one example. This was frustrating, since ONI relied on the diplomatic courier service and consular agents for assistance in the dispatch of war news to Washington, but an indiscreet diplomat in a neutral area might compromise information and hinder the flow of strategic military data—or worse, endanger the lives of naval observers and belligerent informants. "This has to be stopped," the usually taciturn Admiral Robert L. Ghormley warned Stark from his post as special naval observer in London.[27]

The presence of "British Observers" in the United States caused further differences between Anderson's office and the State Department. The passage of a revised Neutrality Act of November 1939 permitting cash-and-carry of war supplies brought a flood of British technical, scientific, and military observers to the United States under the British Purchasing Commission. In December, FDR created the President's Liaison Committee to coordinate purchases by all Allied governments and at the same time to ensure adequate supplies for American armed forces. This process involved ONI because of its cognizance over the visits of foreign representatives to naval facilities and to factories building naval weapons. DNI Anderson personally escorted Sir Henry Tizard and Frederick Lindemann, British scientists and architects of the now famous Ultra wireless intelligence, around the Navy Department. In arranging such visits, ONI and the State Department consulted. Inevitably views differed. When Rear Admiral Raymond Spears, navy representative on the President's Liaison Committee, asked whether British technical observers could fly armed American warplanes in test flights, ONI agreed, but State vetoed the project as "inconsistent with the neutrality of the United States if made for the purpose of training and instruction."[28]

By late 1940, though, this interpretation of Anglo-American collaboration had become difficult to uphold as staff consultations and exchanges of information became more frequent and intimate. In this movement toward naval and military collaboration, the U.S. naval attaché in London assumed a central position, benefiting most fully from the increased flow of vital war news and technical data provided by the British. In the months ahead, the information gathered by scores of ONI personnel in Britain and naval observers with British forces would compensate partly for an otherwise disappointing performance in Europe, Africa, and Japan by the U.S. Navy's neutral observers during the first full year of World War II.

CHAPTER THIRTEEN

ALUSNA LONDON

Between 1939 and late 1941 the United States moved cautiously toward a commitment to defend Great Britain. The decision was not easy for FDR, who unlike Woodrow Wilson never admired the British slavishly and believed the English to be a selfish people. Nevertheless, common heritage and similar national interests in the face of eroding world stability during the 1930s drew the president toward Britain. The turning point came, perhaps, at the futile London Naval Conference of 1935, marking a collapse of postwar arms limitation efforts and leaving Britain as America's only friend. "I must say that our relations with the British have improved remarkably since last year," Norman Davis, chairman of the U.S. delegation, wrote FDR in January 1936.[1]

American resolve to assist Britain appeared fully only after the Nazi blitz of Western Europe and the collapse of France, however. Then the secret correspondence between Churchill and Roosevelt, begun when Germany invaded Poland in September 1939, became more cordial, and months of Anglo-American military contacts moved toward collaboration. During this interval, the U.S. Office of Naval Intelligence provided vital contacts with British officials through its naval attachés in London, and while not nearly as dramatic as the Roosevelt-Churchill secret wartime correspondence, they served to accelerate closer ties and cement practical implementation of Anglo-American military planning.

Ever since 1882 when Commander Chadwick had arrived in London as the first permanent U.S. naval attaché to any overseas post, the British attachéship had remained ONI's most important, profitable, and desirable overseas assignment. Known by its cable address ALUSNA London, the post in the world's leading maritime, colonial, and naval power had served as a center from which to gather data about the latest international, technical, and nautical developments. Chadwick and his successors down the years had forwarded information, hundreds of blueprints, and samples of equipment to assist the U.S. Navy in constructing a modern fleet. Consequently, unlike most other intelligence billets, naval officers welcomed the opportunity to serve in London. "There are a few shore jobs I would rather have had but not many," Captain Russell Willson, the naval attaché in 1938, observed.[2]

U.S. naval attachés had expressed favorable impressions of the British over the years despite occasional tensions and rivalries between the two English-speaking nations. When the United States entered the First World War, naval attaché and force commander Sims promoted intimate Anglo-American collaboration, and after the war Niblack wrote in the Naval Institute *Proceedings* that Britain and the United States had identical interests, despite their momentary postwar economic and naval rivalry. ONI representatives continued this theme throughout the interwar period, and after Dudley Knox expressed one of the rare anti-British statements emanating from the intelligence office, naval attaché Captain Nathan Crook Twining rushed a letter to Knox from London urging a moderate tone and maintaining that Britain wanted American friendship and cooperation. Perhaps McNamee summed up ONI's attitude best in an address to the General Board in 1925. "Now, I think that once and for all we can dismiss

Best known as a mild-mannered naval historian, Dudley W. Knox, seen here leaning over FDR's shoulder, operated behind the scenes for several decades to develop ONI doctrine, and probably as the president's inside man in naval intelligence. (Courtesy UPI Acme)

the possibility of Great Britain ever going to war with the United States," he insisted.[3]

ONI contributed more than moral support for Anglo-American cooperation in 1928 when intelligence officers on duty in Asian waters exchanged views with their British counterparts on a possible joint strategy for the Pacific and Far East in the event of an Asian war. Several years later naval attaché Arthur L. Bristol discussed with Admiralty officials the desirability of Anglo-American collaboration to curb Japanese expansionism. The Far Eastern crisis and Sino-Japanese War in 1937 accelerated consultations, including the dispatch of War Plans Director Captain Royal Eason Ingersoll to London to discuss informally steps to develop a common response to the Asian situation. Naval attaché Willson and his assistant, Commander William Keen Harrill, escorted the director to conversations with the British, adding advice when requested and recording all proceedings for CNO Leahy. The naval attaché reported Ingersoll's activities in separate, confidential dispatches to ONI as well, not an unusual practice but perhaps reflecting early the infighting between War Plans and ONI that would explode in 1940. Though Ingersoll's instructions from the president permitted no concrete arrangements, the conversations led to an exchange of confidential information and naval codes, all through ALUSNA London.[4]

Despite this promising beginning, Roosevelt was reluctant in 1937 to move closer to Britain. Moreover, the British still remained strong enough to bargain as an equal partner with the United States, knowing that the U.S. Navy wanted details on British ASDIC, radar, mine warfare doctrine, and other developments almost as badly as the Admiralty needed U.S. cooperation in patrolling the world's oceans. This was the situation in June 1939 when Captain Alan Goodrich Kirk arrived as the new U.S. naval attaché. A somewhat nervous but enthusiastic officer, Kirk seemed equally excited talking about the beauties of Ascot Racing Week with Air Chief Marshal Sir C. L. N. Newall or on "any subject" with John H. Godfrey, the brilliant and clever director of the Naval Intelligence Division (NID). From the outset Godfrey enchanted Kirk and took the impressionable American naval officer on a tour of the Admiralty's top-secret bomb-proof operational intelligence center, war rooms, and direction-finder stations. Kirk wrote Anderson about how he had accompanied Godfrey through a labyrinth of subterranean corridors lined with watertight doors labeled Japanese Room, Italian Room, Code and Signal Room, and so forth. Unaware that this tour was prearranged as part of a carefully orchestrated program designed to cultivate American sympathy—which included the coincidental visit to Washington and Hyde Park by the King and Queen of England and a secret staff meeting in Admiral Leahy's house—Kirk believed the display was an offer to collaborate with ONI and a promise to open those sealed steel doors to the U.S. naval attaché. "It appears to me evident that a close liaison can be established if it is desired," Kirk told his DNI.[5]

Cautiously Anderson took the bait, recommending visits by British officers to the previously restricted aircraft carrier, the *Saratoga*, to observe the operation of arresting gear to recover planes at sea. In return, the British allowed Kirk to peek at their new antisubmarine boom defense system. Though restrained by official Washington neutrality, Anderson encouraged Kirk to pursue more creative enterprises, although within the guidelines set forth by naval attaché doctrine. "There are no strings tied to you other than the inherent limitations that go with the job," he wrote Kirk. "It goes without saying that no definite commitments of any consequence can be made by an attaché without specific instructions."[6]

The outbreak of fighting in September added new importance and excitement to the London attachéship. Kirk and several assistant naval attachés hurried here and there to keep tabs on damaged British warships docked for repairs. The Admiralty was anxious to have him observe certain ships, such as the *Ark Royal*, so that his report could counteract Nazi claims that the big warship had been sunk by U-Boats. Moreover, the British released selected data to keep Kirk happy, such as information about a captured German magnetic mine sown in English waters from a submarine. However, promise of floods of information failed to materialize. For one thing, Kirk's staff proved too small to follow each lead, and for some reason two of his four assistants provided absolutely no help. At the same instant, the Admiralty became suddenly reticent, forcing Kirk to admit that he could obtain nothing about British operations against German surface raiders or U-Boats, or torpedo damage to British ships. Worse still, the British misled him about the completed submarine net system securing the Home Fleet at Scapa Flow. No sooner had the American officer assured ONI that the British measures were complete than the *U-47* slipped into the anchorage and torpedoed the giant battleship *Royal Oak*, sending her to the bottom in two minutes.[7]

Recognizing that Kirk needed help to collect data, Anderson worked from his end to have a naval observer attached to the British fleet. However, the DNI warned Kirk not to expect the department to extend reciprocity by giving the British similar privileges. Unfortunately, the British demanded a trade before they allowed observers with the fleet, requesting either the Norden Bombsight or the attachment of a British naval observer to the U.S. fleet during Fleet Problem XXI, to be carried out just west of the Hawaiian Islands. Kirk begged Anderson to give the British something, but reflecting Washington's neutral policies, the DNI responded: "There is nothing doing on this for reasons which I cannot elaborate."[8]

Finally, Nazi envelopment of Anglo-French forces, the Dunkirk evacuation, and Winston Churchill's assumption of the prime minister's post changed the atmosphere surrounding Anglo-American naval cooperation. Now Churchill needed U.S. aid to save the British Isles from a feared Nazi invasion and to provide some defense against the German air blitz. In a secret note to FDR on 15 May, the prime minister pleaded for the loan of forty or fifty old destroyers, several hundred fighter aircraft, antiaircraft batteries, munitions, and steel. The ingenious British wartime leader suggested without much subtlety that he might not be able to prevent the British battle fleet from falling into German hands unless he received such material. Meanwhile, the British Passport Control Offices in New York City and in Bermuda aided Churchill's efforts by working with a group of anglophile friends of the president, including Astor, Kermit Roosevelt, and Winthrop Aldrich, to press FDR for more aid to Great Britain. More importantly, Churchill dispatched his confidential agent "Intrepid," Sir William Stephenson, to the United States for months of intrigue designed to promote Anglo-American collaboration.[9]

Somewhat reminiscent of British naval intelligence director "Blinker" Hall's campaign during the First World War, which included release of the infamous Zimmermann Telegram, Godfrey indoctrinated Kirk. First the NID liberalized the release of information about the U-Boat and mine war, damage information, and other combat data, then new Deputy NID Captain W. D. Stephens ingratiated himself to the American naval attaché. This program to convince Kirk of the serious situation in the Atlantic that required U.S. aid worked only too well, as in near panic Kirk rushed his china, linen, and silverware home and poured pessimistic warnings of England's inevitable collapse and occupation back to Washington. Probably reflecting also the overly negative impressions of Britain's slim chance of survival held by U.S. Ambassador Joseph Kennedy, Kirk reported the lack of British defense measures, the supposed attitude of defeatism, and the suspected infiltration by a sinister and effective Axis Fifth Column. "To me it is hard to understand why martial law has not been declared some time ago," he cabled Anderson. "The countryside swarms with German Jews, Poles, Belgians, Dutch, French—everything under the sun."[10]

Despite his obvious overreaction to the situation, Kirk produced the results desired by British intelligence; he advised Washington to strengthen the Atlantic defenses and guard the Panama Canal and Caribbean rather than focus on the distant Philippines or Far East. On 11 June, Kirk warned Anderson that as soon as Hitler conquered Western Europe and occupied the British Isles, he would cross the Atlantic Ocean and attack British territories in the Western Hemisphere. "After they have finished over there this summer, they will be prepared to take time by the forelock and move in on South America and the Caribbean, or perhaps, even Canada, so rapidly that we won't realize what is happening," Kirk wrote excitedly. Undoubtedly Anderson, who met three times a week with FDR, brought the attaché's opinions to the president, and these reports reinforced the remarkably identical statements expressed at the same instant by Churchill in his direct correspondence with Roosevelt. Both pressed the U.S. president to adopt an Atlantic-first strategy.[11]

Before a nervous FDR made any definite decisions on overall strategy, however, he needed more information from abroad than that supplied by the London naval attaché and British naval friend Churchill. Thus in July, Roosevelt turned to his favorite policy of dispatching private confidential agents to gather intimate data for his eyes only. With the advice of new Secretary of the Navy Knox, Roosevelt selected a tough Irish war hero and former law school classmate, William J. Donovan, as his secret observer to report on Britain's prospect for survival. A firm defender of administration foreign policies, Donovan received unrestricted authority to investigate conditions in the war zone. But just to make certain, a few weeks after Donovan left Washington for London, FDR sent yet another personal envoy, Admiral Robert Lee Ghormley, to gather facts on the naval situation. Without much thought about existing organizational guidelines, Roosevelt designated Ghormley as the naval attaché to London.[12]

The arrival of the two presidential agents embarrassed Kirk and angered Ambassador Kennedy, used to serving as the primary source of information about the war in England. Kennedy opposed Donovan's mission from the outset, while naval attaché Kirk found Ghormley's designation as another naval attaché especially disconcerting since ONI had neither recalled nor transferred him. Nevertheless, apparently the charming Donovan cleared the air momentarily with fellow Irishman Kennedy, and brought Kirk, whom he had known earlier, into his confidence as the two visited the proper Admiralty and Air Ministry offices. "I have enjoyed very much renewing an old friendship with him," Kirk wrote Anderson, "and he has expressed himself as being quite gratified—at least to date." Moreover, Donovan intervened on Kirk's behalf with the White House, supporting ONI's effort to get Ghormley redesignated as a Special Naval Observer (SPENAVO) rather than ALUSNA. "It leaves me free and also saves face," Kirk told Donovan, "which is quite important over here."[13]

In any case, the rush of events subordinated petty jealousies. Pressed by Hermann Goering's Luftwaffe and struggling for survival in Europe, North Africa, and the Mediterranean, Britain extended even the most secret data to American naval observers, including technical information on ULTRA short-wave radio transmission, direction finding, radar, ASDIC, and minesweeping. The Admiralty eased restrictions on U.S. naval observers as well, and ONI poured assistant attachés, technical experts, air combat observers, amphibious warfare experts, and antisubmarine warfare students to England, to operating units at sea, and to the most remote

British Commonwealth possessions around the world. "The decision to send the extra officers here to study all the ramifications of the German mine, mine sweeping, and De Gaussing," Kirk wrote the DNI, "is very gratifying."[14]

At the same time, Donovan received even better treatment, gaining access to the most secret intelligence sections, upon which later he would model his own Office of Strategic Services (OSS). Donovan's tour so impressed him that upon returning to Washington he told Roosevelt that Britain would fight on even if the U.S. supplied only a few old, four-stacked destroyers, which were built during the First World War and were long since relegated to the mothball reserve fleet.[15]

After Donovan's departure, Kirk concentrated on escorting Ghormley and special army observers General George V. Strong and Major General Delos C. Emmons to a series of strategy sessions with top British war planners headed by Admiral Sir Sydney R. Bailey, a former naval attaché to Washington. Bailey's team expected substantive talks, since for months Kirk had promised eventual U.S. cooperation. In fact, the naval attaché had already outlined with friend Godfrey the framework for an Anglo-American naval intelligence network, which would radiate out from London to centers in Ottawa, Washington, and Singapore and would have a string of joint high-frequency radio direction-finding (HF/DF) stations to intercept enemy communications and pinpoint U-Boats. But although Kirk had carried on such conversations with Godfrey in an informal fashion only, either he became a bit too enthusiastic in his promises of collaboration or the British had led him into making such promises. Either way, Ghormley made no such promises, because he believed that his instructions prevented formal joint staff talks.[16]

Greatly disappointed, Kirk asked Washington for a daily bulletin defining the current U.S. position in relation to Great Britain so that he would not be embarrassed again by pledging anything at conferences. At the same moment, he asked for a greatly expanded naval attaché office, implying his need for more authority to carry out American policies in Britain. The Navy Department's response was swift and firm. Stark opposed both the issuance of a daily memorandum and expansion of the attaché's powers, reflecting the advice of his new War Plans Division director Admiral Richmond Kelly Turner, who warned about leaks from the attaché's office.[17]

Kirk's discomfiture resulted at least partly from the larger political problems at home. Facing an upcoming election and wary of powerful isolationist sentiment, FDR refused to rush into any formal joint military understandings. His secret correspondence with Churchill, in which he resisted ardent overtures for closer Anglo-American bonds, reflected this cautious approach. Consequently, the Navy Department waited for firmer

Captain Alan G. Kirk, naval attaché in London 1939–1940, and DNI 1940–1941 (right), escorts the Duke of Windsor out of ONI in September 1941. Kirk served as a vital link in Anglo-American collaborations before U.S. entry into the war.

direction, recalling Ghormley and squabbling over which of the RAIN-BOW plans to adopt as a basic strategy. CinCUS Richardson visited the White House to discuss naval policies but left unhappy that the president underestimated, in his view, the Japanese menace and Pacific security. The General Board reported that the navy seemed less ready to defend both coasts than it had been months before, noting specific weaknesses in the mobilization plan, fleet command concepts, inadequate security, terrible antisubmarine measures, and an outdated electric coding machine.[18]

Finally, in late October 1940 Stark and his War Plans Division prepared a study of overall strategic requirements and options, focusing on Anglo-American cooperation. The memorandum presented four possibilities, including Plan A for the defense of the Western Hemisphere only, Plan B for offensive operations in the Pacific and defensive operations in the Atlantic, Plan C for assistance to the Allies on both oceans equally, and Plan D for an aggressive war in the Atlantic and a holding operation in the Pacific. Stark's paper warned against a two-ocean war and reflected both the suggestions of SPENAVO Ghormley and ALUSNA Kirk for an Atlantic-first strategy. Thus Plan D or Dog was the logical conclusion, and both army and navy war planners endorsed it. But FDR still hesitated to adopt any specific plan.[19]

While Washington debated policy, back in London Ghormley's mission had left some avenues for further Anglo-American naval discussions and had prepared the way for more formal arrangements. In general terms, preliminary plans had been made for allocation of forces, logistical lines, communications and intelligence services, and wider sharing of technical and strategic information, especially about the Japanese. Undoubtedly persuaded by Kirk, Bailey insisted that the American naval attaché remain the "regular Admiralty route" for the exchange of information. Ghormley agreed, explaining that routing through Kirk was probably the best channel. "The process of getting the information obtained here to the technical consumer, on technical questions in complete form and promptly, is one of the most important functions of the work in which we are now engaged," he cabled Stark just before departing for America.[20]

Soon after Ghormley arrived in Washington, Kirk followed to consult with department leaders, leaving affairs in the hands of acting naval attaché Captain Charles A. Lockwood and thirty-five assistants and observers. What Kirk discovered upon arriving in the United States was a much firmer attitude toward Anglo-American collaboration on the part of the Roosevelt administration than had existed during his entire tour in London. Secure in his reelection, Roosevelt had been moved by Churchill's impassioned plea on 7 December 1940 that the English-speaking democracies must stand together; now Stark's Plan Dog gave the president a concrete strategic statement with which to frame such assistance. Thus, when Kirk set foot in Washington, FDR had just established the Office of Production Management and presented his fireside chat of 29 December calling the United States the "arsenal of democracy."[21]

The pace of events the following few weeks quickened further, culminating in the passage of the monumental $51-billion Lend-Lease Act on 11 March 1941. At the same time, FDR extended the security zone of 1939 deep into the North Atlantic to protect the flow of goods under the new law and coordinated convoy routing and patrols with the British government. To assist in protecting lend-lease-laden ships, the U.S. set up a base in Greenland and allowed British escort vessels to be repaired clandestinely in American dockyards. Meanwhile, the first of fourteen sessions of the long-awaited American-British Conversations (ABC) began in Washington on 29 January with Kirk joining Ghormley and "Kelly" Turner and Army representatives Gerow, Sherman Miles, and Stanley Embick at the meeting. It was fitting that Kirk serve as acting secretary and speak for the strengthening of Anglo-American defense measures during the initial session, for no U.S. official had labored more diligently than the naval attaché to prepare groundwork for such conversations.[22]

In addition to duty with the ABC-1 session, Kirk used his time in Washington to visit various departmental bureaus to share observations on captured German weaponry shown to him by the British, including magnetic mines. He discussed as well damage information gathered from visits to British warships. Then one afternoon, former DNI Holmes took him over to see the president, where Kirk explained how the British harnessed their best scientific minds to the development of new weapons and methods to counteract enemy military technology. His conversation with FDR, Kirk insisted later, resulted in the appointment of Dr. Vannevar Bush, president of Carnegie Institute, to head a similar American scientific task force. Next, Kirk lectured the General Board, the Secretary of the Navy, the Undersecretary, and other department officials about his findings in London. "It appeared that Mr. Knox and Mr. Forrestal had been so impressed by my speech before the General Board and all the high brass of the Department," he boasted, "that they'd decided they were going to make me the Director of Naval Intelligence."[23]

Kirk's appointment as DNI seemed a natural outgrowth of his service as ALUSNA London. Many of his predecessors had served in both capacities, including the first naval attaché Chadwick and most recently Anderson. Over the past two years few officers had become as familiar with the larger strategic, operational, and intelligence questions posed by the European crisis. At the same time, Kirk worked well with British officers, an important attribute in the evolving Anglo-American alliance. Furthermore, he had learned from Godfrey about counterespionage and operational intelligence, while at the same time developing some competence with his department's own mechanical ciphering machine. In the months ahead, his ability to transform ONI into an organization similar to the combined intelligence office headed by Godfrey would determine whether or not the U.S. Navy's intelligence office could perform its duties both in securing the naval establishment and in providing adequate and timely information for war planners.

CHAPTER FOURTEEN

INTERNAL STRUGGLES

Several weeks after becoming DNI, Kirk greeted old friend Godfrey and his dashing personal assistant, Commander Ian Fleming, who had arrived most opportunely in Washington as part of a joint staff mission under Admiral Sir Charles Little. Kirk arranged a luncheon for Godfrey to meet FBI director Hoover and intelligence liaison Berle, while apparently Fleming, future author of James Bond spy thrillers, slipped off to a quiet rendezvous with Colonel Donovan to draw up the charter for a secret American intelligence section. Later, Kirk invited the British experts to tour ONI and lend advice on a proposed reorganization of the U.S. naval intelligence office. The NID team found ONI's coverage of Japanese affairs satisfactory, but were not nearly as impressed with the rest of the agency as Kirk had been two years earlier with Godfrey's shop. Particularly disconcerting to the Admiralty professionals was the apparent lack of integration of intelligence, war planning, and operations. They found that Kirk's office was isolated from other divisions of the CNO's office and remote from important parts of the U.S. naval establishment. "It became obvious to the visitors that the Office of Naval Information [sic] lacked prestige," one British intelligence expert noted, "and was in worse shape than the NID had been back in the early thirties."[1]

The British view was overly pessimistic, and what they referred to as lack of prestige was more the usual frustrations of American bureaucracy, red tape, and poor organization. Nevertheless, as the British surmised, Kirk and his organization confronted a difficult situation in early 1941. Partly the problem stemmed from ONI's historical evolution, which at various times had located the office as a minor appendage of the bureau of navigation, the office of assistant secretary of the navy, and presently as one of eleven divisions of the office of chief of naval operations. But no matter where the department had placed ONI on its organizational chart, never had it bothered to delineate intelligence doctrine clearly beyond providing general instructions to collect, collate, and store naval information. From time to time a civilian Secretary or CNO had directed ONI to oversee publicity, security, or a secret operation, but more often the Navy Department had ignored the office as it went about peacetime routine. Inevitably, that routine generated the natural manifestations of any intelligence organization, such as spying, surreptitious entry, communications intercepts, and surveillance. The more complex this side of ONI work, the more the office neglected its primary function to supply the Navy with technical and strategic information.

Most recently Holmes and Anderson had wrestled with and succumbed to the naval intelligence dilemma, leading ONI into broader interpretations of its mission. But when Anderson left the office in December 1940, several of his section heads disavowed their former commanding officer's interpretation of intelligence, directing DIOs to disregard all previous orders to unearth espionage and Fifth Column activity in their districts. "The instructions Nixon and I were required to give you then are not in accordance with my conception of the field of activity of Naval Intelligence," head of ONI's planning branch Bryant informed all DIOs in February 1941, and "they do not agree with the conception of our functions of the present director." But then the present director, Captain Jules James, served merely as a two-month interim DNI until the department settled on Kirk.[2]

In March, Kirk confronted this depressingly redundant situation, only this time during a period punctuated by the complete breakdown of U.S. neutrality, a proclamation of unlimited national emergency, and a paralyzing internal conflict within the Navy Department itself. Thus, the usual period of adjustment was more disoriented and traumatic for Kirk than for any previous director in ONI's sixty-year history. To a certain extent Kirk's early difficulties arose from personal considerations. From the beginning he felt uncomfortable about taking over ONI, fearing that it interrupted the normal promotion process. "I must say it is with some trepidation as it causes me to lose my chance to get to sea," Kirk wrote a fellow officer. "This is the first time I ever changed shore jobs."[3]

Complicating matters, during the first week on the job Kirk fell ill briefly, and administrative head Rood ran the office while Captain Frank T. Leighton wrestled unsuccessfully with Kirk's instruction to draw up a model for an operational intelligence agency based on Godfrey's design. When Kirk returned to his desk, he faced so many personnel and administrative problems that he delayed and later abandoned dreams for ONI reorganization. Of immediate concern was FDR's summons to the White House to discuss the placement of presidential crony Astor as Coordinator of Intelligence for the New York area, to be administered loosely by Kirk from the Washington end. A few weeks later Kirk confronted pressure from Astor, DIO MacFall, and Third District Commandant Admiral Adolphus Andrews to get rid of Anderson's secret agent Phillips.[4]

Worse still, Kirk lost all four of his most seasoned section heads to sea duty, including counterespionage chief Nixon. The latter loss troubled the DNI most, since as naval attaché he had shown little patience with this side of intelligence, finding the simple procedure of securing the embassy safe and codes so difficult that Godfrey had complained about security leaks from the American attaché's office. As DNI, Kirk needed assistance in this field, but above all he required time to study the new position and become acquainted with the different aspects of intelligence. Normally a director took six or more months to adjust to the assignment, which differed from any other commands, shore-based and shipboard.[5]

Unfortunately, during Kirk's first months in ONI the international situation changed at such a maddening pace that he had to plunge headlong into the job without learning the ropes through normal routine. In April, Germany invaded Yugoslavia and Greece. The next month, Hitler's troops seized Crete, poured into Egypt, and battled Britain for control of North Africa. At the same moment in Asia, Japan captured Foochow, expanded the war in southern China, pressed into Southeast Asia, and threatened further advances into British and Dutch territories. Then on 22 June, Hitler shocked all except those with access to secret radio transmissions and codes, by invading the Soviet Union, his nonaggression partner.

All the while President Roosevelt slipped toward total involvement in the world conflict by implementing the Lend-Lease Act of March to supply not only Britain, but China, Russia, and any other nation resisting Axis attack. Convinced that by welding American productive might to forces battling invasion he could protect the national interest and at the same time keep the U.S. out of the fighting itself, actually FDR increased the likelihood of participation in the war. On 9 April, the United States established a base in Greenland, both to block Axis occupation and to protect the northern routes used to convoy some 5,400 airplanes, 400,000 Thompson submachine guns, 3,400 Universal carriers, and 5,500 Oerlikon guns, all of which were released to Britain in late March. Then the president announced that U.S. warships would patrol far out into the Atlantic Ocean as part of an enlarged security zone, using the naval and air bases transferred to the United States from British possessions in the Western Hemisphere as part of a destroyers-for-bases deal in September 1940. On 18 April the navy was ordered to attack Axis ships in this zone as the first step of what by the summer of 1941 became an undeclared and clandestine war against Hitler's navy.[6]

The expanded Atlantic war and threats to the security of the Western Hemisphere prompted Roosevelt to declare on 27 May a state of unlimited national emergency and the next month to freeze Axis assets and close consular offices. In July the president ordered a base in Iceland, and on 9 August met at last with his secret naval friend aboard the cruiser *Augusta* off the Newfoundland coast. This Atlantic conference between FDR and Churchill led to a joint declaration of principles known as the Atlantic Charter and brought Anglo-American collaboration close to a formal military alliance.

Each step between March and August 1941 accelerated the pace of U.S. Navy war planning and preparations. By May the department had settled on RAINBOW V as its major war plan, and the next month Stark solidified the strategy with his Plan Dog. At the same time, the General Board circulated "Are We Ready No. III," outlining needs and deficiencies as well as estimating force levels required to carry out an offensive in the Atlantic and a defensive war in the Pacific. Both RAINBOW V and Ready III defined the U.S. Navy's intelligence doctrine, placing the emphasis on ONI's function in securing the navy against sabotage, espionage, and subversive activity. RAINBOW V outlined various ONI tasks, including the denial of information to the enemy and the preparation of joint intelligence, censorship, and publicity plans with other agencies. Concurrently, the readiness study specified the investigation of civilian personnel with access to classified matter and called for the infiltration into potential enemy regions by naval secret agents. In addition, Ready III recognized ONI's requirement to mobilize and train intelligence personnel in order to investigate labor unrest, which undermined the national defense industries and threatened security in naval facilities. "A great deal of the work of Naval Intelligence should be done prior to war," the study concluded.[7]

Essentially these policy statements envisaged ONI as a security agency. Indeed domestic security, counterespionage, and protection against internal enemies seemed the most immediate and pressing need for Kirk in March 1941. Information greeting the new director indicated widespread attempts to sabotage Italian ships in U.S. harbors. The problem appeared so acute that Kirk contacted the president at his vacation retreat. At the same time, news flooded Kirk's office about alien-owned fishing boats prowling close to U.S. naval training exercises, bases, and key ports, especially in the vicinity of the Hawaiian Islands and Pearl Harbor. Intelligence from the Eleventh Naval District revealed that a fishing vessel had carried suspected Nazi agents from Puntarenas, Costa Rica, to Newport Beach, California, while an FBI report insisted that the entire crew of a merchant ship landed to engage in espionage on the Pacific coast. By August 1941 Commander Keisker of ONI informed the FBI that he believed hundreds of alien-owned fishing boats and other small vessels had easy ingress and egress to any spot along the U.S. shoreline. "Use of such craft for clandestine transportation of persons or material between shore and vessels at sea not only is a possibility," Keisker contended, but "it is a probability."[8]

In the meantime, other security duties arose from the Lend-Lease law. A week after Congress passed the path-breaking legislation, the Navy Department ordered ONI to guard against possible sabotage of navy yards repairing British ships, in ports handling lend-lease material, and in ammunition terminals such as the top-secret facility in Bayonne, New Jersey. In related developments, ONI activated its Coastal Information and Commerce and Travel Sections to scan the Atlantic seaboard and ports for possible incursions of German submarines that might land spies or saboteurs. Commerce and Travel worked with other government offices to check visas, search for possible suspicious persons on board ships in U.S. ports—especially Axis radio operators—and to detect sabotage.[9]

The state of unlimited emergency intensified demands for security, and ONI and district intelligence went on twenty-four-hour watches to monitor any threats to the naval establishment. Meanwhile, the FBI turned over to ONI all inspections of private factories doing naval classified contract work, citing the battle against the Fifth Column as the excuse for withdrawing agents. In order to facilitate this unfamiliar investigative job, Kirk set up a plant inspection school to instruct ONI officers, who then practiced field work at Bethlehem Steel, Glenn Martin Aircraft, and Newport News Shipbuilding and Drydock companies and at the Washington Navy Yard and Indian Head naval powder works. Furthermore, ONI expanded its file-card system, adding a merchant marine suspect list and drawing liberally from indexes of suspected dangerous internal enemies compiled by FBI director Hoover and from biographical files accumulated by the Dies Committee, the latter filled with what one veteran investigator insisted was "more hearsay than accurate information."[10]

Clearly domestic security, counterespionage, and police work dominated Kirk's attention in early 1941. Intelligence expert Zacharias tried to warn Kirk to avoid overemphasizing this aspect of ONI duty. "Purely investigative activities," Zacharias wrote Kirk, ". . . are only a small segment of a military operational function, therefore these activities must be kept on the proper plane if the tail is not to wag the dog." The stubborn director ignored Zacharias's unsolicited advice, instead succumbing completely to the investigative and narrower interpretation of naval intelligence. In a lengthy letter to Lockwood, his successor as naval attaché in London, Kirk revealed his obsession with domestic security. The United States crawled with Fifth Columnists and alien agents, he told Lockwood. "Here we are in about the same state of mind that Holland was in about two weeks before she was invaded last Spring." Kirk believed that labor unrest, strikes, and propaganda activities by the America First Committee and other isolationists had "all the earmarks of being part of an organized plot." He admitted that he had no legal proof, "yet, I am pretty certain this is the case." The director asked Lockwood to warn the department in a separate dispatch about the dangers posed by Fifth Columnists and Axis agents. "There is, as yet, no rally cry for the American people to take up," he worried. "It is the greatest need of the moment."[11]

Like Anderson earlier, Kirk turned to the omnipresent FBI director for assistance in combating internal enemies. "I have enjoyed meeting Mr. Hoover, who sent kind messages to you," he wrote Anderson. "He has a most interesting personality, and I hope my relations with him will be as cordial as yours." They were not. Already in late March Kirk had learned that the FBI violated the delimitation agreement by investigating cases on Guam and Samoa, both under the jurisdiction of naval intelligence. Later Kirk insisted that he ran afoul of Hoover because of larger issues, contending that the conflict stemmed from a long-standing ONI-FBI feud and from Hoover's attempt to dominate all intelligence. As Kirk maintained, overlapping responsibilities and rivalries had plagued relations in the past; however, both Holmes and Anderson had managed to work well with the domineering Hoover. Moreover, the FBI had left most naval investigations strictly to ONI, because the organization was spread too thin to pursue all cases in 1941. Thus the tensions arose more from Kirk's own sensitivities and unwillingness to continue Anderson's policy of accommodation in joint intelligence meetings.[12]

Unlike his predecessors, Kirk never sided with Hoover against MID. Rather, he cooperated closely with army intelligence, especially to counteract the growing influence of "Wild Bill" Donovan, who was made coordinator of strategic information by the president in June. Both service agencies considered Donovan an unwelcome rival in the intelligence field. Already ONI and MID prepared alternate-day intelligence summaries for FDR and key cabinet officers, and both worried that the president would now consult instead the data provided by the new Office of Coordinator of Information. Apparently for a moment Kirk pondered a plan for a combined intelligence office merging Donovan's agency with ONI and MID, where the two service organizations could watch and outvote the civilian intelligence agency. However, the DNI rejected this idea as premature, opting instead for complete ONI autonomy and limiting contact with other bureaus through liaison officers and committees.[13]

In reality, though, it was difficult for Kirk to contemplate any merger or reorganization when his own office lay in near physical disarray. In April he had moved the entire division of 125 rooms, manned by fifty-three naval officers and several dozen civilian employees, to the new Navy Department facility, where for weeks carpenters and electricians installed lighting, airconditioning, and shelves for the storage of confidential documents. When this increased space proved inadequate as well, Kirk looked around for rooms in other government buildings in order to relocate his entire ONI censorship section. More disruptive still were the industrial management consultants from the Chicago firm of Booz, Allen, and Fry, brought in earlier by Secretary Knox to prepare a survey of departmental administration. These civilians wandered about prying into files, the mail room, and offices in an attempt to discover organizational shortcomings. All the while Kirk confronted each change or expansion by recasting ONI's budget estimates and reviewing requests for everything from additional marine guards to the acquisition of two motorcycles with which to rush urgent messages around Washington.[14]

Thus, during the first part of his directorship, Kirk discovered that he had inherited a sprawling organization with poorly coordinated and defined missions, internal tensions, and overlapping authority with other agencies—all of which took attention away from international crises and world war. Although unaware that he had become another victim of the so-called intelligence dilemma, Kirk did recognize that he faced a basic contradiction between his position as a professional naval officer and that of an intelligence chief. "As you know better than I," he confided to former DNI Anderson, "the task here is varied, confining, and of course, to me, *covering fields not within the ordinary ken of naval officers.*" (Italics added.) This contradiction complicated his primary task of providing strategic information to the Navy Department from the European theatre and from the increasingly dangerous Far Eastern war zone.[15]

Kirk tried to fulfill traditional information-gathering services for the navy by expanding foreign personnel. Hundreds of technicians, experts, and observers accompanied lend-lease equipment overseas, coming under the direct cognizance and clerical province of his office. By mid-summer Kirk directed several hundred observers in Britain alone, 130 of these in the aviation section under Commander Ralph A. Ofstie. Naval aviators such as Commander William E. G. Taylor, USNR, accompanied RAF fighters and watched interception methods. "I made frequent reports of what I had learned to the American Naval Attaché, London," Taylor explained. Other navy personnel aided British pilots in establishing long-range patrol wings equipped with PBY-5 Catalinas from bases in Scotland. Marine Corps aviators Edward Colston Dyer and Walter Greatsinger Farrell, a former Olympic swimming champion, observed British air operations in North Africa and in the Mediterranean. Inevitably American casualties occurred, and in May 1941 Lieutenant Eugene Edward Davis became the first naval observer killed when his plane crashed off the Portuguese coast. Later, the foreign war touched ONI more closely still when a plane carrying Captain Sherwood Picking and an intelligence team disappeared with all hands over the Atlantic Ocean.[16]

More fortunate were Lieutenant Commander Robert S. Quackenbush and USMC amphibious warfare expert John Crawford McQueen. Quackenbush studied British photographic intelligence methods and doctrine, especially air intelligence over Nazi occupied Europe, and returned to press for a naval photographic intelligence school in Washington. McQueen worked with the Royal Marines at Inverary to develop training doctrine and to test landing craft. Then the Navy Department assigned McQueen to escort a shipment of most secret radio direction gear from London to Washington. McQueen arrived safely in New York City only to be accosted by plain clothes detectives claiming to work for ONI and demanding possession of the secret equipment. Needless to say, the tough marine refused to turn the set over to these sleuths and accompanied the shipment personally all the way to ONI's mail room in Washington.[17]

Kirk placed naval observers and attachés in other strategically important areas in mid-1941. In late March he drew up with Foreign Section head Bode and General Miles of G-2 a plan for North African observers, which assigned army personnel to Algiers, Tunis, Petit Jean, and Oudja and naval intelligence officers to Casablanca, Oran, and Bone. For the Azores and Canaries, he relied on several seasoned World War I intelligence veterans activated especially for the job of watching pro-Nazi activity on these vital Portuguese islands. The DNI ran into trouble, though, when he replaced popular Captain Ben Harrison Wyatt as naval attaché in Madrid. The new officer proved indiscreet. "His criticism of the British and their conduct of the war is 'copious' and 'defeatist,'" Undersecretary of State Welles informed Stark in June.[18]

Hitler's invasion of the Balkans and then Russia widened the scope of ONI's observer system. FDR urged naval intelligence to reassign a naval attaché to Turkey, a post left vacant recently because of State Department opposition and infighting with the WPD. The latter insisted that Commander Rufus King, the officer selected by ONI as naval attaché for Turkey, was of far more value to the service as war plans officer in the Tenth Naval District. At the same time, placing an attaché or naval observer in Russia posed a complex and troublesome enigma. Ever since Nimmer's withdrawal in 1935, both the Soviet government and the cautious U.S. State Department had blocked efforts by ONI to send another naval attaché to Moscow. In April 1941, prior to the Nazi invasion and FDR's extension of lend-lease aid to Stalin, Secretary of the Navy Knox suggested that since the Russians had sent several assistant naval attachés to Washington in recent months, the Navy Department needed some representation in Moscow. But the diplomatic branch opposed the move, citing lack of adequate housing and the risk of angering the Soviet regime.[19]

Kirk determined to get a man in Moscow, meeting with Acting Chief of the Division of European Affairs Atherton and his assistant Henderson. Naturally the diplomats repeated the earlier advice, but Kirk insisted that since the Soviet Union seemed destined to play an important part in the war, the U.S. Navy should have an observer on the spot. However, it was more lend-lease policy than Kirk's arguments that eventually opened Russia to ONI personnel. In July the Navy Department pressed for the dispatch of Lieutenant Commander Ronald H. Allen and Lieutenants Frankel and George D. Roullard for duty in Moscow and Vladivostock. This time the Soviets had to accept, but in an early expression of wartime distrust insisted that all U.S. naval observers remain in Moscow and refrain from travel in Russia.[20]

While concentrating on the European war in 1941, Kirk's people continued to monitor developments elsewhere. In August the DNI sent Thomason on a ten-week trip to coordinate naval intelligence throughout Latin America. "I made a three months' tour by air of the whole damned place," the petulant intelligence officer told his friend Zacharias. "Now, God help me, I'm an expert." More temperate were the observations of Rear Admiral Stanford Caldwell Hooper, pioneering U.S. Navy radio communications officer and former ONI staffer. After visiting Mexico, Hooper reported to Kirk that secret radio direction-finding equipment was needed to monitor German communications. "The Naval Attaché is in urgent need of a small additional sum to assist in obtaining information, which is easily available for cash, such as keeping track of suspicious characters and shipments of Nazi and Japanese material."[21]

When rumors reached the office about Nazi agents stationed in Vichy-administered French Guiana posing a threat to the nearby bauxite mines in Surinam, Kirk sent marine intelligence specialist Major Theodore A. Holdahl to investigate. Holdahl found the bauxite mines unguarded and a tempting target for any Axis saboteur. When attachés or observers were not enough, the director resorted to other methods of observation. To cover the strategic passage around the tip of South America, he relied on the vice consul at Punta Arenas after the Chilean government refused to permit the stationing of a U.S. naval observer. Fortunately, the vice consul was a Naval Academy graduate, who forwarded useful shipping news and naval information to Kirk's office.[22]

Each additional observer and report increased the amount of raw information arriving in Kirk's already overworked office. Though several hundred reservists had enrolled during the past year, most required further indoctrination in the varied operations of plant protection, coastal watch, and security investigations, as well as training in the basic collection, collation, and distribution of information. These data came from many sources, including naval observers and attachés, FBI informants, radio interception, confidential diplomatic reports, and handouts from British Intelligence. The material varied in value and reliability, and had to be sorted, analyzed, and weighed by Kirk's staff before being presented as a synthesis of incoming intelligence each day at the Secretary of the Navy's morning briefing. In order to facilitate this process, the DNI issued a circular letter in May requiring a reliability rating on each intelligence report, such as an A-Rating for unimpeachable sources or a D-Rating for questionable information that could be used only as a comparative index to supplement other data.[23]

Care in the presentation of accurate data had become more critical for Kirk in recent days as he battled the WPD for control of the U.S. Navy's intelligence policies and product. During 1941 Admiral Turner tried systematically to squeeze Kirk and his organization out of the entire business of estimating, evaluating, and projecting information into a finished intelligence synthesis. In order to convince departmental leaders of ONI's continued value, and perhaps to save the office from eventual absorption by WPD, Kirk determined to improve the informational side of his organization's mission.

Turner's attack was not a personal vendetta. A strong-willed, dedicated officer, "Kelly" Turner determined that War Plans was simply the most important division in the office of the CNO and a natural base to direct all subsequent naval expansion, war planning, and intelligence estimates. Turner considered himself an expert in the last field, although he had never served in ONI. He believed that he could estimate the intentions of Japanese leadership better than most, Kirk noted sarcastically, because he had been to Japan for ten days as commanding officer of the *Astoria*, which carried Japanese Ambassador Saito's ashes back to Tokyo for burial. In fact, Turner's information-gathering experience was more impressive. In the 1920s as Asiatic Fleet Aircraft Squadron commander, he had employed his six Martin seaplanes to collect photo-information in the Philippines and along the China coast. He had forwarded twenty intelligence reports to the Navy Department in 1929 alone. Once, Turner had used a two-week leave to consult with the naval attaché in Tokyo about how to prepare intelligence estimates. Then, as commanding officer of the heavy cruiser *Astoria*, Turner had gathered data about Saipan, Rota, and even heavily guarded Yokosuka naval base—all this despite the disparaging and unfair criticism made by Kirk.[24]

However, Turner had no practice in turning raw data into a finished product as refined, synthesized, or analyzed intelligence as, for example, an officer would have acquired serving as the head of one of ONI's desks or to a lesser extent as one of the naval attachés abroad. Nevertheless, as soon as he moved into the War Plans Division in October 1940, he assumed a patronizing tone and attempted to dominate ONI. Not that his attitude was unfounded. Glaring weaknesses existed in the intelligence office's daily routine. Once two officers dispatched by Admiral Ghormley to ONI to research a technical question had discovered "some very important secret reports on technical matters locked in a safe where they had been for two weeks as the officer concerned stated he had not had time to get them distributed." The SPENAVO London complained about ONI's failure to disseminate other vital data as well, and ironically the then naval attaché Kirk had endorsed the view that the office failed to provide adequate service. In yet another case, Turner told President Roosevelt that the latest ONI report dispatched to the White House was just a rehash of outdated *New York Times* newspaper articles. The WPD urged FDR to ignore the useless intelligence paper. Indeed, apparently the only source in ONI either respected or consulted by Turner and his boss Stark was the aging historian Dudley Knox, who they asked for advice rather than current DNI Kirk or his staff.[25]

Turner crusaded to subordinate Kirk's organization to nothing more than a Navy Department lending library and archive. Perhaps ONI could serve the navy adequately in this limited function, but not if it was cluttered up with the business of evaluating data. A sympathetic CNO and his senior assistant and former WPD Ingersoll, who had recommended Turner as his replacement, supported him. Inclined personally to maintain harmony between his divisions, "Betty" Stark leaned toward the blunt and forceful Turner's opinion that ONI should be limited to the function of a departmental acquisition and lending library. Indeed, one month after Turner's arrival, Stark had issued a memorandum to all ships and stations outlining the CNO's understanding of ONI's proper role.

> It is desirable that the degree of dissemination which the Divison of Naval Intelligence can undertake and currently accomplishes should be clearly set forth, in order that there be no hiatus or failure of desirable dissemination. Certain evaluation can only be made by competent specialists beyond the ability of the Division of Naval Intelligence.
>
> Ultimate dissemination frequently requires such evaluation, and also frequently ultimate dissemination should be coupled with or result in technical directives. Such latter action is, of course, not within the purview of the Division of Naval Intelligence.[26]

Stark's letter of 15 November 1940 confirmed the CNO's support for Turner, and served later as a basis for both RAINBOW V and Ready III's interpretation of ONI's part in war planning. However, as long as Anderson directed the office, met with the president, and continued to present estimations in late 1940, Turner gained no satisfaction. But in December Anderson left and James filled in as director until March 1941 before heading to Bermuda to command the U.S. naval operating base. James tried to maintain ONI integrity, arguing with both Ingersoll and Stark for a continued evaluative role. In fact, in January Ingersoll asked James for an estimation of Britain's war outlook. Personal friendship with the president helped, and in February ONI prepared daily estimates on the world situation for Roosevelt. But James knew that he was to leave ONI soon, and in any case he proved no match for Turner.[27]

Kirk's arrival in March forecast conflict. Bringing with him a fundamental philosophy of intelligence garnered from conversations with Godfrey and through observations of the Admiralty's combined intelligence and war planning organization, he promised to reassert ONI's authority. Kirk dreamed of creating an American naval planning center serving the operational needs of commanders at sea and making strategic estimates. In many ways his views coincided with those of Turner, but unlike the war plans director, Kirk believed that ONI should be the nucleus for such an agency, not the War Plans Division. But momentary illness and return to an office dominated by security questions set Kirk back in his fight with Turner. Moreover, his early attempts at preparing analytical studies for the department were not always successful. When Stark requested an evaluation of the desirability of expanding lend-lease aid to China, Kirk waffled. He endorsed the increased aid, but admitted that he had no recommendations, no details on earlier assistance to China and suggested that the CNO contact special presidential adviser Lauchlin Currie for information on lend-lease to China. Disappointed by this sloppy performance, Stark scribbled in the margin of Kirk's memorandum a terse comment that Currie had absolutely nothing to do with this question.[28]

Such a report reinforced Stark's negative opinion about ONI, swaying him toward Turner's crusade against the office. By mid-1941 the war plans director had assumed almost total control over strategic intelligence, ordering personally such measures as the issuance of a fortnightly summary of intelligence for the fleet. In July, Turner lost all patience with Kirk, complaining that War Plans had been trying unsuccessfully for months to pry anything of value from his office regarding the location of British merchantmen sunk or attacked in the Atlantic Ocean. He wondered how Kirk expected the War Plans Division to analyze the strategic situation without such information. Such delays, Turner snapped, meant nothing in peacetime. "However, in preparation for entrance into the war, one should leave nothing undone to establish methods which will give us information of the most exact character."[29]

Worse still, Turner issued his own intelligence estimates without consulting the latest ONI data that arrived almost hourly from scores of naval attachés and observers worldwide. "The War Plans Division would prepare a dispatch and send it out without reference to or even consideration by ONI at all," intelligence officer McCollum claimed. At least in one case, this neglect led Turner to misestimate grossly Japanese intentions, predicting an attack north against Russia rather than a southern advance into Indochina.[30]

Kirk considered Turner's evaluation of the northern strategy so incorrect that he decided to endanger his career by defying the war plans director openly. "Kirk certainly wasn't any weak sister," McCollum noted approvingly. "He immediately went to bat and he and Turner were on the mat all the time." After studying information in his office, the director insisted that Japan planned an invasion of Burma and Southeastern Asia, and refused to defer to Turner's judgment. Kirk went to Stark, demanding a resolution to the entire question of ONI's responsibilities. But "Betty" evaded the issue. "Admiral Stark said he realized that it was a function of ONI to talk about intentions, it was in the manual, and all that," McCollum recalled, "but he thought that in the interests of coordination, it ought to be coordinated, and that Turner was the man to do the coordinating."[31]

Though Stark upheld his war plans director, Turner resented the junior officer's action in running to the CNO. He determined to make life miserable for the DNI, and according to Kirk blocked his promotion until after he had left ONI. "We were clashing right along," Kirk insisted. "It wasn't a very happy time there for me."[32]

The War Plans Division was not the only office contesting ONI for authority during 1941. Director of Naval Communications Admiral Leigh Noyes, whose division intercepted and broke Japanese codes through the MAGIC decryption process, claimed responsibility for delivering these messages to departmental leaders and to the president. However, Kirk's office, particularly McCollum and Egbert Watts, translated the Japanese messages into workable English, and rather than return the translated

Captain Richmond K. Turner (left), who battled for control of naval intelligence with ONI between 1940–1941, in a more quiet moment with Japanese Foreign Minister Arita and U.S. Ambassador Joseph Grew.

material to Noyes for retransmission and dissemination, Kirk maintained that they became ONI property and should be sent directly from his office. Kirk carried them to the secretary's morning conference, and sent Lieutenant Commander Alwin Dalton Kramer with the selected translations over to the White House. Noyes complained to Stark, and the struggle created further tensions, inefficiency, and unhappiness in the embattled intelligence division. "There was some harassment in this office of mine, Naval Intelligence, because we had charge of what was called Magic," Kirk contended.[33]

Feuding over MAGIC reflected the larger concern for security that settled over the department in 1941. Each division guarded jealously its prerogatives and data, fearing that another might leak information or receive credit for an important bit of news. Such a situation hit ONI harder than other divisions, because its central function and business was to sort through and distribute all the news and data to others. It seemed as though every corner of the naval bureaucracy placed obstacles in the way, however. The Bureau of Navigation sent over personnel regardless of their suitability for intelligence duty. In one case, Kirk exploded that the reserve officer provided by the bureau for an attaché billet in Eastern Europe was an absolute idiot. "You can't give a man like this to me," he roared. "He is just out of St. Elizabeth's [mental hospital]. He's a paranoiac." Coming on top of his fight with Turner and Noyes, frustrations with ONI's domestic security program, and the entire dilemma of naval intelligence, minor grievances such as this incensed Kirk, leading to moments of raging anger against everyone, apparently including FDR. The DNI would have been even more agitated and perhaps a little paranoic himself had he known that at that very moment someone in his organization was spying on him for the president of the United States.[34]

CHAPTER FIFTEEN

ROOSEVELT'S SPY

At the height of Kirk's battle with Turner for control of naval intelligence, FDR received a highly confidential memorandum about the DNI. The document revealed Kirk's extreme dissatisfaction with his treatment by the Navy Department and by the president. According to this secret report, Kirk complained continually about his superior's refusal to provide a congenial assistant, failure of either Stark or Roosevelt to review strategic matters with him, and the growing influence over intelligence policy by Colonel Donovan. Apparently the latter disturbed Kirk the most, since Donovan had replaced him as the closest contact with British naval intelligence. Although the memorandum of 30 July 1941 failed to reveal the source of this inside information, it had been prepared for FDR by former State Department employee and now syndicated Washington journalist John Franklin Carter, who added his own cryptic conclusion to the report: "Kirke [sic] is regarded as an able officer and a fine man by those who know him. I do not."[1]

Why was a private citizen spying for the president on an officially appointed head of a government intelligence agency? The answer to this question explained partly why ONI continued to slip in prestige and effectiveness on the eve of America's entry into World War II. While the intelligence dilemma created contradictions within the office and the departmental inter-division feuding paralyzed Kirk, Roosevelt's personal spies diminished earlier White House sympathy with and reliance on the legally constituted intelligence agency. "Jack" Carter headed FDR's semiofficial intelligence unit, but was merely one of a number of amateur sleuths, private eyes, and personal agents employed by the inquisitive president during his entire tenure. He resorted to personal informants partly out of dissatisfaction with regular channels of news, but more directly because of a deep-seated fascination with intelligence and spying. As Anderson observed simply: "President Roosevelt was quite Intelligence-minded." Indeed, for years he had employed confidential agents who communicated privately and directly to the White House—such as Bullitt, Long, and Robert Murphy. "Roosevelt delighted in ignoring departmental procedures in this way, preferring to work informally through men chosen by him and responsible directly to him," diplomat Murphy recalled. In this fashion FDR learned intimate little things about personalities and events within the governmental hierarchy as well as personal views and observations about foreign conditions, which never reached official State Department eyes.[2]

With Roosevelt's use of private agents for personal diplomacy, it was expected that the president would adopt this technique for personal naval and military intelligence as well. He had dabbled in naval intelligence first while Assistant Secretary of the Navy, and the clubby, athletic Ivy-Leaguers hired as naval reserve intelligence officers during the First World War bore the unmistakable Roosevelt connection. One close Boston friend had become ONI's Aide for Information in the Second Naval District while another had served as a Branch Intelligence director. Above all, he had influenced ONI policy, and Assistant DNI Edward McCauley insisted in 1916 that the young assistant secretary had initiated naval investigative services and undercover agents in Latin America.[3]

As president, FDR resumed his interest in intelligence. Thus in 1935 the president had considered a project suggested by naval intelligence officer Captain Bruce L. Canaga to place a bunch of secret agents posing as colonists on the tiny Pacific islets and atolls of Jarvis, Howland, and Baker Islands, claimed for years by the United States. Presumably this fake colonization would block any similar efforts by Japan. From time to time, Roosevelt recommended that the government employ famous people as spies, including author John Steinbeck, who he wanted to send to spy on Mexico under the ruse of collecting data for a forthcoming book. Roosevelt's main effort, though, centered on next door Hyde Park neighbor, old family friend and multimillionaire William Vincent Astor, a naval intelligence volunteer and reserve officer.[4]

FDR's relationship with Astor began during the 1920s when Astor invited him to use the heated indoor swimming pool at his Rhinebeck estate a few miles north of Hyde Park to rest his polio-stricken body. Later during the hectic presidential campaign of 1932 and after the assassination attempt on Roosevelt in Florida the following year, Astor provided a sanctuary aboard his magnificent motor yacht, the *Nourmahal*. For the next few years, the president returned to Astor's craft to watch the America's Cup races off Newport, to fish on Long Island Sound, and for an occasional carousing cruise into the Caribbean with Astor, Kermit Roosevelt, Judge Frank Kernochan, and several other intimate buddies. The shipmates were brought together by their common social, yachting, and fishing interests, but something else bound them together—attachment to a mysterious secret organization called the ROOM.[5]

Founded in 1927 by Astor and Kermit and Theodore Roosevelt, Jr., the ROOM became the monthly meeting place for a band of wealthy, prominent, and active New Yorkers—including Kernochan, explorer C. Suydam Cutting, banker Winthrop Aldrich, journalist and world traveler Marshall Field III, inventor Charles Lanier Lawrence, and some twenty others. Although FDR never joined the ROOM, all members were well known to him through New York political and social circles and the Harvard University connection, and of course he joined the three most active members on the *Nourmahal* cruises. Most likely it was during one of these jaunts that Kernochan, Kermit Roosevelt, and Astor discussed the existence of their clandestine information group, which was composed of a number of former and perhaps still active intelligence officers. Kernochan told FDR that his group could supply any information that the president required.[6]

Undoubtedly, the thought of having the bankers, journalists, explorers, world travelers, and assorted intelligence veterans at his personal disposal interested FDR; in the early 1930s, however, he decided to use only Astor for intelligence gathering. Of all the ROOM members, Astor remained most active in the interwar years through his contacts with the Third Naval District intelligence office and ONI headquarters, where he was considered a slightly naive but enthusiastic and valuable volunteer informant. ONI

FDR prepares to leave on Vincent Astor's yacht *Nourmahal* with ROOM members (from right to left) Astor, Kermit Roosevelt, and Judge Kernochan and others. (Courtesy Wide World Photos, Inc.)

records mentioned Astor's transmission of information from the Caribbean and Pacific Ocean at least from January 1930, and in 1936 Puleston contacted him directly for volunteer intelligence work. Astor shared this information with friend Roosevelt as well, and after ONI and other regular agencies seemed unable to penetrate the mysteries of the Japanese mandates, Roosevelt turned to Astor and his yacht.[7]

Accompanied by distant presidential cousin Kermit Roosevelt, Astor journeyed out into the Central Pacific in 1938, circulating among the Marshall Islands and gathering data on docks, fuel stores, and air strips on Eniwetok and Wotje. "The information gathering side of our cruise has proved interesting, instructive, and, I hope, will be helpful," Astor cabled the president. He had never landed on these forbidden islands, he admitted, but had seen enough to predict that Japan intended to develop military facilities and bases in the mandates.[8]

With the outbreak of war in Europe and the declaration of U.S. neutrality, Astor's value increased as a private intelligence resource. FDR wanted information about the espionage activities in the U.S. of neutrals and belligerents without compromising his own neutral policies or carrying out illegal acts directly. Astor and the ROOM provided the answer. As a managing director of the Western Union Telegraph Company, Astor could order the covert interception of cable messages sent by Axis agents in New York to Latin America without exposing the Roosevelt administration to violations of federal codes against such interceptions. Moreover, ROOM member Aldrich managed the Chase National Bank where the Soviet espionage cloak Amtorg Corporation kept their account. Other members sat on the boards of similarly valuable enterprises. Furthermore, all of Astor's group held intimate school, family, and even marriage ties with Britain and could be expected to cooperate clandestinely with British intelligence people without compromising U.S. official neutrality.[9]

So Astor and his band of volunteers, referred to in correspondence with the president as the "club," went to work in September 1939 to provide the kind of data the administration could not obtain through regular legal channels or government agencies. By October Astor informed Roosevelt that he had two men monitoring all frequencies from Mexican, Cuban, and Swiss radio stations. "Tomorrow, I am starting to work on the banks, using the Chase as the Guinea Pig," he wrote the president. "Espionage and sabotage need money, and that has to pass through the banks at one stage or another." Astor expanded his operation in early 1940, contacting Sir James Paget and Walter Bell of the British Passport Control office in New York City, which directed British Intelligence in the United States. "Shortly after the 'club's' formation," Astor confided to Roosevelt, "it occurred to me that Paget and Bell might from time to time obtain leads useful to us." At first the arrangement proved fruitful, but then somehow the U.S. State

Department learned about the connection and pressed Britain to maintain proper channels of communication. Apparently Astor had better luck with Sir William Stephenson when he arrived in New York City a few months later as the British Security Coordinator. The two secret agents cooperated to stop the Vichy government from employing the Western Union company to set up a communication system for Axis agents on St. Pierre off the Newfoundland coast.[10]

Whether or not Astor began to dream of one day making the club a central intelligence agency, his undercover work for the president generated a tendency to expand operations and try more creative enterprises. "When you return to Washington," Astor wrote his friend in the White House, "I do hope that I shall have a chance to come down and talk with you for a little while about the 'club,' which I am up to my neck in; and also about the suggested Chase Bank mission to Japan." At the same time, the wealthy New Yorker used contacts with "cafe society" to investigate the theft of the top-secret Norden bombsight, supposedly by Nazi agents.[11]

While pursuing some of his schemes, Astor never bothered to keep DNI Anderson fully informed, although he was technically under ONI direction. In late June 1940, the director called Astor to Washington to explain his independent intelligence operation. "Maybe I shall need you to protect me from a firing squad," Astor kidded FDR just before leaving for the capital. He worried unnecessarily, since his yachting companion and Hudson River neighbor not only insulated him from Admiral Anderson, but gave him a new, enlarged, and official intelligence position. FDR explained his decision in a memorandum to Stark on 26 June.

> I asked Vincent Astor to drop in and see you. I simply wanted to let you know that I requested him to coordinate the Intelligence work in the New York area, and, of course, want him given every assistance. Among other things, I would like to have great weight given his recommendation on the selection of candidates because of his wide knowledge of men and affairs in connection with general Intelligence work. Please pass this on to Walter Anderson.[12]

FDR's memorandum gave Astor more authority but also new headaches, rivalries, and complications. In early 1941 Roosevelt's spy Astor bumped into Anderson's spy Phillips in New York City. Perhaps this was the first evidence to the somewhat trusting and naive Astor that he was not alone in the local intelligence field and that others pursued the same duty for ONI and FDR. Astor considered Phillips an unwelcome competitor. He held no personal animosity against him, Astor assured the White House, but thought FDR ought to recognize that Phillips was doing some very mysterious work reportedly under authorization of the Navy Department, and if word ever got out it might compromise U.S. neutrality. Showing a little jealousy, Astor pressed for more authority, and after lunching with

FDR, Berle, and new DNI Kirk, Astor received their support for his appointment as local coordinator of intelligence.[13]

Finally, in March 1941 Berle told Kirk that the president wanted him to draw up orders for Astor, giving him sweeping authority. "In order to coordinate the interested activities and to eliminate duplication of effort, it has been decided, with the concurrence of the Departments concerned, that all intelligence and investigational activities undertaken in the New York area by the representatives of the Departments of State, War, Navy, and Justice shall be coordinated through a single agency—to be known as the Area Controller." Orders for the area controller would be transmitted through ONI. On 19 March Roosevelt reviewed Kirk's letter of instruction to Astor while traveling on the presidential special train through North Carolina, immediately advising his secretary to: "Tell Captain Kirk I approve memorandum about intelligence activities." In response, the director rushed a secret communiqué to the commandant of the Third Naval District outlining Astor's responsibilities, warning that no one must learn about the existence of an area controller and requesting office space and clerical help for Astor in the district intelligence office at 50 Church Street. Kirk explained that under the presidential directive, all agencies "will consult the Area Controller before making any new contacts and shall feel themselves to be free to discuss with the Controller such contacts as may already be in existence."[14]

Thus, Astor found himself in a unique position. He boasted intimate and frequent contacts with the president. He possessed a written directive that gave him authority over all other intelligence agencies. He held extensive international contacts, liaison with British intelligence, and a devoted band of intelligence enthusiasts, which as members of the ROOM had been meeting monthly since 1927. For several months Astor rushed ahead as though director of central intelligence, holding conferences in Washington to coordinate departmental intelligence services and dropping down to Bermuda to discuss counterespionage and antisubmarine warfare measures with British officials. He pursued covert and illegal duties as well. "In regard to the opening of diplomatic pouches in Bermuda and Trinidad," he wrote Roosevelt, "I have given my word never to tell anyone, with always you excepted."[15]

His moment passed quickly, however. He found the field cluttered with rivals, intrigue, and deception, and his health declined. Although Anderson had left ONI months earlier, his secret agent, Phillips, still prowled about through ONI, MID, and FBI files and offices. Phillips had unlimited naval funds, Astor told FDR, and selected agents without security checks. "What worries me is that all this is being done by a man who has no commission but only an appointment from a former Director," he complained. Perhaps Astor might have absorbed Phillips's organization of over

150 agents into his own, but he ignored the outsider, unlike the opportunistic Donovan, who hired Phillips to run his London secret operations in 1942. And barely two months after Astor's appointment as area controller, it would be the tough, free-spirited Donovan—not the proper, reserved Astor—who became FDR's favorite spy. As Coordinator of Strategic Information and then head of the famous OSS, Donovan would direct not one local area but a worldwide operation. "Wild Bill" satisfied FDR's insatiable appetite for information far better than Astor, or for that matter better than ONI, and gradually both faded into the background.[16]

Finally, in October 1941 Astor's health broke and he entered the hospital for a stomach operation, probably brought on by the burdens of the spy business. From his bed, Astor continued to worry about his job, fearing that his organization would fall apart and be unable to serve the president. His usefulness as the president's secret agent had slipped already, however, and hospitalization merely diminished his service further. In fact, shortly after Astor resumed his duties as area controller, Roosevelt sent White House snoop Jack Carter, fresh from spying on DNI Kirk, to New York City to check up on Astor.[17]

His work known only to a select few who were closest to the president, Carter had served as a source of confidential information nearly as long as Astor. Roosevelt found Carter particularly useful, because as a syndicated journalist he had privileged access to the entire National Broadcasting Company short-wave radio network, contacts with leading foreign correspondents, and as a Washington-based reporter could come and go at the White House without causing any unusual comment or suspicions. By late 1941 Carter drew $54,000 annually from the President's Emergency Fund to hire secret agents and to perform "certain specialized investigative work." To keep his job secure from any prying bureaucrat or congressman, Carter drew all funds as appropriations for scholarships under the Coordinator of Commercial and Cultural Relations Between the American Republics. Thus he hired agents at will, most notably Canadian citizen Curtis B. Munson, who provided data on the Vichy Fifth Column in Martinique and roamed the West Coast and Hawaii in search of potential dangers from and racial uprisings among Japanese-Americans. By the end of the Second World War, Carter had prepared 660 studies for Roosevelt and directed several secret projects.[18]

In early 1941 Carter became the vital link in FDR's convoluted and expanding private intelligence network. Anyone who wished to bring any intelligence-related matter to the president's immediate attention, Berle noted in July, simply needed to ask Carter. Carter operated as Roosevelt's troubleshooter to ferret out unhappy government employees such as Kirk and to investigate background material on members of Roosevelt's team. Shortly before his mission to investigate Astor, Carter had completed surveillance on Dr. Henry Field, an expert on the Mideast, employee of the Field Museum of Chicago, and currently working as an ONI analyst. FDR wanted Field for other work, and required Carter's background check for loyalty and reliability.[19]

Carter's investigation of Astor was more sensitive than his earlier cases because of Astor's close ties with the president, his attachment as area controller, and his long-time loyal service to the Navy Department. In fact, somehow ONI discovered Carter's mission and warned Astor. "The whole matter is somewhat mysterious and, to my mind, unsatisfactory," the DNI cabled Astor, "since it seems to be an extra-departmental agency without real responsibility." Nevertheless, Carter completed his investigation, phoning the White House that Astor was very confused and suspicious "about the whole problem of investigation in the New York district." Shortly thereafter someone leaked Astor's cover, ending once and for all his usefulness as Roosevelt's spy. Astor continued as area controller until 1944, but his job consisted mostly of procuring fishing trawlers as auxiliary patrol boats, both to locate enemy submarines and to protect convoys and other defense measures connected with the Eastern Sea Frontier.[20]

As Astor's position as FDR's personal agent declined, Donovan's rose to the top. Successful information-gathering trips for the president to Britain and to the Balkans and Middle East prepared the way, while his appointment in June as Coordinator of Information secured his place. As COI, he hired brilliant, creative, and controversial assistants. He became close friends with Fleming and Churchill's superspy Stephenson, achieving unprecedented access to the very good British secret services. He stepped on the toes of other intelligence agencies, bypassed regular channels, and created interdepartmental jealousies—the kind of approach understood and admired by FDR. However, the older intelligence organizations resented Donovan, fearing that he might attempt to form a central intelligence agency that would submerge or even erase their organizations. ONI appeared most perturbed by the competition from the fast-moving civilian. While Holmes and Anderson had frequent access to the White House, rarely was Kirk invited or consulted, eroding morale already weakened by the ongoing internal struggle. The final blow came when FDR sided with Donovan in his battle with Kirk for the services of William A. Eddy, a retired USMCR officer, college president, and leading expert on North African and Middle-Eastern affairs.[21]

ONI had been trying to assign a naval observer to North Africa and the Mediterranean area for months to fill one of its most glaring information gaps. As usual, the State Department blocked these efforts, warning ONI not to pester the Vichy government, Franco's Spain, or right-wing Portugal for the privilege of assigning naval officers in their territories. But as Axis forces pressed Britain for control of North Africa in 1941, the need for U.S.

intelligence in these neutral regions grew. For once, ONI jumped ahead of other bureaus when it selected Eddy as naval attaché to Cairo. Born in Syria of missionary parents, Eddy spoke Arabic, French, and a variety of local dialects and understood thoroughly the cultures and history of the Near East and Saharan Africa. "No American knew more about Arabs or about power politics in Africa," diplomat Robert Murphy insisted. In addition to this expertise, Eddy was a veteran intelligence officer, serving in World War I. Consequently, unlike most naval reservists selected for attaché or observer posts, Eddy fit every ONI criteria for such an appointment. "From the moment of your arrival," Kirk confided to Eddy, "I have been convinced that yours was the perfect assignment."[22]

But then Donovan, who had already secured Phillips and his people from ONI, decided that he wanted Eddy for a proposed North African undercover operation that he had discussed recently with British naval intelligence expert Fleming. Like Kirk, Donovan recognized that the Marine Corps reserve officer was the ideal choice to run an espionage network composed of consular and shipping officials at such hot spots as Tangiers, Oran, and Casablanca. Donovan went directly to his Columbia Law School classmate Roosevelt and asked for Eddy, and no sooner had the naval attaché debarked in Cairo than he received urgent orders to return immediately to Washington. Kirk was apoplectic. "I beg you to do everything possible to have these orders canceled," he pleaded with Assistant Secretary of State Breckinridge Long. "Owing to his special qualifications and superior ability I consider Eddy's services here absolutely unique and I cannot envisage any other assignment for him to which these considerations would apply," Kirk raged. The response came the next day in a blunt note from the top. "Decision made for definite reasons and presently irrevocable," Secretary of State Hull told Kirk.[23]

This was the last straw for the embattled and humiliated naval intelligence director. Ignored by Stark, attacked by Turner, passed over for rear admiral by the department and now subservient to a civilian intruder, Kirk visited Undersecretary of the Navy James V. Forrestal and asked for transfer to sea duty. Though in the normal course Kirk might serve in ONI another two years, his request for a transfer occurred at an opportune moment, since the department hoped for a more senior officer to head ONI and chair the forthcoming meetings of the recently organized Joint Intelligence Committee. His disillusionment made removal easy. Even after Kirk left the office, he refused to remain quiet, however, and in a parting note to the State Department vented his frustration and anger over the Eddy affair. "He seemed to be the perfect assignment," Kirk repeated, "and I deplore his departure wholeheartedly."[24]

Kirk took Eddy's transfer as a personal insult, but in reality it was just another manifestation of the ruthless and frustrating world of intelligence.

Roosevelt's employment of personal agents intensified the situation and caused conflict and rivalry between private and legally constituted intelligence organizations. Perhaps Roosevelt knew no other way to run affairs and generate information, but as State Department intelligence liaison and presidential confidant Berle told him, this practice could cause trouble. "If it is your desire that the Executive Departments develop intelligence services of their own, without reference to the State Department or to other services operating there, there is no reason why the passports should not issue [to agents spying on the Vichy government in Martinique]," Berle advised FDR. "But the difficulties of overlapping work of this kind are obvious."[25]

For ONI the implications of this presidential conduct were devastating. Already emasculated by departmental power struggles and confused by the naval intelligence dilemma's divided security and strategic priorities, ONI could not stand neglect and mistreatment by the president. The organization became increasingly defensive and cautious, anxious not to diminish further its value to department and president. Taken together, these factors resulted in a disillusioned, frustrated, and uncertain group of naval intelligence personnel in Washington, which hindered the effective operation of ONI and contributed finally to the greatest intelligence failure in U.S. history.

CHAPTER SIXTEEN

FAILURE OF INTELLIGENCE DOCTRINE

"It was a bad day all around; and if there is anyone I would not like to be, it is Chief of Naval Intelligence," Berle recorded in his personal diary on 7 December 1941. All that day information had dribbled into Washington about a sensational Japanese sneak air attack on the U.S. base at Pearl Harbor. By evening, news from the Hawaiian Island facilities indicated the worst. Most of the U.S. Navy warships and Army aircraft had been destroyed or severely damaged, and casualties to American military personnel appeared heavy. It was a day that no one who lived through it would ever forget, especially those in naval intelligence.[1]

The surprise Japanese strike brought to reality the constant nightmare hanging over any intelligence organization that somehow a potential enemy would evade all efforts at surveillance to devise and carry out a secret operation against one's own forces. Seemingly, the successful Japanese masking of their plans meant that all the hundreds of man-hours spent in pouring over radio intercepts, attaché reports, and other data about Japan had been for naught. All the counterespionage work, decryption by MAGIC, surreptitious entry, and use of informants had failed to provide the key signal, the moment of warning required to save the ships and personnel at Pearl Harbor. As Berle suggested, part of the burden for the greatest intelligence failure in U.S. history rested heavily on ONI and on its director, Admiral Theodore Stark Wilkinson.

Bright, charming, and popular, "Reg" Wilkinson had replaced disgruntled classmate Kirk as DNI in October 1941. He seemed a good choice. Wilkinson had made no enemies and had many friends, working pleasantly with any and all from the gruff Kelly Turner to closer comrades such as Captains Schuirmann, Director of the Central Division, and John R. Beardall, FDR's naval aide. From time to time he served as Undersecretary of the Navy Forrestal's enthusiastic tennis partner. Fellow officer George C. Dyer thought him an honest and manly shipmate, while Kinkaid recalled that "he was a man with a fine mind." Even bitter Kirk praised the incoming director's promotion to flag rank. "It is fitting that number one in his class, should be first promoted to admiral," he wrote Wilkinson.[2]

The road to this promotion had been smooth and uncomplicated, a career any officer would be proud of from graduation at the top of his Naval Academy class in 1909, where he had initiated intercollegiate tennis, to heroic conduct during the Vera Cruz landing in 1914. Less sensational but equally rewarding were tours as General Board secretary, member of several arms limitations conferences, and director of a top-secret project in 1936 to develop a pilotless plane for the navy. In some ways it was surprising that the department wasted such a fine officer on the troubled and seemingly inconsequential intelligence office, but Stark felt that Wilkinson had all the qualifications to establish a central intelligence group and coordinate intelligence as the senior member and chairman of the new seven-member Joint Intelligence Committee.[3]

It would take all the ability, charm, and tact at Wilkinson's disposal to run ONI in October 1941. Kirk had left him an organization that lacked pride, purpose, or mission. Kirk tried to warn him indirectly that everything was not running smoothly. "There are a good many changes of personnel going on in this division," he wrote the incoming director on 24 September, "which will have some bearing on the celerity with which you take the reins." For another thing, ONI had moved portions of its operations to new office space four different times between August 1940 and September 1941, each move benefiting other divisions more than naval intelligence. Sections became so scattered that one intelligence officer recalled how he spent time locating and visiting other sections just to keep in touch, and so that he would not operate in a complete vacuum.[4]

As the CNO had hoped, Wilkinson recognized some of ONI's limitations at once; he began a housecleaning and studied reorganization plans. ONI needed to be more responsive to departmental needs, he insisted. "This would be, I thought, particularly important in time of war and it was one of my concerns when I became Director of Intelligence, to endeavor to improve that," he testified later at the Pearl Harbor inquiry, "so as to be better prepared in the Fleet and ashore for the collection and dissemination and analysis of combat intelligence."[5]

One of the first moves was to bridge the gap that Kirk and Turner had created, and Wilkinson approached Ingersoll quietly about the War Plans Division's monopoly over estimates, suggesting some ONI participation. Stark's assistant repeated the usual line about War Plans' cognizance over such work, but at the same time agreed to let Wilkinson prepare little analytical summaries for the department to be attached to weekly general information reports. This was a major concession. Next, Wilkinson increased ONI's access to both Turner and Stark, using his assistant Captain Samuel N. Moore as an intermediary. The DNI maintained that "when news of importance appeared, particularly toward the end of the period prior to December 7, Captain McCollum would go direct with me, if I were at hand, or alone if not, to Admiral Stark and tell him what news he had and what conclusions he had reached." McCollum agreed that "in almost every case we had direct access to both Admiral Turner . . . and to the Chief of Naval Operations, himself."[6]

Thus in one stroke the tactful director bridged the difficult and paralyzing communications gap that had existed between ONI and the CNO during the past two years. Under Wilkinson, the office presented estimates to Turner and Stark directly and regularly. This very success in placing intelligence material before department leaders, though, opened the office to criticism that might be directed later at Stark about conversion of information into intelligence.

After restoring some ONI confidence by opening new communications within the immediate war planning organization, Wilkinson tried to subordinate Donovan's new agency. In a heated exchange with research analyst Professor James P. Baxter III, the DNI warned against interference in naval intelligence and war planning missions. Donovan's man, a tough college history professor, refused to have some naval officer lecture him on his responsibilities under the Coordinator of Information. Baxter maintained that Wilkinson failed to understand the new office's purpose. "None of us, as you know, seeks to operate in the field of strategy or to usurp in any way the proper functions of War Plans or of the Joint Board," he insisted. Unmoved, Wilkinson advised the department not to cooperate with these civilian upstarts. "They must NEVER be shown any War Plans," he shouted.[7]

While it was understandable that Wilkinson did not want competition from the newcomers, his stubborn refusal to take advantage of what Baxter explained was an impartial study center developing educated strategic hypotheses for military planners narrowed ONI's already constricted world view even further. Wilkinson needed assistance from any and all directions in late 1941 to study the implications and future actions of potential enemies brought about by the undeclared Atlantic war and increasing tensions in the Pacific and East Asia. Some of Donovan's bright young intellectuals, foreign policy experts, and professional historians might have presented a wider perspective on the international situation, which was slipping rapidly beyond the control of American naval estimates and policies.

Everywhere evidence pointed to imminent American entanglement in the fighting war. During Wilkinson's first week as DNI, news arrived within a 24-hour period of a U-boat attack on the U.S. destroyer *Kearny* in the nearby Atlantic and a report from across the Pacific that warlike Hideki Tojo had become Japanese prime minister. Several weeks later the destroyer *Reuben James* went down under submarine attack in the North Atlantic, and FDR ordered the arming of merchantmen. Intelligence officer Ben Wyatt expressed the excitement, pressures, and single-minded purpose of naval intelligence that swirled about Wilkinson and his staff. Forgetting that the United States was still neutral, the Madrid naval attaché demanded immediate sea duty. "I cannot sit by while we are actually at war and look on from the side lines without at least doing all possible within my power to get into action," Wyatt cabled ONI.[8]

Although not actually at war for another ten weeks, many in Wilkinson's office during the fall of 1941 expected American entry at any moment, most likely prompted by a Japanese attack somewhere in the South Pacific or Southeast Asia. ONI intensified efforts to exploit the rich variety of sources of information from Asia that had been built up over the interwar period through contacts with businessmen, journalists, former U.S. naval officers living in Asia, an occasional wandering scholar, and most successfully from commercial attachés and consuls such as Gerald Kreutz in Mukden and Willys R. Peck in Nanking. More recently McHugh and Gregon Williams had developed extensive Chinese contacts. Though more restricted, Smith-Hutton, Jurika, and others managed to gather critical data about Japanese air power, fleet strengths, and political conditions, predicting in early

The Pearl Harbor attack shocked DNI Theodore Wilkinson and affected his performance as the navy's top intelligence officer during the months following the Japanese sneak air strike. (Courtesy Franklin D. Roosevelt Library)

March 1941 that Japan planned to attack Malaya. In addition, ONI had listening posts in Siam, Batavia, Sandakan, Medan, and an undercover agent in Hanoi.[9]

The urgency of the situation prompted ONI to bend some rules of proper conduct for its naval personnel overseas. When in October McHugh raised the possibility of inappropriate conduct by sitting on the board of directors of China National Aviation Corporation, a Pan American Airway's affiliate, ONI defended his actions as necessary to monitor the movement of lend-lease supplies in China. McCollum assured the State Department that in normal times the navy would never permit its personnel such privileges with a private company. "Under present conditions, however, with the continual threat of war with the Japanese," he insisted, "there is a feeling here within the Navy Department that we should not be too closely bound by considerations which would be conclusive during normal peace time." Indeed, McHugh was not the only naval intelligence officer permitted such privileges; assistant naval attaché Roy Pearce McDaniels in Lisbon continued to make extensive business investments in Portugal while serving on active duty.[10]

In addition to informaton funneled to ONI from regular channels in late 1941, Wilkinson's office received material about Far Eastern affairs and Japanese intentions from the Fourteenth Naval DIO and from communications intelligence. These sources became more important as the others began to dry up when the United States embargoed the shipment of strategic goods to Japan in early November. Not only did this remove American ships from the area, where their merchant captains had long provided data for the navy, but led to a tightening of Japanese security measures as well. As the overseas avenues of information closed, ONI turned more fully to its DIO in Honolulu, Captain Irving H. Mayfield, his counterespionage expert Lieutenant Commander William B. Stephenson, and investigator Lieutenant Donald Woodrum for news about Japan. Mayfield developed better than usual liaison with the FBI zone office in Hawaii and with G-2's Hawaiian department, while Stephenson carded several hundred Japanese suspects on the island believed to pose a threat to U.S. security, and placed Japanese consular officers under surveillance to watch for signs of document burning that might forecast a break in diplomatic relations and war. More fruitful was Woodrum's detective work, which included telephone taps on the lines of the Japanese consulate in Honolulu and on the private home lines of Japanese vice consuls. "The telephone tapping work done by ONI was kept extremely secret," Woodrum explained. "Only a handful of persons in the District Intelligence Office, who were directly concerned with the information gained thereby, were even aware that such work was being done."[11]

A potentially more valuable source for news about Japanese intentions and activities came from radio intercepts made by Asiatic Fleet intelligence under Commander Redfield Mason, Pacific Fleet intelligence under Commander Edwin Layton, and from a network of radio direction finder stations such as Commander Rudolph J. Fabian's twenty-six receivers, direction finders on Cavite, and the DF station at Pearl Harbor under Commander Joseph J. Rochefort. These intercepts were sent on, deciphered, and passed to ONI by Lieutenant Commander Laurance Safford's naval communication's team in Washington. In addition, Safford's people collected plain-language broadcasts from Tokyo, reportedly at the DNI's specific request, looking for what those on the inside called the "Winds Message," a false radio weather report indicating the direction of Japan's next great offensive.[12]

Whether or not ONI received all the pieces and intercepts, language experts McCollum, Hartwell C. Davis, Egbert Watts, and various others translated the radio communications for the department during Wilkinson's first month in office. Moreover, whereas Kirk had battled Noyes for control of the finished product, Wilkinson established his office's authority by preparing a daily book of radio intelligence, decrypted by Magic, for the White House, Knox, the CNO, and War Plans Director. Furthermore, while an earlier security leak in March had forced Kirk to limit the release of this summary to a nearly paralyzing level, Wilkinson and his close friend Beardall resumed a full flow to the White House.[13]

Heavy reliance by ONI on the interception of Japanese communications required the strengthening of the office's language capabilities—always one of its shortcomings. Early in the century, ONI had cast about for months trying to find just one translator of the Japanese language, and in the interwar years relied largely on aging linguist Dr. Haworth and his wife to read Japanese material and to aid in decoding. By 1940, however, ONI had begun to prepare for the impending confrontation. Shortly after naval intelligence had lost track of the Japanese fleet for a day in July, the CNO had ordered all officers proficient in Japanese to be reassigned to intelligence work. Consequently, Martin R. Stone went to Tokyo, Rochefort to Hawaii, Layton to the Pacific Fleet, Watts to ONI, Edward S. Pearce to the CNO's office, and Joseph Finnegan to the Asiatic fleet. Though this was a beginning, many of the other sixty-five naval personnel who had taken the three-year Tokyo course since 1922 were judged inadequate, and ONI launched an effort in February 1941 under McCollum and Al Hindmarsh, a former Harvard government professor and long-time civilian secret agent in Asia, to develop an Oriental language school to train naval officers as translators. After a difficult beginning—including the rejection of the Harvard University course, which stressed only literary and scholarly techniques—Hindmarsh developed a school first at Berkeley and later in Boulder, Colorado. By October, two months before Pearl Harbor, ONI's program was well under way.[14]

Not only were ONI's sources and quality of information about Japan numerous and its ability to translate that information improving, but by late 1941 Wilkinson's office managed to disseminate it on time to war planners and operational personnel. Every officer who was questioned at the several Pearl Harbor hearings and inquiries during and after the war affirmed his indebtedness to ONI. Assistant War Plans officer Lynde D. McCormick claimed that routine publications and special ONI studies were available at once to the fleet and the department, while Fleet Aviation officer Arthur C. Davis insisted that the intelligence office did its very best to keep him informed. Director of Ship Movements Division Roland M. Brainard concurred, admitting that his division had plenty of data from ONI and naval observers, while commanders at sea, including Admirals Wilson Brown and William Halsey, agreed that they received ONI bulletins on time. Even ONI's adversary Turner praised the collection and dissemination of data. "I think our intelligence regarding Japanese activities and intentions was quite good," he testified. "It was adequate for the preparation of war plans and for the direction of affairs."[15]

In addition to supplying adequate and at times superior coverage of Japanese and Asian affairs, Wilkinson's organization possessed one of the most thorough and definitive bodies of information and thought about Japan in any U.S. government agency. Over the years ONI had collected volumes of data on Japanese capabilities, intentions, weapons, and national characteristics. While some of this information varied in quality and usefulness to the navy, there was one consistent and accurate thread of thought that had permeated reports from naval attachés and intelligence officers ever since the Japanese surprise attack on the Russians at Port Arthur in 1904. And that theme was that Japan considered the surprise attack on the enemy's main military facility before declaring war a primary aspect of war planning. Time after time this observation had appeared in ONI reports until it became what former U.S. intelligence officer William Corson referred to as intelligence doctrine, a consistent body of evaluated experience.[16]

This evaluated experience started soon after the end of the First World War when Admiral Gleaves had warned from his Asiatic station that Japan might strike the United States without warning. Several years later Commander Robert A. Theobold made a similar ominous prediction, arguing that: "It would seem conclusive that the Japanese formal declaration of war would be preceded by some offensive military action." Throughout the next decade, this theory was expanded to include the opinion that Japan might deliver such a sneak attack by carrier-based aircraft. Indeed, during

Fleet Problem XIV in 1933, umpires Schuirmann, Kirk, Kinkaid, Clement, and Virgil E. Korns had judged as technically feasible a Japanese air raid against Oahu. These umpires served at various times in prominent intelligence positions throughout the 1930s. In 1936 Puleston reviewed his files and determined that the Japanese liked to launch aircraft just before dawn, considering this the ideal moment for sudden attack. Two years later Tokyo naval attaché Bemis noted that Japan's current naval building program emphasized offensive operations at some great distance from the home islands. "By this is meant that Hong Kong, Singapore, Dutch East Indies, Philippines, Borneo, Guam, Aleutian Islands and *possibly the Hawaiian Islands* would be in jeopardy depending upon who challenges her efforts at Asiatic domination," Bemis estimated clearly and firmly. (Emphasis added.)[17]

Nor did ONI keep this doctrine to itself. In 1937 the War Plans Division advised Leahy that: "History shows that Japan strikes without warning." Reflecting Puleston's views, the division concluded that "Under existing conditions and limitations of the Naval Intelligence Service our Fleet is exposed to surprise attack even in our own waters and our naval shore establishments to sabotage." Above all, War Plan ORANGE, the navy's only well-developed contingency plan, estimated that war with Japan would be precipitated without notice and would most likely require a rapid defense of U.S. bases in Asia, Hawaii, and the Panama Canal Zone.[18]

For some time, ONI had also been monitoring Japanese interest in the Hawaiian Islands, probably as early as the Sino-Japanese War of 1894–95 and the Hawaiian annexation movement of the 1890s. Recent evidence was more revealing. "There are voluminous reports available concerning the visits of Japanese tankers, Japanese training ships, Japanese training squadrons to the Island of Oahu and to other islands in the Hawaiian group," one intelligence officer noted. "It was well known that officers attached to these groups made 'sightseeing trips' of the islands, including such vantage spots as Aiea Heights [which overlooked the Fleet anchorage at Pearl Harbor]." Occasionally a report reached ONI about a Japanese submarine lurking near the approach channels to the Pearl Harbor facility, perhaps keeping an eye on the U.S. Fleet for a more distant Japanese operation, or making an advance reconnaissance for an attack on the base itself—a possibility that had been reported in recent days to Ambassador Grew by a Peruvian diplomat in Tokyo.[19]

When the State Department forwarded Grew's report to ONI, though, McCollum and other analysts labeled the report too fantastic and filed it away. Given the situation in late 1941, such a response was understandable. "Because of Japanese water-tight security there was no evidence of their attack on Pearl Harbor," future DNI Thomas B. Inglis insisted years later. Indeed, the cocktail conversation of a Peruvian diplomat made at an embassy party comprised the only specific ONI reference to a current Japanese plan to attack the Hawaiian military installation. Volumes of other intelligence signals, which according to historian Roberta Wohlstetter were more than ONI could digest, suggested that Japan's main interest was an attack into Southeast Asia, the Southwestern Pacific, or against the Philippine Islands or Guam. Naval intelligence never expected the attack, McCollum testified later. "The ONI was not an omnipotent and over-all intelligence center."[20]

At the same instant, Japan was not ONI's major concern! During late 1941, Wilkinson's staff worried more over the immediate threats to the Atlantic coast from Nazi U-Boats, saboteurs, and spies, and from suspicious fishing boats lurking around the Panama Canal waters. In some ways, it seemed more important to track the Fascist-owned, transatlantic LATI airliners, which pinpointed Allied convoys for German submarines, than to keep an exact plot of each Japanese aircraft carrier in the remote Sea of Japan. Above all, ONI still suffered from difficulties with organization, communications, and personnel, which meant that even if Wilkinson's staff had concentrated solely on Japan and wished to study sneak attack doctrine, they would have had to search through old files that had been moved about several times, with the pre-1921 material lying in forgotten boxes in the National Archives.

Taking this situation and other evidence into consideration, the various investigations held after the Pearl Harbor attack that sought the reasons for the lack of adequate warning of a secret Japanese operation unanimously absolved ONI from blame. Down through the years this conclusion has been supported by historians and participants, who while pinpointing one or another guilty party—including Kimmel, Stark, and even the president—never suggested that Wilkinson shared the responsibility. Most recently, former DNI Inglis, whose office in 1945–46 prepared material for the hearings, cautioned against being a "Monday morning quarterback" in judging past ONI performance and events. Nevertheless, a study of ONI's history and its response to the crisis of late 1941 raised some disturbing questions about whether the U.S. Navy's intelligence director and agency had provided their best effort.[21]

No other government office or official, including the State Department, held in their files or records more strategic and military data about Japan than Wilkinson and ONI. From 1904 on, nearly every intelligence officer in the navy had focused on Japan—whether overseas, at the Naval War College, or in ONI headquarters—mostly to provide constant data for revisions of War Plan ORANGE. For years the intelligence office had sought ways to uncover Japanese activities on the mandated islands, had helped intercept and decode communications, and had broken into Japanese offices in the United States. From time to time, secret operations such as Worton's mysterious trip in 1937 had been undertaken to probe the secrets of Japan.

Of all agencies in the U.S. government in 1941, only ONI held enough of the puzzle pieces to predict the Pearl Harbor attack as *one* strong option. Instead of simply labeling Grew's report on Pearl Harbor as too fantastic to consider, ONI should have researched the possibility and reawakened its earlier doctrine on surprise attack. The major American base in the Pacific was not Guam or Cavite, but Pearl Harbor. Estimating a potential attack required not an omnipotent agency as McCollum asserted, but an office imbued with its most basic and traditional function as a research agency, retrieval library, and filing center. There was plenty of evidence of the Japanese doctrine of sneak attack. With war perilously close, every option required analysis and discussion. But ONI performed two-thirds of its job, leaving the fatal third unfinished, or, as intelligence officers claimed later, to others who had cognizance over estimates and analysis. At the very least, a good intelligence office and director would have developed internal estimates. "It's fellows who are usually in the basement who do the work of filing away and having cross files, cross indexes, and careful analyses who come up with the proper answers," naval intelligence expert William Sebald once observed.[22]

Sebald might have added that the fellows in the basement had to possess some historical perspective as well. Unfortunately, the technically brilliant Wilkinson, like many of his shipmates, lacked an historical sense of the larger setting, criticizing as naive those historians in Donovan's office who presented broader strategic hypotheses. Wilkinson saw the present and struggled with the future, becoming totally oblivious to ONI's own recent past. Incredibly, at the Pearl Harbor inquiry, in response to the question "was there, Admiral, during the month or so preceding December 7, 1941, any discussion in which you participated concerning the likelihood of a Japanese move toward Pearl Harbor?" Wilkinson replied sadly, "Unfortunately, no!"[23]

The DNI found many excuses for ONI's failure to discuss that likelihood in his subsequent testimony before Admiral Kent Hewitt's inquiry in 1945. Mostly he resurrected the communications gap that had existed during Kirk's tenure, claiming that the job of estimating, analyzing, and discussing the possibility of a Pearl Harbor attack was not in ONI's province but under the cognizance or responsibility of someone else. Thus, in response to a question about what information ONI forwarded to Admiral Kimmel, the unfortunate commanding officer at Pearl Harbor, Wilkinson replied: "I don't know. That was in the province of the Chief of Naval Operations." However, he expressed ignorance also of the most basic aspects of communications intelligence, security measures, or Magic— despite the fact that he was one of the few naval officers privy to top secret matter and was constantly in attendance in Stark's office and at top level conferences every day preceding Pearl Harbor.[24]

Was Wilkinson involved in a great Pearl Harbor cover-up? No one ever presented evidence to support this, and indeed the DNI was too honest and forthright an officer to resort consciously to such tactics to defend his or the navy's reputation. Yet perhaps it was his perfect character and unblemished record before 7 December that led to these lapses of memory and inconsistent testimonies later. Despite a distinguished record in Pacific Ocean combat after he left ONI in 1942, in his testimony three years later Wilkinson reflected a gnawing realization that somehow his performance as DNI had contributed to the greatest intelligence failure in U.S. history. Nowhere was this sense of tortured guilt clearer than in his conduct as naval intelligence director in the months immediately following the Pearl Harbor attack.

CHAPTER SEVENTEEN

ON THE DEFENSIVE

"How in hell did those yellow barstuds get in?" Lockwood wondered from his London attaché post. "Where was Kimmel? Resting at the Sub. Base, no doubt. If we lose him as well as two battleships we actually gain quite a lot," the agitated naval officer wrote in his private diary the day after Pearl Harbor. Lockwood's views reflected the mixture of shock, grief, recrimination, and bitterness that permeated the naval establishment on 8 December. Nor was the gloomy week following the disaster any better. "For ten days, we stayed glued to the radio, tensely reading the scant war news in the papers, while the Japanese bombed Manila, Baguio and Cavite Navy Yard, landed in Malaysia, shelled the California coast from a submarine, invested Wake Island and sank the *Prince of Wales* and *Repulse* north of Singapore," former CNO Standley recalled.[1]

Soon Japan seized Guam, surrounded beleaguered American defenders on Bataan and Corregidor, and attacked in rapid succession Burma, Hong Kong, Singapore, and the Dutch East Indies. Australia and New Zealand appeared open to ultimate invasion as well. At the same moment, the situation in the Atlantic Ocean and Europe appeared equally precarious. Though England had resisted invasion momentarily, the Nazis tightened their grip on the rest of Western Europe, grew more bold in attacking Anglo-American shipping, and endangered the security of the entire Western Hemisphere. Simultaneously, German armored columns moved relentlessly into the heart of Soviet Russia. In North Africa Erwin Rommel, the brilliant tank strategist, prepared to launch a devastating offensive against British Commonwealth defenders, which if successful would secure strategically vital Egypt and the Suez Canal and open the oil-rich Middle East to Nazi domination.

The rapidly worsening world situation following the surprise air attack on Pearl Harbor bred uncertainty, disorientation, and momentary panic in Washington. "The Hawaiian Islands are in terrible danger of early capture by Japan," Stark warned. Despite months of undeclared Atlantic warfare, lend-lease deliveries, and constant international and domestic tension, no one in the United States really expected such a sudden and final thrust into the war. On the other hand, once the administration and nation recovered from the initial shock, they regrouped, united, and confronted the business of fighting total war. The Japanese act of war against the United States had ended abruptly the isolationist schism and pacifistic tendencies that had plagued the country throughout the interwar years, something that the FDR government could never have done alone.[2]

By mid-December, the Roosevelt administration moved rapidly to mobilize the economic and military resources of the nation. The critical moves for the U.S. Navy came on 17 December when Admiral Chester W. Nimitz took command of the wounded U.S. Pacific Fleet and on 19 December when FDR authorized Admiral Ernest J. King to assume the position of both CNO and CINCUS, the first officer ever to hold simultaneously the top administrative and operational commands. Referred to as the Commander in Chief of the Navy or COMINCH, King wielded tremendous authority over naval policy and operations during the war. His appointment occurred just in time to represent the navy on 24 December at the Arcadia Conference, the first of many top-level gatherings to plan for coalition warfare. At this initial gathering in Washington, Churchill, Roosevelt, and their military leaders discussed measures to contain Japanese expansion and to overcome the shortage of ships for lend-lease and war supplies, and made plans to unify command under a Combined Chiefs of Staff, which would begin meeting in late January.[3]

While Anglo-American leaders organized the machinery for planning and fighting total war, rumors swept through the United States that other surprise air raids would occur on Pearl Harbor or some other strategic point. The DIO in San Diego warned that a radio intercept from Tokyo indicated another attack at any moment on the Hawaiian Islands in conjunction with strikes against Alaska and the Panama Canal Zone. Underscoring the threat to the Pacific Coast, on 23 February a Japanese submarine managed to lob twenty-five shells at an oil refinery near Santa Barbara, leading to the blackout of all lights and the decision to relocate and intern local Japanese-Americans in concentration camps.[4]

Meanwhile, British Intelligence in New York, working intimately with the FBI, reminded the U.S. government that while everyone watched the Pacific Ocean and Japan, the European dictators had declared war on the United States as well and posed a more immediate threat to the Atlantic Coast. One report alleged that the Nazis planned to attack South America and New York City in conjunction with the Japanese offensive against the British base at Singapore. Reinforcing the impression that the major threat came in the Atlantic, the FBI's Miami office warned of a possible concentration of enemy submarines and warplanes on Vichy-controlled Martinique in preparation for an attack on the Florida Keys. Donovan joined his British and FBI friends in spreading the spectre of danger to the Atlantic Coast by passing on to ONI the report of a mysterious cottage on Baker's Island in Salem harbor that reportedly signaled to enemy U-Boats. The Coordinator of Information (COI) tried to put the Salem matter in perspective, however. "It may be a 'witchhunt'," he snickered to Wilkinson, "but I thought you should have it."[5]

Despite such witch hunts, the menace to the Atlantic Coast was very real. German submarines prowled the coast at will from Maine to the Caribbean, even attacking ships silhouetted against the Atlantic City coastline or off the Carolina Capes. Reminiscent of the first months of the Spanish-American War, paranoia and fear spread throughout the eastern seaboard, leading to more rumors of enemy cruisers, submarines, agents, saboteurs, and individuals signaling some unseen enemy far at sea. Reported strange sightings flooded district intelligence offices and ONI, including mysterious lights, hidden airfields, painted signals, strange footprints on the beach, and sinister black-hulled vessels surfacing suddenly in front of some startled bather off Martha's Vineyard. Perhaps reflecting memories of the First World War when German agents used the radio station at Tuckerton, New Jersey, to signal their comrades at sea, numerous rumors came from New Jersey about Nazi activity. "It is reported to be common gossip at Sea Girt, Asbury Park and nearby places that enemy submarines are being refueled by fishing boats from local resorts," ONI revealed to the DIO in Philadelphia.[6]

Desperately anxious not to be caught off guard again, Wilkinson was receptive to all such information and reported every substantial and silly rumor to the department. One memorandum for the harassed Secretary of the Navy noted that Japan planned to attack the seals on Pribilof Island. "In addition to a valuable catch of fur," Wilkinson advised with much gravity, "the Japanese could hope to derive a not inconsiderable supply of edible meats and fats from the seal catch." In a similar piece of intelligence, one of Wilkinson's assistants warned that the *Luftwaffe* was going to blitz New York City. "It is visualized that the next jolt which the Navy receives may not be at Pearl Harbor, but at Hampton Roads or New York Harbor, and position plots of aircraft (not submarines and surface vessels as at present) will be required," ONI determined in late January 1942. Certainly Wilkinson's staff knew that Germany possessed neither the aircraft carriers nor the long-range bombers capable of an air strike against the Atlantic Coast, but the evaluation reflected the aftershocks of Pearl Harbor that rocked ONI.[7]

Wilkinson suffered especially in the weeks following the Japanese raid from the implications that his intelligence office had failed to provide adequate warning. The once-confident, newly promoted admiral, who had become DNI in September, now had become a self-effacing, apologetic officer. In January he wrote DIO Mayfield in Honolulu about his concern that the department would eventually investigate ONI's role, asking Mayfield to collect his thoughts about naval intelligence activity before the attack. "Please understand that no one here is at all critical of your activities," Wilkinson assured him, "but I think for your good name and ours as well some such report ished be available here." The director needed Mayfield's help because he had been unable to explain the overall intelligence picture of 7 December to Secretary Knox. "It has been somewhat difficult for me to draw the line for him between the local Intelligence, of the district, the Operating Intelligence or information procured by the operating forces by air search, etc., and the general Intelligence obtained by radio interception and Direction Finder."[8]

In a similar humble letter to Admiral John Hoover, commandant of the Tenth Naval District, Wilkinson begged him not to ask for any advice or direction about how to set up the local district mobilization scheme. "I do not, of course, know the general difficulties of your area and I am very green at this Intelligence business as a whole," the Director of Naval Intelligence appealed, "and I cannot at this long range prescribe any details."[9]

Wilkinson's expressions of uncertainty and humility made difficult the task of aggressively chairing the Joint Intelligence Committee and of checking the ambitious Coordinator of Information, one of the qualifications that Stark believed Wilkinson held. In the meetings that began on 12 December, the admiral remained silent, passively watching as his nemesis Donovan dominated early sessions. "Bill Donovan wants to take over the FBI Work in South America and Canada," JIC member Berle recorded after the 6 January meeting. Donovan's grandiose schemes of centralizing intelligence, which he had presented to the joint body, Berle suspected had been orchestrated by the secretive British Security Coordinator Stephenson. But regardless of who motivated Donovan, the State Department liaison troubled: "You can never quite pin him down to saying what he really does want to do."[10]

Wilkinson showed no inclination to pin Donovan down, cooperating humbly with the COI instead. Unlike his tough stance with Baxter in November, now the DNI praised the many reports produced and sent to ONI by Dr. William Langer's Research and Analysis branch, including studies on Axis propaganda in the Moslem world, the Burmese at war, the Falange Party in Spain, neutral Sweden, and a survey of political instability in Latin America. Indeed, Wilkinson almost begged the Harvard historian to mention ONI in a footnote to one of his reports. Similarly, the naval intelligence chief asked if ONI might participate in the collection of motion picture material and supported Donovan's decision to add a new Branch of Foreign Nationalities to his rapidly expanding office of strategic information. "In my opinion," Wilkinson admitted to Commander Francis C.

Denebrink, his liaison with COI, "ONI should concentrate on Naval Intelligence and leave the study of political situations to other Departments and men who are better equipped and trained to delve into this field."[11]

This veneer of diffidence cracked once in a while, though, as the DNI strained under the incredible tension of intelligence duty in early 1942. When one officer questioned the strange information sent to him by ONI about alleged Axis ties to the Military Order of Knights of Jerusalem, Wilkinson snapped that his office sent out only correct information. "It would seem that if there were information available in the fourth Naval District that was contrary to the information distributed by the ONI," Wilkinson shouted, "the preferable procedure would be to furnish the ONI with that information and allow it to correct its own faulty material." The nervous exhaustion showed up as well when Wilkinson and his special warfare expert, Lieutenant Commander John L. Riheldaffer, stumbled into an anti-isolationist hate session instead of the expected lecture on British psychological warfare. The embarrassed DNI stormed out.[12]

ONI's constant critic Turner was quick to seize upon Wilkinson's apparent post–Pearl Harbor inability to cope with the intelligence job. In a memorandum to Stark, the War Plans Director insisted that ONI failed to get proper information to naval commanders at sea, to the president or even to the American people through its public relations office. He claimed that ONI and its army counterpart failed to provide the Joint Intelligence Committee with the necessary information on war planning and operations; therefore, the JIC summaries for the president were neary useless. The JIC, Turner concluded, should limit itself to "factual summaries of the strengths and distribution of the forces of the Associated Powers and of the enemy, similar to some of the summaries heretofore prepared by ONI and MID."[13]

Feebly Wilkinson answered Turner's attack by circulating an internal paper to all the CNO's division directors that reminded them that ONI held authority over the distribution of information. He explained that unless his office maintained cognizance over this function, ONI could not collate and check reports for accuracy before disseminating them to other parts of the department. He urged fellow directors to clear data through his office. But if they decided to ignore ONI, Wilkinson wondered if at least they might allow him to peek at their dispatches to ascertain whether they contained the most complete information available in the intelligence division.[14]

Wilkinson's meek defense of his division led to a more blunt reply from Turner. The War Plans Director wondered how Wilkinson could expect cognizance over such a large area as information policy when he spent most of his time restricting, not sending, data. "Rather than a list of 'don'ts,' I believe a few 'do's' would help," Turner lectured the DNI. In yet another candid memorandum, this time endorsed by King's acting chief of staff Admiral Richard S. Edwards and presidential naval aide Captain John L.

McCrea, Turner concluded that ONI and MID were not doing their jobs. "They are supposed to show the worldwide military situation, but generally exclude political information," he complained. "I personally do not think very much of their product."[15]

Apparently others shared Turner's opinion. Unhappy with his intelligence agencies' recent performances, Roosevelt instructed special White House spy Carter to investigate naval and military intelligence around New York where poor port and travel control plagued the U.S. war effort from the outset. He also dispatched former DIO Paul Foster on a private mission to inform on naval security and intelligence in the Panama Canal Zone and Alaskan defense frontier. Concurrently, FDR told Astor to keep presidential instructions from the eyes of Wilkinson and ONI, apparently fearing leaks from that end. Worse still, Secretary Knox lost faith in the intelligence office, ordering some clumsy ONI investigators to stop following him around, detaching the publicity office and placing it under former DNI Hepburn, and hiring a private civilian consulting firm to thoroughly evaluate the navy's intelligence office in Washington. And finally, Knox jarred Wilkinson by ordering him to get rid of deadwood, especially older officers. In response to the latter order, the DNI apologized sadly to Admiral William T. Tarrant in the First Naval District for removing his experienced but aging intelligence officer. "At this point, please be assured that I am not gunning for your excellent man," Wilkinson explained, "but I am simply asking if you have any Reserve officer in your District whom you believe would make a satisfactory District Intelligence Officer."[16]

Not entirely satisfied, Knox next sent special civilian assistant Adlai Stevenson around to see whether some of ONI's reservists had been attached to naval intelligence because of wealth and social connections rather than ability. There seemed reason for this concern. "We are swollen enormously," Latin American chief Thomason admitted in early February 1942, "never was there such a haven for the ignorant and well connected." But Wilkinson denied vigorously any impropriety. "My predecessors and, in my short tour here since October, myself, have been most anxious that we should take on only earnest, capable, serious-minded and intent officers for duty under this office." Then, Stevenson wondered whether ONI discriminated against Jews in their search for reserve officer material. Once again Wilkinson defended his besieged office, forwarding to the secretary's civilian assistant a list of some thirty-five "Hebrews . . . who are doing excellent jobs in the Intelligence Organization." At the same time, Stevenson failed to inquire after ONI's attitude toward Negroes, who because of their alleged ties to Japanese espionage, were refused consideration for any naval intelligence billet during the war, except for three minor clerical jobs.[17]

Given the amount of criticism, fault-finding, and unhappiness expressed by everyone from the president to local district intelligence officers with ONI's performance in the months following Pearl Harbor, it was remarkable that the Navy Department allowed Wilkinson to continue as director instead of relieving him of command or pressing for a transfer. But then, ONI's relative role and importance probably seemed too insignificant to bother much with the loyal and until now flawless Wilkinson. More to the point, on 23 December the COMINCH assumed the most vital and essential aspects of naval intelligence work, diminishing the need to shake up ONI. In time the department could scrutinize the office, but for now the business at hand was intelligence for operational planning and combat directed by King's office and action agencies in the field, such as advanced joint intelligence centers.[18]

King's decision to run his own intelligence division left ONI's wartime role somewhat vague, and in order to clarify his duties the DNI met on 17 January 1942 with the COMINCH and Admiral Stark. Stark set the tone for the entire conference by opening with a long argument on why ONI should no longer direct naval missions in Latin America, urging the separation of yet another function from the fading intelligence office. King, however, believed that ONI could serve a valuable role in the war, especially in providing information for long-range planning, such as monographs and technical reports. As in the past, ONI would compile, collate, and disseminate ship and aircraft identification and characteristics manuals, studies on enemy fleets and naval officers, foreign ports, and maritime commerce. In other words, King stressed the usual emphasis on ONI as an archive and lending library. Even Turner conceded that Wilkinson's staff could perform this limited job, consenting to have ONI staple together some information folders for the staff of the Commander Southwest Pacific Area, where the U.S. was preparing the first great drive of the war against the Japanese.[19]

Desirous of redeeming his office, Wilkinson met with senior staffers Captains Howard Kingman, William A. Heard, John B. W. Waller, and other intelligence officers to map out the information program. They determined to work through the new Fleet Identification and Characteristics and Fleet Intelligence sections to prepare the best possible product. Aerial views of Japanese warships, the director informed Stark, would include "actual target angles instead of correct ones" to assist pilots in attacking the enemy. These and other ONI bulletins would have removable, loose-leaf pages for immediate posting on walls, wardrooms, or in the cockpits of fighter aircraft. New weapons or modifications in enemy equipment would be added at once to ONI silhouettes and descriptions sent out to commanders at sea. And finally, the "ONI Weekly Information Bulletin" would include photographic material, summaries of the war's progress, combat information, and historical background data to better prepare naval officers for war.[20]

It was not sufficient merely to collect and prepare data for the department, and Wilkinson determined to improve ONI's product for the JIC, the new Combined Chiefs of Staff, and various subcommittees studying enemy oil supplies, manpower, and weapons. And there were other government agencies anxious for information about the enemy, such as the National Defense Research Committee or the Economic Intelligence Division of the Board of Economic Warfare under former DNI Puleston.[21]

ONI's informational role revived Wilkinson. Proudly he showed erstwhile critic Admiral Edwards about the office, focusing especially on ONI's plot room where young reserve Lieutenant G. G. Westfeldt explained how this section gathered and disseminated information about hostile enemy incursions near the U.S. coast. "It was pointed out that such suspicious activities were tied in with our sinking and submarine plots wherever possible," Westfeldt reported. Edwards appeared satisfied. Another senior officer praised "Ping" Wilkinson for reviving a "more or less dead outfit" and distributing information of value to the service. The director's resurrection also influenced the JIC, where Berle noticed a decided improvement in leadership.[22]

But Wilkinson's problems continued. Some lay beyond his powers to correct, stemming from the contradictory nature of naval intelligence. While responsible for disseminating information, as part of its security function the office was obligated as well to restrict the circulation of data and information. This negative role covered everything from warning sailors against loose talk about ship movements to censoring mail from personnel in cooperation with Byron Price's Censorship Bureau, established by FDR on 19 December. As usual, Turner lectured the DNI on what the department considered classified data, advising Wilkinson not to release to the press anything relating to the sinking of U-Boats, enemy combat strength, location of U.S. forces, or rumors and speculation about forthcoming operations. At the same time, Stark ordered ONI to stem leaks about Admiralty trials, arising after collisions or disasters at sea, that might reveal losses to the enemy.[23]

The effort to curb the unauthorized release of military information led Wilkinson's office into several sensitive operations, such as snooping about government agencies and investigating U.S. civilians and journalists. When ONI learned that casual comments by a member of the U.S. Maritime Commission jeopardized convoys, the office launched a probe of the board membership to discover the guilty party. Somewhat heavy-handedly, Heard told the commission liaison Huntington T. Morse that if the member failed to cooperate, ONI would step in and ensure secrecy. The most controversial incident occurred several weeks later when a published article by Chicago *Tribune* reporter Stanley Johnston revealed that the U.S. Navy had broken Japanese codes during the Battle of Midway, citing a Washington intelligence spokesman as the source of his classified information. Johnston's article kept the Navy Department in ferment for weeks, and buffeted ONI especially, since it was a potential source of the leak. Wilkinson rushed down to the enraged King's office to assure the COMINCH that Johnston had learned absolutely nothing from the intelligence office. Then Wilkinson became involved in a very tricky investigation of the incident. It included the danger that in prosecuting Johnston the navy would reveal some of its most secret Magic methods, and the probability that such a prosecution would lead to the accusation that Secretary of the Navy Knox, owner of the Chicago *Tribune*'s major newspaper rival, used his authority to destroy competition in the city. Wilkinson sat on the navy board to consider these issues, and supported the departmental decision to drop the entire case.[24]

Meanwhile as part of ONI's responsibility to censor naval news, Wilkinson championed efforts by other security agencies to achieve passage of a wiretapping law to investigate offenses "broadly relating to the national security." The DNI requested as well a general directive allowing his investigators to examine the files of telegraph and cable companies. In the case of ITT, a company long very cooperative with ONI, however, Thomason assured its vice president that naval intelligence had no intention of interfering with company business. "It seems to me important that, while we should take all practicable steps to deny communication to Axis nationals and agencies," Thomason assured, "we should do nothing to jeopardize the franchises held by our American controlled companies."[25]

Before ONI stumbled too deeply into this legal tangle concerning censorship, interference with the press, and cable communications and wiretapping, the department removed censorship from Wilkinson's office, and then in June the remainder of ONI's cognizance over any phase of communications intelligence. The loss of communications intelligence to the rapidly expanding Office of Naval Communications, which had taken over the buildings of an old girl's school on Nebraska Avenue, hit Wilkinson's assistant Captain Kingman particularly hard, since he had worked on and off in ONI in this capacity since 1925. "He was just crushed when this decision was made to take it entirely out of ONI hands," McCollum recalled, "because here we'd worked on this thing together for all these years. . . ."[26]

Now without a chance to help translate decoded radio interceptions, ONI became almost completely isolated from the actual warfare. "Of course, it meant that ONI lost a certain amount of face and prestige and so on, that's true, and that wasn't very pleasant to contemplate," McCollum sighed, "but when you're fighting a war you have to put up with some of these things." Anyway, there were ways to get around the roadblocks, and McCollum pieced together hot battle reports by taking intercepted material, delivered for a quick reading only, into his office against regulations to copy it down before the courier finished his rounds in ONI. Moreover, there was at least one benefit to the office from the separation; the source of the Johnston leak could not be ONI, which did not know about the Battle of Midway until after the reporter learned the details.[27]

Deprived of communications intelligence, ONI came to rely more on information from the COMINCH and an exchange of data developed daily through conversations between McCollum and King's intelligence officer Captain George Dyer. But the COMINCH jealously guarded information of immediate war value, and as a British intelligence visitor noted, gave ONI nothing on current operational intelligence about the U-Boat war in the Atlantic. Finally, Wilkinson asked why daily dispatches about enemy submarine movements never reached his office, explaining that ONI maintained a coastal information section, and wished to analyze data about all enemy activity and disseminate evaluated information to the rest of the naval establishment. Assuming his earlier diffidence, he admitted that unlike the COMINCH his interest lay in long-range patterns rather than immediate tactical tracks, but he believed still "that all information regarding enemy submarine attacks or sightings of our coast [should] be made available to this Section." COMINCH's response was not satisfactory and reflected the sorry state of the U.S. Navy's antisubmarine warfare in 1942, which led eventually to the creation of the shipless Tenth Fleet to battle Nazi U-Boats in the Atlantic Ocean.[28]

Restricted in collecting and disseminating data and squeezed out of the field of action' (operational and combat) information, Wilkinson's office slipped back into the dirty business of surveillance, snooping, and security—a job no one else in the navy wanted or seemed to care much about. After the first careless weeks of war when almost anyone could gain access to government buildings without serious scrutiny by a guard, security began to tighten in Washington and naval facilities generally, and blackout curtains, marine sentries, and scrambled telephone lines became the rule. Secretary Knox reminded Wilkinson of his obligations in this direction. "It is a function of the Intelligence Service, and all problems relating to the determination of actual or probable jeopardy resulting from espionage, subversion, or sabotage are under the cognizance of the Office of Naval Intelligence," he proclaimed on 7 January. And four weeks later Wilkinson, Hoover, and MID director Raymond E. Lee signed a revised delimitation agreement that reemphasized ONI's investigative duties during wartime.[29]

The sensational fire on the converted ocean liner *Normandie* in New York Harbor on 17 February accelerated security measures, especially waterfront control, port security, and boarding patrols to interrogate passengers and search incoming vessels. In cooperation with other agencies, ONI prepared a joint survey of New York Harbor, and in a less overt operation began to send agents into the city's seamy world of prostitution, organized crime, and racketeering in search of America's enemies. Reportedly, from March 1942 ONI cooperated with local crime syndicate leaders including Charles "Lucky" Luciano and "Socks" Lanza to locate leaks of convoy information along the waterfront and infiltrate the fishing industry with ONI agents. Naval intelligence probed Harlem in search of alleged Negro affiliation with Japanese espionage and kept watch on a male bordello near the Brooklyn Navy Yard, a known spot for Nazi sympathizers and possibly for the chairman of the U.S. Senate naval affairs committee as well.[30]

For a moment, when an informant revealed that four Nazi agents had landed from a U-Boat on Amagansett Beach on Long Island, this avenue of investigative work promised to bring credit and recognition to Wilkinson's office. ONI sleuths from the DIO in New York City performed much of the early leg work, but after they had broken the case, Wilkinson had to turn it over to Justice Department operatives, who unlike naval officers had legal power to arrest suspects. Immediately J. Edgar Hoover went on the radio and announced dramatically that the FBI had solved the spy case single-handedly. Frustrated, DIO MacFall complained bitterly about Hoover's failure to mention ONI assistance. Wilkinson calmed him. "As to credit, I'm sorry you feel disturbed as to the lack of it, but as you may know we have always kept in the dark and allowed FBI to take the bows (and the kicks!), which earns us their gratitude and support and permits us to pursue our sometimes devious ways unsuspected."[31]

Wilkinson's response was characteristic. He had learned to soothe his disappointments and those of others, to explain away failures, and to justify the limited contributions made by this office in the early months of the war. Stoically he had watched Admiral King assume all the important aspects of naval intelligence. Patiently he had suffered periodic tongue lashings from Turner and criticisms by Knox. Resolutely he had accepted the loss of one ONI responsibility after another, from public information releases to translation of radio intercepts. The agony ended in July as Wilkinson went on, ironically under Admiral Turner's command, to a distinguished war-time record in South Pacific amphibious operations. Nevertheless, he remained a tragic figure in the shadow of Pearl Harbor, fumbling to find the right answers at the investigative hearings, and in 1946 he abruptly ended his career when he drove a borrowed car to his death off the end of the Norfolk-Portsmouth ferry boat and into the Elizabeth River.[32]

CHAPTER EIGHTEEN

THE MAN WHO WANTED
TO BE DNI

Wilkinson's departure in late June 1942 left the DNI post vacant for the fifth time in twenty-six months of continual international crisis and naval expansion. As usual, the shuffle of ONI leadership occurred at a critical stage when the war had reached a dangerous turning point. Although checking Japan momentarily at the great carrier battle near Midway in June, the U.S. Navy still confronted a powerful opponent entrenched in many Pacific island bases and free to attack across the ocean anywhere from the Aleutians to Australia. Worse still, Nazi submarines roamed through the Atlantic Ocean devastating Allied supply convoys and planning to sow destructive mines in American waters. In North Africa, recently promoted Field Marshal Rommel's forces pounded Allied defenders, while Nazi armies in Russia captured Sevastopol and moved toward total victory along the eastern front.

This time, at least, the Navy Department brought to ONI a naval officer who would not need six months to familiarize himself with intelligence duty. This officer was the most accomplished and experienced intelligence expert in the U.S. Navy—Captain Ellis Mark Zacharias, a man who wanted to be DNI. Zacharias had devoted his career to naval intelligence the way other officers pursued advancement up the promotion ladder through sea duty or nice comfortable staff billets. While most steered clear of unglamorous intelligence work, Zacharias eagerly sought any assignment connected with it. Even his personal life reflected that of another naval intelligence officer made famous in fiction by Ian Fleming. Like Bond, Zacharias enjoyed a tense card game and kept his wits about him at all parties, drinking one dry martini so that he could gather information from others who drank more and hence talked too much. Of course, here the similarities ended, as intelligence work for the U.S. Navy was not nearly as glamorous or creative for Zacharias as it was for Fleming's preposterous hero.

Interest in naval intelligence began for Zacharias as a young language officer in Tokyo in 1921 when he had gathered information about Japanese attitudes toward arms limitations. Recognizing his unusual talent for this job, Galbraith had invited him to work in ONI in 1925, especially in mysterious Room 2646 where the Navy carried on top-secret decryption of Japanese codes. During this tour in Washington, Zacharias fulfilled the assistant director's judgment by leading successful surveillance against the espionage-minded Japanese naval attaché. The next year, aboard the cruiser *Marblehead* in Asian waters, he had headed the first comprehensive radio communication interception unit, monitoring Japanese carrier and fleet training radio communications. This experience determined Zacharias's future. "At last I was an intelligence officer in name as well as in fact," he observed in his autobiography, "one of the very few who regarded intelligence as a permanent assignment and career."[1]

Between routine sea duty during the next decade, Zacharias served as head of ONI's Far Eastern section under Puleston and as a district intelligence officer in San Diego. The latter tour in the Eleventh Naval District brought Zacharias fully into the world of counterespionage on the West Coast where Japanese, Communist, and Axis agents threatened the security of both the U.S. Fleet and the extensive California defense industry. Among his accomplishments in the DIO at San Diego, Zacharias developed a network of informers and labored to convince Washington to place naval spies on board ships of the Pacific Fleet to watch for subversive activites. Of most concern was the anti-navy propaganda efforts of the local Young Communist League, but "Zack" worried as well about Japanese secret agents penetrating U.S. military secrets in the guise of college students.[2]

When not working for ONI, Zacharias maintained constant interest in and contact with the office, never tiring of sending advice to current ONI personnel. "As you know, I have been connected with the organization so long," he wrote Kirk in 1941, "that even though I am afloat I consider myself an intimate part of it and keep in touch with the Districts whenever I am in port." While some did not always listen to the eager officer, Thomason carried on a warm correspondence, unburdening himself about the office's weaknesses. Thomason's loyalty exemplified the circle of sympathetic intelligence enthusiasts who gravitated around Zacharias. His admirers included Puleston, McCollum, Coggins, Sebald, Worton, and retired Army Intelligence officer Colonel Sidney Mashbir. "He was probably, in my humble opinion," Worton insisted, "the foremost intelligence officer the United States had." Smith-Hutton rendered a less effusive but favorable judgment. "He impressed me as being a very energetic officer, with many unusual ideas: perhaps slightly eccentric, but talkative and good company."[3]

Zacharias's energy, eccentricity, and dedication created enemies as well, however. Always bluntly outspoken and disturbingly zealous in pursuit of spies and information, he upset more conservative and traditional naval officers, as well as those who considered him a rival. As assistant naval attaché in Tokyo during 1927, without permission he assumed all responsibilities of naval attaché George McCall Courts, temporarily abed with bleeding ulcers. When Courts failed to recover quickly, Zacharias told friends that the attaché was dying or insane, and he worked with Mashbir, then an assistant military attaché in Tokyo, to draw up plans for an informant network in Japan. Courts had him transferred for obvious reasons, but Zacharias claimed it was a political move. Later as DIO in the Eleventh Naval District, he ran into trouble on a trip to Washington, where he had gone to visit the FBI director to discuss a joint counterespionage system for the West Coast. Hoover thought Zacharias's scheme extravagant, and when the abrasive naval officer persisted, Hoover apparently threw him out of the office and determined to find a way to discredit him in the future.[4]

Zacharias's most bitter fight came with veteran ONI security and foreign section officer Bode, who's resentment of Zacharias verged on paranoiac hatred. The reticent and brooding Bode had served in Anderson's office behind the scenes to orchestrate the office's greatest expansion. Now he watched bitterly as the noisy, ebullient Zacharias arrived, brushed Bode aside, and hurried about with grand ideas to revive ONI's image. "I think most of the fault there was Bode, not Zacharias," one ONI colleague observed, "but they built a wall between them as high as it could be and they didn't want to talk with each other." Soon hostility between the two grew intolerable, leading to rumors that the feuding officers tapped each other's internal telephone lines. Ultimately the fight, along with several tragic sea commands following his detachment from ONI, may have contributed to Bode's suicide in a naval hospital in the Panama Canal Zone during World War II.[5]

It was both Zacharias's controversial personality and undoubted expertise that dominated ONI during the critical months of late 1942 and early 1943. Whether or not, as he claimed, King had selected him personally to replace Wilkinson, when Zacharias arrived in ONI in June as head of the Foreign Section, he expected promotion to the directorship. Wilkinson, Kingman, and several others were preparing to leave for sea duty in two months, opening up the top post. "Awaiting these changes and what seemed to be the probable and logical advancement to the top," Zacharias recalled, "I was given temporary charge of the Foreign Branch, relinquished by Captain Heard, who, too, went to sea."[6]

Confidently the veteran intelligence officer settled into his new berth. His mission was clear. "For a great many years I have watched the weakening processes going on in the Naval Intelligence Service," he lectured a group of admiring junior officers. He abhorred efforts to strip the essential functions away, such as fleet and personnel security, public relations, censorship, commerce and travel control, and operational coastal information. His purpose, he proclaimed, would be to restore "the prerogatives and the functions that have been allowed to drift away in the past few years."[7]

While waiting for Wilkinson to leave, Zacharias bided his time by dabbling with foreign intelligence operations. He planted an agent in Australia to contact exiled Dutch officials in order to learn about their activities behind Japanese lines in occupied Netherlands East Indies. Then he squelched earlier ONI plans to place an agent in Axis-infested Colombia, noting that the area was well covered already. Apparently during this interval, he considered adopting for ONI the plans brought back from London by Lieutenant Commander Ralph G. Albrecht, USNR, for a psychological warfare branch to develop "black" intelligence, such as misinformation, deception, and propaganda. In this regard, Zacharias wrote William L. Clark, assistant Coordinator of Inter-American Affairs, that ONI could supply evidence of Japanese atrocities against female nurses and diplomatic personnel interned in Japan after Pearl Harbor. One incident had contributed to the death of the Brazilian ambassador's wife, Zacharias revealed. He suggested that Clark employ such information to offset pro-Japanese propaganda flooding into Latin America.[8]

Then, barely a month after arriving in ONI, Zacharias received the department's replacement slate for Wilkinson and his team. Instead of DNI, he was listed as assistant director. With a bitterness that lingered years afterward, Zacharias remembered the moment. "On this slate a Captain Harold Train, USN, an officer who had been passed over the regular selection process for rear admiral and who had never had one day's experience in intelligence work (he had attended several international conferences) was named director of Naval Intelligence." For Zacharias, the decision was based on departmental politics, personal animosities, and perhaps a tinge of anti-Semitism, which had appeared in ONI regularly since World War I and had been investigated most recently by Adlai Stevenson. Regardless of the reason, his frustration was understandable; after all, he had devoted his life to improving ONI and the navy's entire intelligence system and expected that his career would culminate naturally as DNI.[9]

Nevertheless, in July 1942 the U.S. Navy neither wanted nor required a brilliant, controversial intelligence wizard to head its intelligence outfit. Instead, the department needed a tactful, cooperative administrator to manage what by early 1943 had become an organization of 1,500 personnel in Washington, 5,500 in the naval districts, and 1,133 on foreign duty, all supported by an annual budget of $4,793,842. Rather than direct some

Mata Hari-like adventure overseas, the DNI would have to assimilate cautiously the first of the 200 Waves who began to enter the office in early 1943. Above all, the new director would need to be courteous and diplomatic in ONI's relations with the vast array of civilian and military wartime agencies. ONI needed extra tires and gasoline for its automobiles from the Office of Price Administration and a permanent seat for intelligence couriers on the Pan American clipper to Port Lyautey. He would have to show patience with the Board of Visa Appeals, which most intelligence people viewed as a group of overly liberal civilians who allowed dangerous aliens into the United States in the name of humanitarianism. He must thread his way delicately among the other intelligence and security agencies, cooperating with Hoover, Donovan, Berle, and the rest. How could the sometimes impudent and haughty and always impatient Zacharias perform these tasks? And how could an officer who insisted that other intelligence agencies come for advice to the older, better-established ONI, and who once had been kicked out of Hoover's office, smoothly synchronize naval intelligence with the larger intelligence field?[10]

Train was better suited than the effusive Zacharias to adjust to the larger strategic atmosphere enveloping Washington in July 1942. That month FDR had appointed Admiral Leahy, back from his sensitive post as ambassador to Vichy, to chair the Joint Chiefs of Staff (JCS). Increasingly unhappy with the progress of joint army and navy planning for amphibious operations in North Africa and the Pacific, Roosevelt expected Leahy to provide a steadying influence and impartial arbitration between conflicting strategic aims and disputes over allocation of resources. At the same time, the president stressed smoother coordination of combined Anglo-American war planning, sending King, Army chief of Staff George C. Marshall, and presidential troubleshooter Harry Hopkins to London to iron out details about opening a second front. He was also concerned about the distribution of war material, which in the summer of 1942 was spread dangerously thin, as the U.S. was trying to simultaneously aid Stalin's forces, the British, and Chiang Kai-Shek and pursue its own operations against the U-Boat in the Atlantic and Japanese island strongholds in the Pacific.[11]

King and Marshall responded to the emphasis on joint planning by pushing closer liaison between the various agencies and offices in their respective services. This meant more intimate ties between ONI and MID, and the JCS established several working committees, including a Joint Intelligence Subcommittee to study possible amalgamation of the two intelligence services. Harmonious relations between the DNI and head of G-2 would facilitate such work. Thus Zacharias, whose closest comrade in army intelligence was the eccentric, retired Colonel Mashbir, was a less desirable DNI than Train, who considered as one of his best friends the current director of MID, Major General George V. Strong. "We thought alike, kept each other informed of developments in our respective services, never had any disagreeable arguments," Train claimed. This nearly perfect relationship between the two chiefs promised to reduce conflict to a minimum in the reorganization of military intelligence, in joint interrogation of POWs, in the preparation of joint intelligence reports, in production of Joint Army and Navy Intelligence Studies (JANIS), and the rapid development of Joint Intelligence Collection Agencies (JICA) in Algiers, Cairo, and New Delhi.[12]

The Train-Strong team stood together as well in the daily business of the Joint Intelligence Committee, where MID, ONI, OSS, the State Department, the FBI, and any number of other experts met to discuss common policies and problems and to make recommendations to the JCS. Despite months of operation under Wilkinson's chairmanship, the committee had not lived up to expectations as a central intelligence sounding board. In late July 1942 Berle complained that the JIC focused only on defensive strategies and responded to outside events rather than initiating war plans and fresh ideas for planners. "I have been trying to give some direction to the Joint Intelligence Committee," he noted in his private diary.[13]

With Train's arrival the JIC found new life. Of course, FDR's reenergizing of the JCS and war-planning apparatus helped, as did Donovan's promotion in June to head his own Office of Strategic Services. No longer did he need to use the JIC as a forum to advance his own position rather than collaborate with other intelligence chiefs. But Train's presence contributed to the improved morale as well. Not only did he work comfortably with friend Strong, but developed good rapport with Berle and Ray Atherton. Moreover, unlike Zacharias he coexisted successfully with the temperamental FBI director, making every effort to consult with Hoover and assisting in yet another delimitation letter in December 1942, which removed some of the parochialism and jealousy between agents in the field.[14]

Train's attitude toward cryptanalytical security and the dissemination of communications intercepts to all members of the JIC reflected his broader perspective. "Admiral Train stated that the O.N.I. has no intention of excluding any agency from obtaining intercept information which is pertinent to its mission," the committee minutes noted. Unlike beleaguered Wilkinson, Train encouraged the extension of this material to a wider audience, although trusting that the JCS would keep its distribution to a minimum number of war planners.[15]

While adjusting ONI to the joint planning machinery, Train responded as well to FDR's call for better relations with other members of the wartime coalition fighting the dictators. Thus he smiled most graciously and extended courtesies to the droves of British, Russian, Free French, Dutch, and other united nations naval representatives coming to ONI for favors or mingling at official receptions. In the actual release and exchange of information, however, Train made a definite distinction between the pushy Russians or troublesome de Gaullists and the loyal British.[16]

ONI files during Train's directorship indicated an accelerated rate of exchange of technical information with the British Central Scientific Office, the Air Commission and Admiralty Delegation in Washington, as well as with the British Security Coordinator in New York City. In the field, Train's office urged naval liaison officers to cooperate with British consular security officers. The director frowned upon officers who showed little enthusiasm for the Anglo-American collaboration, criticizing one who did "not seem to have had the word about the complete and free exchange of information between the British and ourselves."[17]

The accelerated combined operational planning and interagency cooperation put a new strain on ONI's obsolete organizational structure, which still focused on topical sections while MID had moved to geographical divisions. The present ONI structure would not last through the war, warned Lieutenant John T. Harding, USNR, a precocious Georgetown University graduate and former commercial attaché enrolled in the Mail and Dispatch Section in 1941. "Under the present system of filing," Harding explained to Assistant Director Kingman, "a person inquiring, for example, about Otto Helveg, a German-born naturalized American citizen, United States machinery exporter to Latin America who travels extensively and is an amateur yachtsman, would find information on Otto Helveg in files currently maintained in" fifteen different ONI desks.[18]

Departmental administrators knew about the problem already, marching a seemingly endless parade of management consultants and efficiency experts through the office in search of flaws and to make recommendations for reorganization. The most devastating evaluation came in early 1943 from Secretary Knox's personal Chicago friend Rawleigh Warner. Coming as part of a power struggle between King and Knox over restructuring the department (and against the background of an internal ONI conflict between those who wanted an action agency and more traditionalist officers who advocated a static role), the Warner Report recommended that ONI turn over all investigative work to the FBI, combine all foreign intelligence with army intelligence and the Research and Analysis Branch of OSS, and leave operational, combat, and communications intelligence to the COMINCH.[19]

The Warner Report, Train realized, almost terminated the Office of Naval Intelligence. He fought back, answering each recommendation in an effort to save his organization. In a memorandum to Warner on 30 March 1943, Train explained that the FBI could not investigate the naval establishment. "A civilian law enforcing agency, built up with traditions of years in this sort of work," he argued, "is apt to find it extremely difficult to recognize the Naval Interest in events or subjects, that on the surface, have no apparent connection with the Naval effort, but which, upon investigation, from that point of view, prove to be of considerable interest and importance to the Navy." Usually the FBI would not enter a case until a crime or violation of the law had been committed, Train continued; thus how could the FBI protect naval property from acts that were about to be committed, such as sabotage. Nevertheless, Warner's report received a sympathetic hearing in the department, and only Train's contention, supported by VCNO Frederick Horne and to a lesser extent by Admiral King, that the middle of a war was a bad time to tamper with ONI prevented efforts to implement parts of the Chicago management expert's recommendations.[20]

The Warner investigation, subsequent report, and further efforts to reduce ONI propelled Zacharias to the front of a movement to strengthen and perhaps save the office from reduction and absorption by other agencies. While Train argued with bureaucrats and administrators, the assistant DNI determined to make ONI indispensable to the service. Instead of sitting back and receiving information passively, Zacharias wanted ONI to carry the war to the enemy through psychological warfare, special operations, counterespionage, black propaganda, and operational intelligence. Thus he advanced two action offices in ONI, the Special Activities or "Z" Branch and the Special Warfare or "W" Branch, the latter organized in extreme secrecy. "I conducted preliminary negotiations with the staff at my home and then gave instructions to regard the new branch as secret," Zacharias recalled.[21]

Z Branch, under former General Motors salesman in Europe Riheldaffer, interrogated prisoners of war, liaised with OSS, and developed operations to acquire and process captured enemy equipment, technical documents, and other material. The Special Warfare Branch was the navy's euphemism for psychological warfare, since the term drew opposition in some quarters. Organized by Commander Coggins, W Branch planned operations with Elmer Davis's Office of War Information, earlier part of the Office of Coordinator of Information and which had become autonomous after Donovan formed the OSS. Filled with eccentric, unorthodox but capable intelligence specialists, including author Ladislas Farago, Curt Reiss, and Professor Stefan T. Possony, W Branch fed misinformation and bred deception and confusion among the enemy. It prepared material for Mayor Fiorello La Guardia's radio broadcasts to Italy and worked with the JCS's Psychological Warfare Plans Group. Perhaps the branch's biggest contribution lay in the development of the Commander Norden broadcasts, designed to undermine the morale of German U-Boat crews by spreading gossip, rumors, scandals, and news of losses that were gleaned from POW interrogations, radio intercepts, and other classified material. Eventually over 300 broadcasts were aired by Commander Robert Lee Norden, the cover for ONI's POW interrogator Commander Albrecht.[22]

More important to Zacharias than these creative branches was the entire idea of transforming ONI into an action agency contributing a constant flow of operational intelligence to war planners and field commanders. "Our goal is to have the Naval Intelligence organization adjacent to Operations not only to evaluate information coming into Operations," Zacharias maintained, "but also to obtain for them through our unlimited sources the information that they might require." Such work called for carefully trained intelligence officers indoctrinated at basic and advanced intelligence schools run by ONI and then sent to operational theatres for six months before returning for a six-month tour back in Washington or in the districts. These officers, Zacharias trusted, would contribute directly to the war effort and win recognition for ONI. "We hope that [operational intelligence] will serve to bring to the attention of the Naval Service the broad activities of the Naval Intelligence Service, and enlist their support rather than the skeptical and derogatory attitudes that have existed in the past."[23]

In a limited way ONI had performed operational intelligence when it mobilized Coastal Information Sections in early 1941. From the outset, section head Lieutenant Commander Charles F. Baldwin back in Washington understood that the district network served this function, providing immediate data to army air patrols, destroyer scouts, Sea Frontier commands, operating bases, and district intelligence offices about sub sightings, wrecks, mines, driftwood, ship movements, or suspicious waterfront activity. But in practice, poor organization, lack of doctrine, and inadequate patrol equipment prevented a successful coastal information system. The head of the section in the Western Sea Frontier at Pearl Harbor complained to ONI that not only did the Advance Intelligence Center Pacific Ocean Area assume its own duties, such as communications intelligence, but took over his job as well. Admiral Adolphus Andrews in New York explained the issue more clearly. "It has come to the attention of the Commander, Eastern Sea Frontier that upon many occasions escort vessels, as well as patrol vessels have put to sea without first having been informed of the latest combat information."[24]

For Zacharias, the solution to these problems lay in assigning better trained ONI personnel to coastal information and operational intelligence positions. The first step in the training was attendance at a basic intelligence school at Frederick, Maryland, and then on to an Advanced Naval Intelligence School (ANIS) in New York. There, intelligence candidates would learn how to collect, evaluate, and disseminate information of military value, as well as how to identify ships and planes; they would also study travel and commerce control and other aspects of operational in-

telligence. The first students, Zacharias insisted, must be selected carefully, since these graduates would determine the success of the whole
program.[25]

While the first class completed their course, pressure for a more positive
ONI role increased. In planning and implementing the North African and
later the Sicilian and Italian invasions, war planners needed the latest
information on enemy order of battle, beach terrain, hydrography, local
geography, meteorology, and any number of other requisites. TORCH,
the North African operation, convinced Baldwin that the time was at hand
for an Operational Intelligence Branch in ONI. "This raises the basic
issue," he wrote Zacharias in January 1943, ". . . that a decision as to
whether an Operational Intelligence Branch should be formed in ONI, or
whether some other administrative steps to meet the problem should be
reached as soon as possible."[26]

Two months later Baldwin had his Operational Intelligence Branch as
part of the first complete regrouping of ONI's sections since its original
creation in 1882. In a plan approved by VCNO Horne on 18 March and
adopted on 14 April, a deputy director (Zacharias) linked the DNI with
three assistant directors heading Services, Intelligence, and Counterintelligence Groups. Modeled after the army's intelligence agency, ONI's Intelligence Group included geographic theatres of operations for Europe-
Africa, the Far East, Latin and North America, as well as new sections for
statistics, evaluation and dissemination, planning, foreign trade, intelligence plots, and, of course, operational intelligence. The Counterintelligence Group, which incorporated much of the old "B" Branch, was the
most important reorganization. For the first time, one officer would be
responsible for counterintelligence both inside and outside of the United
States, precluding the employment of people such as Phillips. Like the
Intelligence Group, Counterintelligence now had a more active mission "to
protect our war operations" from enemy espionage, sabotage, and propaganda. It was hoped that the new structure would provide a better overview
of domestic and foreign aspects of the naval interest, preventing entrapment
by the perennial intelligence dilemma.[27]

Reorganization and the creation of operational intelligence machinery
generated some action. Suddenly everyone wanted an operational intelligence officer. The Advanced Intelligence Center South West Pacific
Force ordered eight, the Motor Torpedo Squadron wanted one for each
vessel, and Zacharias's disciple McCollum headed for operational intelligence duty in Brisbane, requesting dozens of operational intelligence
officers for the Southwest Pacific war theatre. After the commanding officer
of U.S. Navy forces in the South Pacific asked ONI for officers in April,
Zacharias wrote excitedly to a friend: "As this is the first request we have
received for Intelligence Officers to serve aboard ships of the fleet, we are

extremely anxious that the officers selected for these billets make a good impression, and we are trying to find the officers who appear to be best qualified to do this work." Back in Washington, the reorganization impressed both Knox and King, who commented on the improved ONI briefings, miniplots, and the better media displays with maps and data sheets. Similar progress developed in the districts, where operational intelligence school graduates collected local photographs, postcards, maps, and books from libraries or college archives and interviewed missionaries, importers, and travelers to foreign lands to provide ONI with items of information. One such item was the complete groundplans of a Japanese chemical plant on Formosa, obtained from a former engineer.[28]

At last by the summer of 1943, the ONI revival seemed to be going according to Zacharias's best hopes. But obscured by his success was an undercurrent of unrest and disillusionment. Several senior intelligence officers, including most of Train's own section heads, opposed the changes, and some went their own way obstructing the performance of operational intelligence missions. Moreover, despite the new emphasis, one sympathetic officer admitted that not much had changed. "Once the operations began, ONI was pretty much out of it and the thing was handed over to CinCPac and they handled the thing on their own," he wrote. "It was only when something came to ONI's attention that they thought would be helpful that they would send the stuff out."[29]

Apparently oblivious to or intolerant of any opposition, Zacharias plowed ahead, lecturing Train in May 1943 that any delay in the full implementation of operational intelligence resulted from a total ignorance of ONI's mission. "I feel that some of the problems which we have encountered recently result from a lack of knowledge of what the Naval Intelligence Service is doing and what it should be expected to do in the future," Train's deputy argued. "I feel it is our responsibility to go as far as we can in removing any such misunderstandings." But in pressing ONI's case, Zacharias seemed to go too far. At least that was his impression when suddenly he was ordered out of the office. "All of my subordinates were amazed that I should be sent back to sea just when I was at the top of my successes and was planning new ones," Zacharias insisted years later. "It will have to be credited to the fact that I was moving too rapidly, and was becoming too strong for the good of more ambitious individuals and agencies."[30]

Admiral Train's version of Zacharias's removal differed somewhat from the tale of martyrdom to the intelligence cause. Train claimed that his deputy had never ceased coveting the top spot in ONI. Reminiscent of his efforts earlier to unseat Courts as naval attaché in Tokyo, he had worked clandestinely to undermine Train and seize the position of director. According to Train, he had learned about the plotting upon his return from

Harold Train battled throughout 1942–1943 to keep ONI on an even keel, and to prevent his closest subordinate from taking over his job. (Courtesy Franklin D. Roosevelt Library)

an inspection trip of the district intelligence organization in late 1942, when both his friend Strong and the vengeful Hoover revealed that Zacharias had tried to get Train's job. "I watched him carefully, very carefully, from then on," Train confided, "I wanted him to commit himself so I'd have definite proof." His opportunity came after Zacharias penned a letter allegedly disloyal to the director and others, which found its way to the director's desk. Upon Train's appeal, King ordered Zacharias out of ONI and to a minor district intelligence post that he had held ten years before. However, Train contended that the slippery deputy appealed to his friends in Congress that he had been axed for anti-Semitic reasons, and rather than cause a scandal Knox gave him command of the battleship *New Mexico*, leading to promotion as a "tombstone admiral." Zacharias caused his own troubles, his ONI boss concluded, because "he was so ambitious and so determined to be Director of Naval Intelligence and to be promoted to flag rank that he would stoop to any methods to obtain his ambition."[31]

Whatever the explanation, Zacharias's removal led to the immediate, although temporary, abandonment of operational intelligence. Succumbing to pressures from Captains Adolph von Pickhardt, Nathaniel Pigman, and several other section heads, Train issued an order on 11 September announcing a complete change in the curriculum of ANIS, canceling operational intelligence courses and substituting a general program. Train's order indicated the predicament he found himself in between two factions with different interpretations of ONI's major function. With the forceful leader of one group gone, the director supported the other. This ability to balance, pacify, and appease had allowed him to guide ONI through a most perilous year. Certainly the harmonious team handed over to incoming DNI Schuirmann in September 1943 differed completely from the shattered organization inherited from Wilkinson the previous summer. But maintaining harmony in ONI and with the Navy Department affected Train's health. Apparently the suppression of the turmoil and tensions of his office caused a bad case of high blood pressure and led to his early resignation as DNI.[32]

CHAPTER NINETEEN

GLOBAL AGENTS

While ONI experienced what seemed an interminable internal crisis back in Washington, its overseas agents carried out distant missions during World War II with varying degrees of expertise and success. Nothing exemplified the global nature of the war more clearly than the worldwide distribution and assignments of these U.S. naval attachés, observers, and liaison officers. Though of less importance than combat and operational personnel, intelligence officers became, nevertheless, an integral part of the strategic, logistical, and diplomatic functions of the U.S. Navy during the Second World War. They operated on every continent, served in every important and many smaller ports, watching Allies, neutrals, and enemies around the globe.

Unlike the informal and indifferently organized ONI overseas network during 1914–18, between 1942–45 through improved radio communications and air travel, the agents in foreign posts were more closely tied to Washington and in general better prepared and equipped to carry out duties than their predecessors had been twenty-five years before. Theoretically, their reports, if viewed together, would present the overall picture of the war situation and international affairs and assist policy makers in strategic decisions. In practice, however, bureaucratic tangles, uneven quality of personnel, different strategic values of each post, and reluctance by planners to utilize or consult such sources consistently combined to diminish the broader implications. Ultimately, just as in World War I, the contributions of ONI's overseas team lay in individual accomplishments and specific cases rather than through a coherent network.

Though their numbers varied from time to time during the war, at the height of the fighting in early 1943 ONI directed twenty-nine attaché posts manned by 156 officers (mostly reservists), twenty-two observer posts with seventy-nine officers, forty-three liaison offices with eighty-four officers and thirty-five men attached as shipping advisors, assistant consular officers, petroleum observers, or some such cover designation. No matter what the title, each officer received from ONI a little kit including a Hoey Position Plotter, various stationery and supplies, a .38 revolver, belt and holster, a *World Almanac*, fifty rounds of ammunition, and sometimes a gas mask and steel helmet.[1]

ONI's original overseas agent, the naval attaché, occupied the most institutionalized and usually the most important foreign station, reflecting Allied diplomatic and military considerations of the assignment. The attaché's mission included promoting the united nations concept and the strategy of coalition warfare through diplomatic, social, and military contacts. The department's unusual wartime practice of encouraging attachés to bring along wife and family to the overseas post reflected the social side of the officer's mission. There were fourteen naval attachés in Latin American capitals, as well as one each in British Commonwealth centers at London, Ottawa, Melbourne, Wellington, Capetown, and later Cairo. At the same time, naval attachés represented the U.S. government in the Allied capitals of Chungking and Moscow (or Kuibyshev), and for France, Poland, and other governments-in-exile, the navy posted one attaché in London. At different times during the war, naval attachés resided as well in Ankara, Lisbon, Madrid, Tangier, Algiers, Teheran, and Stockholm. These offices included any number of assistant attachés, who specialized in everything from air war and communications interception to filmmaking and photography.[2]

When no ambassadorial or ministerial office existed, or when a government for diplomatic reasons prohibited an attaché, the navy attached naval observers. Unlike the attaché, the naval observer had no tradition or well-developed doctrine to follow and often expressed uncertainty about his duties. And though he paid "due deference" to the wishes of the chief foreign service officer at his post, the naval observer owed primary loyalty to the navy and often ran into conflict with the diplomats. Finally in early 1942, the CNO explained that the naval observers performed functions identical to those of the naval attaché, keeping in touch with all naval and merchant marine authorities, making daily ship movement reports, studying communications problems, and maintaining liaison with local intelligence and security organizations. Broadly speaking, the CNO instructed these officers to obtain a progressive knowledge of all naval, air, military, and merchant marine operations at their scattered and distant stations.[3]

Naval observers appeared and disappeared with the course of the war and the strategic value of an area for the navy. Consequently, after Pearl Harbor larger defense considerations prompted the immediate dispatch of two observers and a clerk to Talara, Peru. "It is considered needless to stress the strategical importance of this oil field and distillery not only in relation to the defense of the Canal Zone, but to the economic life of Central and

South America," Heard insisted on 17 December. At other times naval observers popped up in such widely dispersed and variously vital locations as Casablanca, Aden, Suva, Martinique, Basra, Colombo, Rangoon, Guayaquil, Halifax, Georgetown, Paramaribo, and Dakar. More permanent was the network of forty-five reserve officers assigned as observers along the strategic Brazilian coastline from stations at Bahia, Belém, Natal, Recife, Santos, and others.[4]

The designation "naval liaison officer" arose from war experience, probably at the behest of the British as part of a ship routing agreement. Thus liaison officers worked from offices in Adelaide, Brisbane, Perth, and Sydney; Bombay, Calcutta, and Karachi; Alexandria and Suez; Mombasa, Durban, and Gibraltar; and Belfast, Liverpool, Gourock, and Loch Ewe. The department employed liaison officers as well in Chile, Cuba, and Mexico, where the term "naval observer" was considered offensive.[5]

In addition to the common titles, ONI representatives operated under several other euphemisms, usually in sensitive political areas where local governments wished to mask cooperation with the Allies or with the U.S. Navy. Thus in Las Palmas, the naval agent assumed the cover of petroleum observer, while in Lourenço Marques, Pointe-à-Pitre, Barranquilla, and Izmir they became consular shipping advisors or assistant to the consul, although the State Department vetoed plans for a consular shipping advisor for the Balearic Islands. The primary task of these officials was shipping control, and usually they did not wander into larger information-gathering fields or counterespionage work. In these cases ONI instructed such officers to wear civilian clothes, use "Mr." rather than naval titles in all correspondence, and to "scrupulously refrain from any mention of their naval status." These precautions failed to please everyone, however, as the ever-troublesome Soviet allies often refused to accept any of these designations.[6]

Recruiting competent personnel for these posts posed a problem for ONI. The best officers, both active and reserve, applied for and were most needed in the fighting war itself. The better ones remaining in naval intelligence received assignments to Washington headquarters or to the fleet, district, or combat intelligence networks. Reflecting upon the shortage, one U.S. diplomat discovered a solution—the assignment of "some rather elderly Naval man who looks imposing and whose presumptive shortcomings from the point of view of mobility could be compensated by the assistance of his juniors." Unfortunately, at times the navy followed this recommendation. For the Brazilian attachéship, ONI selected the nearly invalided Admiral Beauregard, who upon arrival in Rio de Janeiro fell seriously ill. "He told Capt. E. E. Brady [the assistant naval attaché] that he would die here rather than leave at this juncture," U.S. Minister Jefferson Caffery told the State Department. In this case Beauregard's wish was fulfilled. However, age made no difference to World War I veteran Tracy

B. Kittridge, who was rejected as too old by one office and went on to become a vital and valuable link to the French government-in-exile as part of the SPENAVO's staff in London. Nor did age trouble sixty-three-year-old Galbraith, who served as the head of ONI's American desk for much of the war.[7]

When retired or active-duty personnel were not available, ONI dipped into the reserve officer pool to come up quickly with the right man for the right post. Finding and identifying suitable prospects was tedious business. An ideal agent combined a good reputation, college education, proficiency in a foreign language, and travel or knowledge about foreign lands. The credentials of Ensign Leo E. Haughey, USNR, selected as an assistant naval attaché for Santiago, exemplified the successful blend. Educated in the Spanish language and in law at the University of Kansas, Haughey became a legal representative in Venezuela for the Standard Oil Company and after Pearl Harbor an expert on economic intelligence for the Board of Economic Warfare before joining the U.S. Navy. The credentials of Lieutenant Arthur J. Campbell, an assistant naval attaché in Chungking, fit the model as well. After graduating from Georgetown University, Campbell edited a weekly shipping journal before becoming a special Treasury Department customs agent in Hong Kong. Interned in 1941 and exchanged on the *Gripsholm* the next year, he joined the navy and served in ONI's Far Eastern section until the Chungking assignment.[8]

Experience was not enough, though. ONI's global agents needed to possess the ability to get along in the foreign post with both American diplomats and local officials. In a way, this intangible art of getting along was the most important attribute for a reserve intelligence officer attached to an overseas mission, overriding other considerations, and when the naval liaison officer in Valparaiso complained that the eccentric U.S. consul was impossible to work with, ONI ordered him to defer to the "unusual personality" anyway. Meanwhile, Minister J. C. White in Haiti told Washington that despite years of U.S. Marine Corps intervention in local affairs on the island, a USMC officer was entirely acceptable as naval attaché because he would know how to get along. "If an ex-Marine has friends among the Garde, and is a likeable person and tactful, he is a good selection for this country, as the Marines still enjoy considerable prestige with the Garde d'Haiti," White insisted.[9]

Unfortunately, not every officer sent abroad during the war as a naval attaché, observer, or liaison officer was a likeable, tactful, or able person. In fact, some were unhappy selections. Here and there reports of corruption, ill-manners, drunkenness, disdain for local sensitivities, dereliction of duty, and immorality tarnished the record. While such conduct might be absorbed in combat zones and battle areas, it stood out starkly when going beyond military circles and affecting diplomatic or political relations with host governments. In Wellington, New Zealand, authorities warned the U.S. naval attaché repeatedly about his drunkenness and traffic violations. To no avail. Finally, after his fifth major violation local officials demanded that this inebriated intelligence officer be expelled. Such conduct could be dangerous as well as embarrassing. The consular shipping adviser at Buenaventura (Colombia) became so drunk at a party in Bogotá that he revealed his cover as an ONI operative, drawing the director's condemnation that such "indiscreet disclosures may inflict injury upon the national interest."[10]

Others lived too well, taking advantage of their position and department intelligence funds. Cavalierly, the naval observer in Georgetown ordered ONI to restring his two tennis racquets and send down a new racquet press to British Guiana. Another entertained lavishly, including an expensive banquet for foreign naval officers. Finally in December 1944, the department ordered that funds for the collection and classification of information could not be used for dinners, luncheons, and entertainment. Temptations could lead even further, though, and one intelligence officer in Turkey allegedly ran a prostitution ring and fenced stolen jewels and gold, while an officer returning from North Africa arrived back in the United States with thirty packing cases of foreign weapons, leading to an ONI recommendation for court-martial.[11]

While not always venal, other personnel were simply lazy or incompetent. The oil observer at Las Palmas forwarded one report in three months from this strategic Portuguese possession frequented by Axis agents, and ONI found that single correspondence inaccurate. He was recalled. Another officer stationed in Chile refused to take seriously his instructions from the American Republics section to complete a Chilean monograph. "The majority of the intelligence reports submitted by the U.S. Naval Liaison Office, Concepcion, between the dates 15 December 1942 and 30 September 1943," DNI Schuirmann criticized, "are casual, fragmentary, and insufficiently detailed." Sometimes it was not the agent's fault, as in the case of naval observers in the Caribbean whose excellent intelligence reports were not transmitted to Washington by the Tenth Naval District commandant at San Juan, prompting Train to remove him. In his place Train sent ONI troubleshooter Captain Sidney Souers, USNR, director of central intelligence after the war, to Puerto Rico.[12]

The gravest obstacle confronting ONI personnel overseas during the war was not incompetence, corruption, or criminality, but the same frustrating internal rivalries, cliques, bureaucratic tangles, overlapping agencies, and ill-defined missions that confronted their naval intelligence colleagues stateside. In addition, those on foreign station faced the various political, social, and military troubles presented at their exotic posts. Both issues plagued nearly all attachés, observers, and liaison officers, and at times affected their performance and the type of information forwarded to Washington. The most capable were buffeted about by relations with the OSS, MID, British Intelligence, and any number of apparently unattached agents who surged back and forth through these posts. The seven naval observers in Port of Spain, headquarters for the British Navy in the Caribbean, wrestled with British operatives, FBI agents, Colonel Donovan's people, and FDR's own secret agent to gather information about Axis threats to the area. Complicating matters, White House intelligence chief Carter decided to dispatch to Trinidad his own special informant Henry Field, a former ONI recruit now in disfavor with the intelligence office.[13]

The intelligence tangle in the China-Burma-India Theater was worse still, as "free agents" moved about spying on the Japanese enemy, Indian nationalists, Chinese Communists, or each other. Against this convoluted background of intrigue, the U.S. Navy created its own intelligence conflict by assigning Captain Milton E. ("Mary") Miles as naval observer and head of the Sino-American Cooperative Organization, or Naval Group China, to gather operational intelligence through intimate contacts with Chiang Kai-shek's secret services. Though Miles tried to maintain harmonious relations with ONI, requesting a number of the office's personnel, including photographic expert Raymond Kotrla, his affinity for the Nationalist Chinese brought him into conflict with the naval attaché office, which recommended cooperation with Chiang's avowed enemy Mao Tse-tung and his Chinese Communist partisans battling the Japanese from their secret base in Yenan.[14]

Miles's feud with ONI surfaced after the office had dispatched Lieutenant Simon Herbert Hitch, USNR, one of its Far Eastern section assistants, to Chungking as an assistant naval attaché. Educated at Emory University and for years a representative of the Wrigley Engraving Company in Korea, Hitch left at once for Mao's retreat in northern China, probably on orders from ONI. Following in the steps of earlier visitors such as Evans Carlson, journalist Edgar Snow, Army Intelligence expert David D. Barrett, and a number of OSS agents, Hitch was moved by the sincerity and patriotism of the Chinese Communists. He reported to Captain Henry T. Jarrell, the naval attaché in Chungking, that the CCP would cooperate with the navy in coast-watching operations, but not if they were run by Naval Group China, which Mao's people claimed kowtowed to the "Chungking Government's Gestapo." Hitch's report on the Chinese Communist's potential assistance in the battle against Japan impressed former naval attaché to China and current head of ONI's Far Eastern desk, Captain William L. Bales, USMC, and others in ONI who recommended closer ties. When Miles learned about Hitch's trip, however, he was furious. "Although it is the duty of Naval Intelligence to know things," Miles wrote, "it seemed to me that sending an officer, full-time, to the Yenan Reds was a little like one of our allies sending a man to serve as liaison with the Capone Gang in order to see what they were doing." Ironically, unknown to Miles ONI was indeed working closely in New York with organized crime in gathering data for the Sicilian and Italian invasions.[15]

Internal rivalries plagued the naval attaché office in London as well, especially when Admiral Stark replaced Ghormley as SPENAVO and commander of naval forces in Europe (COMNAVEU). Stark assumed all intelligence functions normally assigned to the naval attaché, perhaps recalling how his boss Admiral Sims had combined intelligence under the London Planning Section in World War I. But in 1942 the London post had more different types of intelligence personnel and missions. Consequently, when naval flight surgeon and medical observer Captain H. H. Poppem arrived in the British capital, he puzzled over whether to report as instructed by ONI to the naval attaché or as ordered by the special medical observer in London, to Stark's office. For a time Captain Paul H. Bastedo, the naval attaché in 1943, battled for his office's integrity. But poor health forced his recall, and Stark merged the office into his organization.[16]

In addition to the other rivalries, ONI personnel ran afoul as usual of State Department officials overseas. Widespread complaints against naval agents by U.S. diplomats during the war made it difficult to sort out valid criticisms from routine jealousies, personality conflicts, or honest differences of interpretation over spheres of interest and missions. Typical was the U.S. minister in Nicaragua's cryptic complaint that the naval observer "does not show necessary discretion and judgment, and that a more capable officer is needed at Corinto." Meanwhile, in a repeat of ONI's clash with Ambassador Joseph Willard during World War I, the office collided with current U.S. Ambassador to Spain Carlton J. H. Hayes, a cantankerous history professor. Under personal instructions from the president to maintain friendly relations with Franco and thus ensure the neutrality of the Iberian peninsula, Hayes worried over the strong anti-Franco opinions of Captain Richard Drace White, the naval attaché in Madrid. White advocated Allied occupation of Spain to forestall a similar Nazi move from France. "I am not prepared to recommend that the Allied Powers should take the first action in this connection," he insisted in June 1942, "but I believe without qualification that sooner or later, one combatant will do so." The doctrinaire Hayes brooked no contrary opinions and demanded White's withdrawal.[17]

In yet another conflict, Minister Spruille Braden in Havana demanded that all naval liaison officers report the names of their informants to him directly. Naturally ONI objected to the compromise of its sources to an indiscreet diplomat. Fortunately, in this incident Berle supported ONI at the JIC meeting. Finally in late 1943, when Ambassador Boaz Long in Guatemala complained that the naval attaché had overstepped his authority by interviewing local businessmen about political and economic conditions, the State Department had grown tired of its own people's constant bickering with ONI. "I doubt that the matter is serious enough for us to raise a fuss about it with the Navy Department," State advised Long.[18]

While bureaucratic flaps frustrated naval intelligence personnel, foreign conditions from friend and foe alike promised worse treatment. In Baden-Baden, Nazi agents kept a close watch on former naval attaché to Vichy Captain A. C. J. Sabalot and his assistant, Commander Thomas G. Cassady, a Chicago banker and friend of Secretary of the Navy Knox. Once the Gestapo entered Cassady's hotel room, pushed him about a bit, and seized some papers. They also restricted his movements. Meanwhile, someone threatened to kill the U.S. naval attaché in neutral Madrid, while ten Italians beat up an assistant naval attaché in North Africa. The gravest danger to ONI people came when the Pearl Harbor attack caught intelligence officers in Asia. For months the office tried to discover the condition and treatment of their interned agents, especially Williams and Harold K. Jackson in Shanghai, who were held apart from the others. In Tokyo, naval attaché Smith-Hutton and other American diplomatic and military internees were confined to the embassy compound, suffered minor indignities and long hours of boredom before being exchanged for Japanese internees on board the Swedish ship, the *Gripsholm*. Indeed, during the exchange process Smith-Hutton, aided by Williams, managed to carry out several intelligence operations, including surveillance of some pacifistic missionaries and the recovery of a propaganda film being smuggled to Latin America in a tube of shaving soap.[19]

Threats, intimidation, and danger to ONI's global observers could be expected in enemy or neutral territory crawling with enemy agents, but relations with uncertain and devious ally Russia posed the greatest threat to the safety of naval intelligence officers. From the outset, relations with the

The interned American Embassy staff in Tokyo shortly before repatriation aboard the *Gripsholm* in 1942.

Soviets ranged from cautious cooperation in lend-lease arrangements to outright deception and hostility concerning the movement of Russian ships or the exchange of military information. Train claimed that during his entire directorship, the Russians never sent ONI one shred of valuable information about Japan, the Far East, or the Pacific Ocean, denying even meteorological data necessary for U.S. Fleet operations. The Russians restricted the movements of any U.S. naval agent and bottled up assistant naval attaché Commander John Young, USNR, and his plane load of films, newsreels, and publications, nearly creating a diplomatic incident. Naturally such secrecy increased ONI's appetite for news from Russia, and in late 1942 the office ordered Commander Carroll H. Taecker, Russian language expert and assistant naval attaché in Vladivostock, on a secret reconnaissance of Soviet harbors and naval facilities. At the last moment, though, ONI canceled the espionage trip after the State Department worried about his safety and the extreme peril to a coalition war effort that would accompany the possible revelation of such a mission. "As you know," Russian expert Loy Henderson warned, "the Soviet authorities are extremely sensitive to endeavors through 'back door' channels to obtain military or naval information."[20]

With the successful Russian defense of Stalingrad and subsequent counteroffensive, ONI's concern for information about the Soviet Union in-

ONI's team in Archangel in 1943 included one of the navy's earliest Russian language experts and wandering intelligence gatherers, Commander Kemp Tolley (extreme left). Others include from left to right Lieutenant Commander Pancratov, naval attaché C. E. Olsen, Lieutenant Commander Sablin, Commander F. Lang, and Lieutenant Commander E. Yorke.

creased. Already there were rumblings that the postwar era would bring a titanic struggle for world hegemony between Russia and the United States. The U.S. naval observer in Basra, a key listening post, thought that at the very least Russia would demand strategic and economic concessions in the Middle East, including a road and oil pipeline from northern Persia to Bandar 'Abbas on the Persian Gulf. Other sources noted how the Russians raced frantically to beat Allied armies into Eastern and Central Europe.[21]

While the postwar situation and possible struggle with Russia began to concern ONI, the months of hard fighting ahead against the Axis in Europe, Asia, and the Pacific required more immediate attention. To assist, many ONI agents were absorbed into operational commands and their observer or liaison office closed. Every resource was put into the immediate victory on the battlefield, leaving postwar political questions until later. Nevertheless, it would be the job of the last two wartime DNIs, Schuirmann and Leo Hewlett Thebaud, to provide not only operational information but also to look to the future by improving ONI's internal structure and by maintaining global agents, who despite the return to peace, could forward information about the potential worldwide Soviet menace.

CHAPTER TWENTY

DEFINING THE NAVAL INTEREST

Roscoe Schuirmann possessed the same patient, cooperative demeanor as his predecessor Train. While Director of the Central Division and Navy Department liaison with the State Department, he had displayed an ability to get along with self-important civilians who liked to tell the navy how to run the war and also with all the members of the JIC. This served as a valuable asset in the waning months of world struggle when ONI had to provide tidbits of data to Combined and Joint Chiefs of Staff, and departmental and other war planners as they worked out grand strategies for the wartime series of top-level conferences—such as Teheran where Stalin, Churchill, and FDR and their staffs discussed a second front in France and Russia's eventual entrance into the war against Japan.[1]

Schuirmann was the type of nearly invisible naval administrator required to bring ONI into line with departmental retrenchment, which was pushed by Knox until his death in April 1944 and then by Forrestal. Entering the office at a peak wartime deployment of 65 officers, 240 enlisted men and women and 124 civilians, the incoming director at once faced requests for personnel management surveys and manpower cutback studies both in Washington headquarters and in the bloated DIOs. Schuirmann's major task, unlike all his wartime predecessors, was consolidation and contraction rather than expansion, change, and new enterprises. He dared not tamper with various departments or press operational intelligence. In fact, he seemed inclined personally to have the office focus on static information, perhaps recalling his experience as a young intelligence officer in ONI in the 1920s when he had assembled tables and charts on warships and port directories.[2]

More importantly, Admiral King provided an apparent solution to internal controversies over operational or static intelligence when in September 1943 he combined Schuirmann's position with that of Assistant Chief of Staff for Combat Intelligence in the COMINCH. Concentrating on his job as DNI and preparing long-range informational services, Schuirmann assigned Smith-Hutton, William Sebald, and three other ONI staff officers to run the operational intelligence side in King's office, where they helped draw up plans for amphibious and other operations and plotted sinkings and submarine sightings in conjunction with the Tenth Fleet's war against the U-Boat. Thus, ONI could contribute to the fighting war through this channel without compromising what Schuirmann believed was the office's primary function to collect technical and strategic information of direct interest to the Navy Department in the form of monographs or combat narratives.[3]

During his brief twelve-month tour as DNI and Assistant Chief of Staff for Combat Intelligence, Schuirmann devoted himself to the business of defining the naval interest for ONI and limiting any activity or new projects to that definition. Such an emphasis had been attempted before. Periodically, past directors and naval administrators had attempted to define the naval interest, but had discovered that the parameters were too vague, slipping into the ever-widening concept of naval intelligence. World conflict accelerated this trend. As one intelligence officer insisted: "You can make a naval interest in almost anything you want in this war." Even the cautious Train succumbed to this larger view the very month he had turned the office over to Schuirmann. In a letter to all district intelligence officers in September, Train had urged the study of national and ethnic groups and surveillance of exiles and refugees in the United States. "Because of the strong Naval interest in development of situations abroad which may create service demands on the Navy and in domestic political trends which may be utilized by persons and organizations inspired by foreign powers to weaken the Navy and its effective power as an instrument of U.S. National Policy," Train argued, "the Office of Naval Intelligence is preparing a series of studies to show the forces that may be considered as dangerous or potentially dangerous."[4]

On the other hand, some intelligence officers went to the opposite extreme, focusing narrowly on ships and naval information as the only ONI business of direct interest to the navy. Such an approach greatly simplified naval intelligence but also led to potentially fatal information gaps. Consequently, when reports of mysterious aircraft landing strips along the Chesapeake Bay reached ONI, the Coastal Information Section watch officer refused to take any action! "The attached correspondence should not be investigated by the Office of Naval Intelligence," he insisted, "since there is no naval interest involved."[5]

Schuirmann made an effort to define the nebulous naval interest. His exercise derived more from immediate exigencies than from any philosophy of intelligence, however. Personnel cutbacks and manpower freezes forced the closer look at the question. The DNI had to eliminate peripheral tasks of questionable naval interest and harvest dwindling intelligence resources by employing as a measuring stick how each job fit the navy's interest. Accordingly, he told DIOs in February 1944 to avoid any subject that had no definite naval interest, such as peace movements, Moslems, Arabs, Irish nationalists, economic espionage, the Gestapo, Pan-Serbs, and Spanish consular agents—all of previous interest to ONI during the war. Furthermore, he directed intelligence officers to observe strictly the delimitation agreement, leaving to the FBI and Military Intelligence all domestic investigations.[6]

And yet Schuirmann could no more escape the temptations of the naval intelligence dilemma than any of the previous DNIs since the First World War. "No hard and fast definition as to what is or is not of direct Naval Interest is deemed feasible," he admitted. In the course of gathering information or providing security for the navy, he wished to be free in certain cases to move into peripheral fields, secret operations, snooping, or extralegal conduct. But he had to avoid embarrassing situations, such as the one he found plaguing ONI when he had entered in September. Apparently several months before, Train's office had placed radio news commentator Drew Pearson under surveillance, tailing him about and tapping his telephone lines, to discover the source of his broadcast about the Axis use of Spanish ships to carry war goods. Unfortunately, ONI's bumbling sleuths had blown their cover, and the repercussions had gone all the way to the White House, which ordered troubleshooter Carter to spy once again on naval intelligence for the president. Although Carter discovered no concrete evidence that ONI had pried into Pearson's affairs, he told the president that naval intelligence was a "clumsy outfit for this kind of work."[7]

After the wartime buffeting experienced by ONI from department, president, and civilian analysts, Schuirmann wanted to insulate the office from further bad publicity. He warned DIOs to be careful in their conduct. "Good common sense must govern any decision, and if there is doubt, the advice of the Office of Naval Intelligence is always available," he proffered. The safe, conservative course recommended by the office was to focus on the naval interest by collecting, collating, and disseminating technical and strategic information. This had been the basic guideline ever since Lieutenant Theodorus B. M. Mason and his obscure crew had assembled folders on steamship boilers and breech-loading cannon as the first ONI team in the early 1880s. Naturally there were many more complex technical matters to sort and collect now. Information arrived from POWs, naval observers, captured documents, the OSS, battle action reports, and many other sources about everything from German V-1 and V-2 rockets to synthetic fuels and electronic gear.[8]

To study the new data, ONI added special sections and subsections for air intelligence, technical intelligence, flak intelligence, target analyses, and liaisons with the joint intelligence reading panels, collection agencies, reception agencies, target and strategic bombing survey teams, committees to assess loss or damage inflicted on the enemy, and the Intelligence Analysis Unit of the navy's Office of Coordinator of Research and Development. An ominous side of the technical intelligence business appeared in August 1944 when King's chief of staff, Admiral Edwards, asked Schuirmann's office to keep an eye out for special German successes in developing atomic weapons. In response, Schuirmann dispatched Captain Henry A. Schade as liaison with ALSOS, a secret team headed by Army Captain Boris Pash, to scavenge liberated Europe for evidence of Nazi research and development of atomic weaponry. According to one naval intelligence officer, however, no intelligence report reached ONI in 1944 about any German project or about America's own Manhattan project to develop an atomic bomb.[9]

When Captain Thebaud replaced Schuirmann on 21 October 1944, he determined to expand ONI's technical intelligence service as part of a decision to resurrect and revive the operational intelligence section. Opportunely, in October the Navy Department accepted the advice of Schade, Stark, and Captain Tully Shelly, the naval attaché in London, to create a Naval Technical Mission for Europe and to exploit German science and technology for the benefit of navy technical bureaus and the Office of Research and Development. In this manner, the U.S. Navy would not have to rely on uncertain handouts from ALSOS, from a similar A-Bomb hunting team organized for the British by Ian Fleming, or from any other intelligence organization. Indeed, once the Naval Technical Mission was organized, naval officers, technical experts, and assorted scientists and enlisted men raced behind Allied combat forces as they rolled through Nazi-occupied France and on into Germany itself to arrive first at any cache of weapons, documents, or research laboratory. Once the Russians entered the eastern part of Germany, the race to grab German secrets became even more intense.[10]

Under a directive of June 1942, ONI administered the navy's captured document and equipment program and hence received the cartons of data sent first by the Naval Technical Mission in Europe and later by a similar mission created for Japan in August 1945. The amount of technical information was enormous, including even crated ME 262 and Arado 234 jet fighter planes. To process this material and information, ONI created a new technical section, and in February 1945 opened a document center at 5th and K Streets under former Frigidaire salesman Riheldaffer to sort and forward captured material to appropriate bureaus.[11]

Thebaud expected all this data processed and disseminated more quickly than before, not only to technical bureaus in Washington but to forces at sea. Unlike either Train or Schuirmann, Thebaud believed in and strongly supported operational intelligence, surrounding himself with sympathetic officers such as veterans Heard and S. A. D. Hunter and newcomer Commander Frank P. Morton, USNR, fresh from combat intelligence experience in the Mediterranean. Overcoming opposition from conservative traditionalists such as counterintelligence chief Keisker and receiving support from King's office, Thebaud promoted an operational intelligence section, restructured the ANIS curriculum—gearing it more fully to operational intelligence than even Zacharias and Baldwin had envisaged in 1942.[12]

In fact, in March 1945 Zacharias returned to head a psychological warfare program against Japan, broadcasting messages designed to weaken Japan's will to resist and at the same time providing subtle reassurance that the United States would not destroy Japanese civilization. Zacharias assembled some of the Norden broadcast team and brought in several Japanese experts, including John Paul Reed, Francis R. Eastlake, and Dennis McEvoy. However, trouble once again plagued the navy's foremost intelligence promoter who, while comfortable with the atmosphere in ONI, ran afoul of Secretary of the Navy Forrestal's civilian agent Ferdinand Eberstadt. "We agreed that Zacharias should cease his use of the phrase 'official spokesman' in his broadcasts to Japan because of the delicacy of current negotiations," Eberstadt wrote after a conversation with Secretary of State James Byrnes in July 1945.[13]

Nevertheless, other aspects of operational intelligence showed great promise during the closing days of the war. ONI prepared a comprehensive watch officers guide for operational intelligence, rotated officers between joint intelligence collection agencies and ONI each six months, began to dispatch an operational intelligence officer to every battleship or cruiser in the service, issued regular operational intelligence notes, and pursued an aggressive program in the districts to collect data of operational intelligence value, such as maps and charts from local libraries and colleges. Nowhere was the progress more evident than in the ANIS curriculum, which featured fifty-two hours of operational intelligence training—including courses on amphibious warfare, plotting, photo interpretation, ship and aircraft identification, aerology, and antisubmarine warfare. It also included a new seminar to prepare intelligence officers for duty with the military governments in conquered enemy territory, especially liberated eastern European countries where Soviet agents had infiltrated already. By April 1945 Thebaud noted proudly that "The Operational Intelligence program has now the second largest strength of the various activities in the Intelligence Service, and new requirements continued to average thirty officers per month."[14]

Thebaud had reason to be pleased with ONI in the spring of 1945. Departmental administrators expressed more confidence in the office than at any time during the war, and Forrestal restored some of ONI's former functions taken away at the outbreak of fighting. "A new section, headed by Captain Vernon Huber, U.S. Navy, is being established under Admiral Thebaud," Forrestal advised Byron Price, "to take cognizance of all matters pertaining to the censorship of civilian communications." At the same time, war planners asked often for ONI assistance, giving the long-neglected agency members a sense that at last they were contributing something to the war effort. Thebaud determined that ONI information should be of a high quality—whether distributed in the form of an urgent memorandum to the Joint Chiefs of Staff, which calmed their fears that Germany had developed a long-range V-3 rocket capable of hitting the United States, or in the form of scholarly studies prepared by Lieutenants Richard Leopold, Carl Bridenbaugh, and other professional historians in ONI's historical section. Most vital was the quality of information provided for the Joint Army-Navy Intelligence Studies (JANIS), which the JCS and theatre commanders alike considered a standard intelligence reference for their war planning. Thebaud reminded his staff of the importance of sharing information with the Joint Intelligence Study Publishing Board, charged with the final production of JANIS. "All personnel of the Division of Naval Intelligence are hereby advised that there should be no arbitrary decision on the part of a custodian of intelligence to withhold information needed by another activity within or without the Division of Naval Intelligence in the prosecution of this important work," Thebaud proclaimed.[15]

ONI's value as an information agency took on more importance as Thebaud's office contributed data for the various committees established to study postwar military unification and centralized intelligence agencies in the fall of 1944. Thebaud considered the creation of a "Central Intelligence Agency" as most probable, expressing concern for his organization's proper place in the postwar structure. "ONI could and should have a small section to liaise with the State Department and other agencies to tie up [the] naval interest," Thebaud and his plans officer Sidney Souers recommended in December 1944.[16]

Tying up the naval interest meant staying away from peripheral questions. Consequently, though worrying that some Japanese agents might be among Japanese-Americans released from internment camps, Thebaud insisted that "the Navy has no primary jurisdiction or responsibility over the movements or activities of alien Japanese or American citizens of Japanese ancestry in the United States or its territories. . . ." For the same reason, the director sought to steer clear of the racial issues confronting the navy during the closing phase of the war, despite one of his assistant's insistence that ONI should pay attention to the "Negro elements insofar as those elements could affect directly or indirectly the personnel of Navy establishments." Thebaud disagreed, contending that ONI had no direct interest in the "Negro element" or in the question of racial segregation in the armed services.[17]

But ONI could not escape the intelligence dilemma. By late 1944 danger signals portended future entanglement in questions that strayed beyond strictly naval interests. The trouble appeared as U.S. forces landed in and advanced through Italy and France, penetrated the inner defenses of the Third Reich, and moved closer to the defeat of Japan in China and the Pacific. "Substantial data already exists," counterespionage chief Captain Wallace S. Wharton advised in November 1944, "which reveals extensive plans by the enemies of the United States to activate 'stay-behind' organizations and networks in territory from which the enemy's armed forces have been or will be ejected." Wharton asked naval officers around the world to report on any organization, group, or individual who might carry out espionage, sabotage, or subversive activity against the U.S. Navy.[18]

But who were these "stay-behind" enemies? Thebaud explained. "While persons or groups serving the German and Italian governments in intelligence, subversive and sabotage capacities cannot be disregarded, the present stage of the war requires placing the main emphasis upon the following: (a) Oriental ideologies; (b) Latin American ideologies; (c) Marxian ideologies; (d) sabotage and (e) Racial and Minority Groups in the U.S." The list suggested several developments in Thebaud's conception of ONI duty. He included category (a) naturally since the fighting war continued against Japan, but the other categories pointed toward postwar concerns and domestic considerations. Of particular interest was Thebaud's change of attitude about ONI's need to keep racial and minority groups in the United States under surveillance, since apparently he had succumbed to Wharton's contention that there was a sinister "centralized direction or control of Negro elements. . . ." Taken together, each category suggested that the current director had begun to focus on the nemesis of every DNI since Niblack's tour in 1919—the menace of world Communism and all its various manifestations both in the United States and abroad. In fact, rather than signifying Japanese militarism, the category on Oriental ideologies suggested interest in data about Chinese Communism.[19]

Surveillance and countermeasures against Communist agents had been difficult over the past few years, since the Roosevelt administration stressed harmonious relations with wartime ally Soviet Russia. Nevertheless, ONI had watched Communists and suspected sympathizers throughout the war, perhaps more closely than agents of the actual enemies. "Having full cognizance of the objectives and activities of the Communist Party and recognizing the danger therein relative to Navy Security, especially because of its record of overnight flip-flops in relation to our Government," ONI's Communist hunter Lieutenant Commander F.C. Caskey observed in late 1942, "it becomes quite evident that it is proper for Naval Intelligence to continue relative to Communists, to know who they are, where they are, and what they are doing. . . ."[20]

When ONI and the DIOs reduced their files on other suspects, they retained and expanded their "Communist File", and in October 1944 launched a survey of Communist activity within the naval establishment. The results of the investigation, one naval intelligence officer told a House Judiciary Subcommittee after the war, revealed thousands of "fellow travelers" in the U.S. Navy, including some with access to secret documents. Apparently one, Lieutenant Andrew Roth, worked in ONI itself and allegedly leaked classified naval intelligence documents to the left-wing journal *Amerasia*.[21]

In addition to the domestic side, ONI concentrated in the waning months of World War II on Soviet Russia and its potential postwar threat to the United States. Major Andrew Wylie, USMCR, head of the Eastern European desk in 1944, prepared a careful estimate of the strength and intentions of the postwar Soviet Navy. Wylie believed that Russia would develop four battle fleets built around capital ships for the Arctic, Baltic, and Black Seas and the Pacific Ocean, with a strong Soviet naval presence in the Mediterranean Sea and off the Korean coast. He predicted also that Russia would subsidize a first-class merchant marine. At the same time, prompted by his desire to have adequate naval preparation for dealing with the Russians at the Yalta Conference in February 1945, Admiral King asked for an intelligence estimate of Russian intentions, resulting in a fifty-page study that concluded simply that Russia was ruthless and could not be trusted under any circumstances. And all the while as Allied armies liberated Eastern and Central Europe from Hitler's occupation in the spring

Convinced of postwar tensions with the Soviet Union, U.S. naval intelligence provided an increasing amount of information about the Soviet Navy toward the end of World War II, despite numerous obstacles placed in their way by the Russians. Here the U.S. naval attaché provided a photograph of a *Leningrad*-class destroyer.

ONI personnel surreptitiously photographed the Molotovsk Navy Yard in Russia from a small motor launch in Nikolske Inlet, near Severodvinsk, June 1944.

of 1945, ONI rushed agents as naval members of the Allied Control Commissions to Rumania, Bulgaria, Yugoslavia, Hungary, and Poland. Wylie went to Warsaw himself.[22]

Back in Washington, Thebaud began the battle against Russia and the Communists in earnest during the summer of 1945. Several factors provided impetus. In June, the sensational *Amerasia* case broke, when the FBI arrested six people, including State Department China expert John Service, Lieutenant Roth, and Emmanuel S. Larsen, an ONI civilian analyst for nine years. Among the cache of documents seized in the editorial office of the journal were classified ONI memoranda, and although the charge of espionage was never proven, both the press and Thebaud's office believed at the time that these two former intelligence officers had leaked the data to Russian agents as well as to the journal, which was said to be a "center of a constellation of Communist zealots and their satellite fellow-travelers."[23]

Another reason for Thebaud's emphasis on Communism was the tense Soviet-American atmosphere surrounding the last great conference of the war, held in late July and early August at Potsdam. No longer led by FDR, who had died in April, the U.S. delegation under President Harry S Truman displayed far more coolness toward Stalin than before. Inevitably, the Soviet-American power struggle, the suspicion, and the political and economic rivalry that grew into the Cold War rubbed off on ONI, where Thebaud and his staff began to see Communist subversion everywhere. When Afro-American sailors rioted at the Portsmouth Naval Prison, Wharton reported that much more than racial animosity and discrimination lay behind the unrest. Reflecting the common wartime ONI theme that Afro-Americans were pawns of Oriental agents, the counterespionage officer merely suggested that Communist rather than Oriental agents were inciting the "Negro element." In the same manner, Thebaud warned naval district commandants that displaced persons, deserters, fugitives, and foreign nationals thrown on American shores by the war might be Communist agents. "It should be borne in mind that the danger of intelligence infiltration always exists and must be guarded against in every manner possible."[24]

Fear of intelligence infiltration increased with the end of fighting on V-J Day, 15 August 1945. The return of peace meant that personnel, funds, and the sense of emergency would be curbed, and instead of pursuing America's potential enemies at home and abroad, ONI would be on the defensive once again. Two days after the Japanese surrender, Keisker issued a statement to deal with the expected postwar reaction against intelligence operations, recommending that Thebaud attach a cover letter explaining the strict naval needs when he requested information about spies, subversives, and saboteurs. "This letter is considered to be one of the safeguards that protects the Office of Naval Intelligence from the unjust criticism often times directed against it as being an organizaion of sleuths and 'snoopers'."[25]

Keisker's memorandum echoed a letter written twenty years before just after the end of the first world conflict in which Niblack had assured potential critics that ONI never used gumshoe methods. Though conditions in 1945 differed in some respects from those in 1919, most especially in increased American involvement in postwar affairs and peacemaking, the issues confronting naval intelligence bore a remarkable and relentless similarity to Niblack's era. Once again the DNI had to go before congressional committees to defend the organization against cuts in personnel and appropriations. Once again a dangerous potential enemy, now Russia instead of Japan, had to be revealed to the department, government, and public. Once again, intelligence reservists and civilian experts returned to civilian pursuits. While Niblack had confronted the Red Scare and Bolshevik menace, Thebaud and Thomas B. Inglis, who took over ONI in late 1945, faced a Communist challenge and Cold War.

There were new issues in 1945 to be sure, including movements to unify the military and to centralize intelligence, the development of electronics, jet propulsion, and the awesome power of atomic weapons, which now made vigilance against sneak attack more critical than ever before. But no matter the changes in environment and external circumstances, the dilemma confronting ONI remained depressingly consistent. On the one hand, the office served the naval interest by providing technical and strategic information about the war potentials and intentions of foreign nations. "That is the mission of Naval Intelligence," Inglis insisted in December 1945. However, on the other hand, ONI had a more obscure mission, which arose from its nature as an intelligence organization, and that was the pursuit of secret operations, surveillance, spying, and extralegal activity. The two missions were not always compatible, and at times the naval mission contradicted the intelligence mission, interfering with the basic collection of data for the navy. Thus, while Inglis stressed the

strategic aspect in December, several months later he warned the department about the internal enemy, which caused strikes on the waterfront,
met in the Communist Party convention in New York, and undermined
American society. "I think our people should be told more forcibly than
they have been told so far of the threat of a Communist Fifth Column *within*
the United States," he concluded. (Emphasis added.)[26]

But in protecting the American people against the internal Communist
menace, would ONI neglect to collect all the necessary information from
widely scattered, potential trouble spots such as Greece, Turkey, China,
Korea, Berlin, or Cuba? Or would the postwar centralization of intelligence, the introduction of computers, and acceleration of the Cold War
prevent any lapse into the naval intelligence dilemma? Most importantly,
would those who directed the United States Navy's strategic war planning
and intelligence policies in future decades pay attention to their organization's own doctrine and history, rich in models of the timeless pitfalls and
potential of the intelligence business? In fact, anyone involved in security,
strategy, and secret operations might learn from the successes and failures
between 1919 and 1945 of the likes of Niblack, McNamee, Ellis, Puleston,
Holmes, Kirk, Wilkinson, Train, and Zacharias; or at least realize that
others had been just as puzzled and frustrated by the United States Navy's
intelligence dilemma.

ABBREVIATIONS USED
IN THE NOTES

BuNav	Bureau of Navigation
CinCUS	Commander in Chief of the U.S. Fleet
CIS	Coastal Information Section Records
CNO	Chief of Naval Operations
CO	Commanding Officer
DCD	Director of the Central Division
DIO	District Intelligence Office(r)
DNC	Director of Naval Communications
DNI	Director of Naval Intelligence
FDR&FA	*FDR and Foreign Affairs* (See bibliography)
FDRL	Franklin D. Roosevelt Library, Hyde Park, NY
GB	General Board
GBR	General Board Records, Operational Archives, Wash., D.C.
IMS	Instructional Material Sent (1938, NA)
IR	Intelligence Report
JCS	Joint Chiefs of Staff
LC	Library of Congress, Manuscript Division
LNA	Limitation of Naval Armaments (GBR)
MR	Map Room File, FDRL
MSS	Manuscript Collection
NA	National Archives, Wash., D.C.
NAtt	Naval Attaché
ND	Naval District
NHD	Naval History Division, Operational Archives, Wash., D.C.
NWCL	Naval War College Library, Newport, RI
OH	Oral History
ONI	Office of Naval Intelligence
ONIAC	ONI Security-Classified Administrative Correspondence
ONICC	ONI Confidential General Correspondence, RG 38, NA
ONIGC	ONI Security-Classified General Correspondence, RG 38, NA
ONIH	Typescript in NHD
ONISC	ONI Security-Classified Correspondence, RG 38, NA
RC	*Roosevelt and Churchill* (See bibliography)

RG	Record Group (number)
SecNav	Secretary of the Navy
SNAR	Selected Naval Attaché Reports Relating to the World Crisis 1937–1943, RG 38, NA, Microfilm Pub. M975
SNCC	Confidential Correspondence, SecNav, RG 80, NA
SNGC	General Correspondence, office of SecNav, RG 80, NA
SP	"Strategic Planning in the U.S. Navy: Its Evolution and Execution 1891–1945" (Wilmington: Scholarly Resources, Microfilm)
SPDR	Strategic Plans Division Records, Operational Archives
USMCL	United States Marine Corps Library, Wash., D.C.
USNIP	United States Naval Institute *Proceedings*

NOTES

CHAPTER ONE   INTELLIGENCE DILEMMA

1. Vice Admiral Paul Frederick Foster, Oral History Transcript, Oral History Office, Columbia University, 1969, pp. 211, 339, (hereafter Foster OH); the Log of Glenn Howell, NHD, entries for 21 May and 25 June 1930 (hereafter Howell Log).

2. Entries 21 May and 25 June 1930, Howell Log.

3. Howell to DNI, 8 April 1929, in U.S. Navy Department, "U.S. Naval Administration in World War II: The Office of Naval Intelligence," typescript in NHD, p. 67 (hereafter ONIH).

4. Foster OH, pp. 385–87; entry 21 May 1930, Howell Log; *also see* "Historical Narrative of District Intelligence Office, Third Naval District, 1945," typescript, NHD (hereafter History 3rd ND).

5. Entry 25 June 1930, Howell Log.

6. Holmes to SecNav, 25 April 1938, Division of Naval Intelligence, Security-Classified Letters Sent "Day File," 1929–45, RG 38, NA (hereafter Day File); "Instructions for Naval Attachés, 1930," p. 81, in Instructional Material Sent to Intelligence Officers and Naval Attachés, 1916–33, RG 38, NA (hereafter IMS).

7. Chadwick, "Opening Address Delivered by the President of War College, June 2, 1902, *USNIP*, 28 (June 1902), pp. 253–54.

8. *See* Dorwart, *ONI*; Spector, *Professors of War*; Costello, "Planning for War."

9. Cotten, "The Lessons of the Russo-Japanese War," *USNIP*, 36 (March 1910), pp. 41–60.

10. Dorwart, *ONI*, pp. 96ff.

11. Murphy, *Civil Liberties*.

12. Memo by Captain Jackson, November 1918, Box 8, ONI Security-Classified Correspondence, 1916–1927, RG 38, NA (hereafter ONISC).

CHAPTER TWO   BOLSHEVIK MENACE.

1. Dorwart, *ONI*, pp. 58ff.

2. Niblack to Daniels, 23 May 1919, Box 91, Josephus Daniels MSS, LC.

3. Gilchrist to Stark, 13 April 1919, Box 146, William S. Sims MSS, LC; Breck to Welles, 2 May 1919, Box 1, Roger Welles MSS, LC.

4. Niblack to all NAtts, 14 January 1920, Box 3, Records of the U.S. Naval Attaché, Rio de Janeiro, 1919–1929, RG 38, NA (hereafter NAtt Rio).

5. Niblack to Sims, 8 January 1920, Box 146, Sims MSS; Niblack, *ONI*, p. 6.

6. Memo on ONI Organization, 29 November 1919, Box 1, IMS; bribery in, Goold to SecState, 30 May 1921, 121.55/776, State Department Decimal File, RG 59, NA (hereafter Decimal File).

7. Polk to Niblack, 13 March 1920, File 20958-Genl A, Box 1, ONI Confidential General Correspondence, 1913–1924, RG 38, NA (hereafter ONICC); Cronon, ed., *Daniels Diaries*, p. 533; also, Newport Investigation File, ASecNav MSS, FDRL.

8. Challener, ed., *U.S. Military Intelligence Weekly Summaries*, VI, p. 1558, IX, p. 1717; Murray, *Red Scare*; Donner, *Surveillance*, pp. 33ff; Jeffreys-Jones, *Espionage*, pp. 151ff.

9. Dorwart, *ONI*, p. 119; Preston, *Aliens*, p. 161; Welles to SecNav, 23 December 1918, 3 January 1919, Box 522, Daniels MSS; Williams Memo for SecNav, 7 January 1919, Louis L. Howe MSS, FDRL; Yarnell to CNO, 6 February 1919, Box 522, Daniels MSS.

10. Danish Situation, in Gade to DNI, 1 July 1919, EL File, Knauss IR, 21 October 1922, NAtt Report, 16 February 1923, Strite IR, 28 July 1924, McNamee to OpNav, 12 December 1921, EN/O File, RG 8, NWCL; also, Rogers to SecNav, 15 July 1921, GB File 420–2, GBR; ONIH, p. 17.

11. Niblack to SecNav, etc., 20 December 1919, Box 91, Daniels MSS.

12. Niblack to Hurley, 10 April 1920, File 20958-Genl. A, Box 1, ONICC.

13. Bristol, "The Situation Abroad," lecture NWC, 20 November 1925, EP File, NWCL; Henderson to Gleaves, 11 August 1920, Box 9, Albert Gleaves MSS, LC; Lansing to SecNav, 15 August 1919, File 20958-Genl. A, Box 1, ONICC; also, Roskill, *Naval Policy, 1919–1929*, p. 184n3.

14. Gleaves to GB, 4 November 1920, GB File 429, GBR.

15. Niblack to State, NWC, etc., 31 March 1920, File 20981-143–A, Box 7, ONICC.

16. Niblack to SecNav, 5 January 1922, File 20996–3409, Box 8, ONICC; Niblack to Sims, 8 January 1920, Box 146, Sims MSS.

17. Niblack to NAtts, 14 July 1920, Box 3, NAtt Rio; Baum Memo, 29 November 1919, Box 1, IMS; Niblack to NAtts, 14 January 1920, Box 3, NAtt Rio.

18. U.S. Congress, *Naval Investigation*; Morison, *Sims*, pp. 435ff; Trask, *Captains*; Harrison to Sims, 21 April 1920, Box 62, Sims MSS.

19. Baum to Sims, 25 May 1920, Box 60, Sims MSS; also, Braisted, *Navy and Pacific, 1909–1922*, pp. 468ff; Dingman, *Power*, pp. 89–104.

20. U.S. Congress, *Naval Investigation*, I, Part 2, pp. 997, 1011.

21. *Ibid.*, p. 1043.

22. Coontz to Niblack, 6 August 1920, Albert P. Niblack MSS, Indiana Historical Society Library, Indianapolis; Jones to Bristol, 9 March 1922, Box 1, Hilary P. Jones MSS, LC.

23. Long to City Bank of NY, 24 February 1921, Box 3, NAtt Rio; Farago, *Broken Seal*, pp. 34–35.

24. Long to NAtts, 28 January, 2 March 1921, Box 3, NAtt Rio.

25. Gibson to SecState, 21 April, 26 July 1922, 121.55/760 and 836, Bliss to Long, 18 May 1921, 121.55/849a, ASecNav to ASecState, 5 August 1921, 121.55K81/1–3, Decimal File.

26. CO *South Carolina* to Long, 23 September 1920, File 433, Andrew T. Long MSS, Southern Historical Collection, University of North Carolina Library, Chapel Hill; Eberle to All Ships, 22 August 1924, File 28642, General File, General Correspondence of the Office of the Secretary of the Navy, 1897–1926, RG 80, NA (hereafter SNGC).

CHAPTER THREE   FALSE INFORMATION

1. Dingman, *Power*, 141ff; Sprout, *New Order*, chs. 7–8.

2. Long to NAtt London, 31 January 1921, Box 3, NAtt Rio; Cole to DNI, 16 July 1921, File 28642, SNGC; Galbraith to NAtts, 21 July 1921, Box 3, NAtt Rio.

3. Niblack to SecNav, 18 September 1921, Box 488, Y (NAtt Paris) to ONI, 24 August, 17 October 1921, NAtt Report Berlin, 31 August 1921, Box 487, QY File, Subject File, 1911–27, RG 45, NA (hereafter Subject File); also, Farago, *Broken Seal*, p. 29; Braisted, *Navy*, pp. 538–39.

4. List of Japanese Delegates, Box 487, QY File, Subject File; Farago, *Broken Seal*, pp. 35–36.

5. Knox to GB, 8 September 1921, Box 1, Dudley W. Knox MSS, LC.

6. Dingman, *Power*; Pusey, *Hughes*.

7. Copy of Secret Message, in Galbraith to NWC, etc., 18 July 1921, Box 487, QY File, Subject File; also, Farago, *Broken Seal*, pp. 30ff; Dulles, *Intelligence*, p. 75.

8. McNamee to Hasbrouck, 11 February 1922, Watson to McNamee, 30 March 1922, File 20996–2916, Box 10, ONISC.

9. Breck to Sims, 5 March 1922, Box 50, Hussey to Sims, 12 December 1928, Box 63, Sims MSS; copy of McNamee Speech, 4 April 1922, Box 8, William V. Pratt MSS, NHD; McNamee to Hasbrouck, 3 May 1922, Box 10, ONISC.

10. McNamee, "Keep Our Navy Strong," *USNIP*, 49 (May 1923), pp. 805–8.

11. Knox, "Public Indoctrination," *USNIP*, 55 (June 1929), pp. 485–89.

12. Knox, *Eclipse*, pp. x, 123; also, Knox to Foss, 29 October 1923, Knox to Beck, 30 October 1923, Knox to King, 28 March 1924, Knox to Father Keller, 4 August 1927, Box 1, D. Knox MSS.

13. Thomson to Knox, 11 December 1923, Box 1, D. Knox MSS.

14. ONI, *Information Concerning the U.S. Navy and Other Navies, 1925* (Wash: GPO, 1925), p. 11.

15. McNamee to Hussey, 19 and 28 May 1923, Hussey to McNamee, 24 April, 12 June 1923, Box 10, ONISC; also, Pratt to Wilbur, 14 July 1925, Box 4, Jones MSS.

16. Niblack to GB, 20 April 1922, GB File 420–2, GBR; Niblack to SecNav, 5 January 1922, File 20996–3409, Box 8, ONICC.

17. Niblack to McNamee, 7 August 1922, File 20996–3409, Box 8, ONICC.

18. Acting SecNav to CinCUS Naval Forces Europe, 27 January 1922, Niblack to McNamee, 7 August 1922, *ibid.*

19. McNamee to all NAtts, 10 November 1921, 24 July, 22 September 1923, Box 3, NAtt Rio.

20. McNamee to Cotten, 21 May 1923, Box 8, Halsey to ADNI, 16 September 1922, Box 1, ONICC.

21. Cotten, "The Naval Strategy of the Russo-Japanese War," *USNIP*, 36 (March 1910), p. 57; Cotten to DNI, 30 December 1922, Box 230, ONI Security-Classified General Correspondence, 1929–1942, RG 38, NA (hereafter ONIGC).

22. Niblack to McNamee, 29 May 1920, File 21000–835, Box 9, Cotten to McNamee, 5 June 1922, McNamee to Cotten, 21 May 1923, File 20996–3397, Box 8, ONICC; LeBreton in, Third Assistant SecState Memo, 25 September 1922, 121.55/844, Decimal File.

23. McNamee to Cotten, 21 May 1923, Woods to State, 12 September 1923, Cotten to SecNav, 20 November 1923, File 20996–3397, Box 8, ONICC.

24. Hulings to DNI, 2 February 1924, Box 230, ONIGC; Hussey to McNamee, 1 February 1923, Box 10, ONISC; Jones to Upham, 5 November 1924, Box 1, Jones MSS; Reminiscences of Rear Admiral Arthur H. McCollum, Oral History Transcript, U.S. Naval Institute, 1970–71 (hereafter McCollum OH); McNamee, "Aviation and the Navy," *USNIP*, 49 (December 1923), p. 2073.

25. Watson to McNamee, 25 April 1922, Box 10, ONISC; NAtt Report, 12 May 1922, Box 8, Pratt MSS; Advanced Base Operation in Micronesia by Earl H. Ellis, USMC, 1921, Box 59, Strategic Plans Division Records, Operational Archives, NHD (hereafter SPDR).

CHAPTER FOUR   THE MYSTERIOUS ISLANDS

1. Niblack to SecNav, 31 March 1920, File 20981–143–A, Box 7; Coontz to DNI, 5 November 1919, Box 16, File 21067–3, ONICC; Williams to State, 15 February 1919, Box 482, QQ File, Subject File; Braisted, *Navy*, pp. 442ff.

2. Statement of Everett E. Clifton, USMC, 23 June 1920, Mandated Islands File, USMCL; NAtt Tokyo to Navintel, 20 December 1920; Navintel to NAtt Tokyo, 17 December 1920, File 21067–3, Box 16, ONICC.

3. Niblack to CNO, 26 April 1920; Daniels to SecState, 3 June 1920, File 21067–3, Box 16, ONICC.

4. Long Memo for CNO, 12 October 1920, *ibid.*

5. Anderson to SecNav, 10 May 1921, *ibid.*

6. McNamee to Burton, 1 October 1921; Burton to Galbraith, 26 September 1921; Assistant to the President to McNamee, 7 October 1921, all in *ibid.*

7. Assistant Secretary of the Interior to SecNav, 5 October 1921; SecNav to Secretary of the Interior, 22 September 1921, File 21067–3, Box 16, ONICC. Another college professor George H. Blakeslee may have worked for ONI in the islands in the 1920s, see Pusey, *Hughes*, p. 477.

8. Long to President U.S. Shipping Board, 23 October 1920; DNI to CO Marine Aviation Detachment, Guam, 14 May 1921, Box 16, ONICC.

9. William A. Worton Oral History Transcript, p. 177, USMCL (hereafter Worton OH).

10. Niblack to MajGen Cmndnt USMC, 4 September 1920, Earl H. Ellis File, USMCL; Niblack Memo for GB, 8 September 1920, GB File 429, GBR.

11. Reber, "Ellis," pp. 53–64; Ellis, Advanced Base, Lejeune to CNO, 10 August 1921, Box 59, SPDR.

12. Reber, "Ellis," pp. 53–64; Zacharias, *Secret*, p. 42; Farago, *Broken Seal*, p. 35; Mashbir, *Spy*, p. 104; NAtt Tokyo, to DNI, 29 December 1922; Chief Special Agent Dept. of State to Navintel, 21 May 1923; McNamee to MajGen Cmndnt USMC, 23 May 1923, Ellis File, USMCL.

13. McNamee to CNO, 24 October 1923, GB File 409, GBR.

14. McNamee to CNO, 31 May 1923, GB File 409, GBR; Lang to Ingersoll, 25 September 1924, File 20996–3364, Box 8, ONICC.

15. Estimate of the Situation of the Size and Composition of the Forces Necessary to Seize Two Bases in the Marshall Islands, 13 October 1927, Box 35, SPDR.

16. McNamee, "Naval Intelligence," copy of lecture, 21 September 1922, GB File 429, GBR.

CHAPTER FIVE   SURREPTITIOUS ENTRY

1. McNamee, "Naval Intelligence"; McNamee to Burns, 29 May 1922, File 20948–184, Box 1, ONICC.

2. McNamee, "Naval Intelligence," *USNIP*, 50 (Sept. 1924), p. 1444.

3. For a different view see, ONIH, pp. 150–52.

4. Report of the Second Committee of the GB, 26 November 1906, Proceedings of the General Board, vol. 3, GBR; Memo of 15 June 1907 and Report of 26 February 1907, GBR; Lammers to ONI, 12 September 1919; DIO 14th ND to DNI, 9 July 1919, File 21067–3, Box 16, ONICC; also, Braisted, *Navy*, pp. 444–45; Dorwart, *ONI*, pp. 99ff.

5. McNamee to Chandler, 23 February 1922; McNamee to Burns, 25 Feb. 1922, File 20962–943, Box 2; Castle to McNamee, 21 February 1923, File 20964–2489; Arnold to Ingersoll, 20 June 1923, File 20964–2495, Box 3, ONICC; Reminiscences of Admiral Royal E. Ingersoll, Oral History Office, Columbia University, 1965, p. 45, (hereafter Ingersoll OH); Farago, *Broken Seal*, pp. 36–37.

6. Arnold to Ingersoll, 20 June 1923, File 20964–2495, Box 3, ONICC; McNamee to CNO, 2 July 1923, Report of Section B to CNO, 9 June 1924, Box 8, ONISC.

7. Jeffreys-Jones, *Espionage*, p. 127; Zacharias, *Secret*, pp. 71–72, 83ff; Hough to Cmndnt 16th ND, 11 November 1924, File 20961–316, Box 2, ONICC; Denby to Rev. Watson, 25 January 1924, File 28642, SNGF.

8. Hough to Pacific Coast Communications Supt., 1 February 1924, Hough to DNC, 18 October 1924, McLean to DNI, 17 July 1924, CO Naval Forces Europe to DNI, 18 December 1924, Hoover to Lang, 18 September 1925, Box 124, ONIGC; Farago, *Broken Seal*, ch. 4.

9. Hough to Pacific Coast Communications Supt., 1 February 1924, Box 124, ONIGC; Farago, *Broken Seal*, pp. 47–52; Zacharias, *Secret*, ch. 10.

10. Galbraith Memo, 22 July 1921, Box 3, NAtt Rio; McNamee Memo for CNO, 22 November 1922, Box 1, ONIGC.

11. Thomas to BuOrd, 30 July 1925, Galbraith to SecNav, 7 August 1925, Box 1, ONIGC; Hepburn to Jones, 15 September 1926, Box 2, Jones MSS; ONIH, p. 186.

12. GB Records Relating to Limitation of Naval Armaments, Series III, NHD (hereafter LNA); Jones to Gardiner, 22 June 1925, Box 1, Jones MSS.

13. Shearer to Chief of Navintel, 5 July 1926, Box 230, ONIGC; Hepburn to Jones, 15 September 1926, Box 2, Jones MSS; see Wheeler, *Prelude*, pp. 64–68.

14. Hepburn to NAtt The Hague, 3 January 1927, Box 5, Records of the U.S. Naval Attaché, The Hague, 1920–1933, RG 38, NA (hereafter NAtt Hague).

15. Taylor, *Search, Seizure, Surveillance*; Murphy, *Wiretapping*.
16. Entry 1 September 1929, Howell Log.
17. Entries, 12, 15 April, 2 June 1930, *ibid*.

CHAPTER SIX   DANGER SIGNALS

1. Stimson and Bundy, *On Active Service*, p. 188.
2. Hoover to SecNav, 22 June 1929, Johnson to GB, 11 March 1929, LNA; DNI to NAtts Paris, Rome and Berlin, 11 July 1929, Box D9, Day File; Corwin to Johnson, 18 September 1929, Box 5, NAtt Hague; Wheeler, *Pratt*, pp. 294ff.
3. Johnson to Sims, 13 January 1920, Box 62, Sims MSS; Wheeler, *Pratt*, pp. 294–303.
4. Wilbur to Hayden, 25 January 1929, Curtis Wilbur MSS, LC; London Naval Treaty File prepared by ONI for Pratt, Box 8, Pratt MSS; Macomb Memo on British Press, 23 October 1929, Biographical Notes on British Delegates, 3 December 1929, Box 488, QY File, Subject File; also, Train to Reed, 9 April 1930, LNA.
5. Intercept of Translation of Telegram Received by Japanese Delegation, 1 April 1930, LNA; Johnson to Taussig, 24 January 1930, Box D9, Day File.
6. Standley, *Admiral*, p. 25; Wheeler, *Pratt*, pp. 312ff.
7. Johnson Memo for all Officers in ONI, 20 December 1929, Box 2, General Files of the U.S. Naval Attaché, Tegucigalpa, Honduras, 1929–33, RG 38, NA (hereafter NAtt Tegucigalpa).
8. NAtt Instructions, 1930, p. 80, Box 1, IMS.
9. DNI to all NAtts, 11 January 1930, Box 2, NAtt Tegucigalpa.
10. Johnson to Longstaff, 24 March 1930, Box 193, ONIGC; Astor, in Baggaley to Howell, 25 January 1930, Box D9, Johnson to Vanderbilt, 31 July 1929, Box D10, Day File; Johnson to Loening, 26 March 1930, Grover C. Loening MSS, LC.
11. Johnson to Corwin, 14 June 1930, Box 5, NAtt Hague.
12. ONI Comments on London Treaty, 9 May 1930, Data for Limitation of Armaments, GBR.
13. Resumé of Conditions in China, 1931, *Panay* IR, 14 April 1931, McVay to CNO, 4 August 1931, Monthly IR *Mindano*, 1 April 1931, Baggaley to CNO, 11 March 1931, Hartigan to DNI, 5 November 1929, Box 275, ONIGC.
14. Sayles to DNI, 14 September 1925, Hartigan to DNI, 10 April 1930, Box 191, NAtt Peiping to DNI, 11 June 1931, Box 275, ONIGC; Manchurian Situation, 26 September 1931, Box 3, D. Knox MSS.
15. Stimson and Bundy, *On Active Service*, p. 189; Corson, *Armies*, pp. 69–71.
16. GB to DNI, 22 April 1930, Memo for DNI, 2 December 1931, GB File 429, GBR; Ellis to Cmndnts all NDs, 4 March 1932, DNI to Professors Naval Science, 21 March 1932, Box D18, Day File.
17. Kilpatrick to DNI, 13 January 1932, ONI to Dept. of Justice, 30 January 1932, Box D18, Day File.
18. Secret and Confidential Matter, June 14, 1932, *Hearings before the General Board of the Navy 1932*, vol. 1, pp. 198, 200, 220, GBR.
19. Baggaley to White, 7 January 1932, Ellis to Lindsay, 3 March 1939, Ellis to all NAtts, 3 March, 24 February 1932, Box D18, Day File.
20. Baggaley to Pye, 27 October 1931, Pye to Spears, 13 January 1932, Ellis to Head Mission Peru, 8 October 1931, Correspondence and Reports U.S. Naval Mission to Lima, Peru, 1929–33, Box 1, RG 38, NA (hereafter Mission Peru); Johnson, in ONIH, p. 576.
21. Ellis to Cook, 5 March 1932, Ellis to Gillis, 8 March 1932, Box D18, Day File; ONIH, pp. 20–21.
22. Ellis to all NAtts and DIOs, 2 August 1932, Box 3, Ellis to Magruder, 11 December 1931, Box 5, NAtt Hague; also, Ellis to Cmndnts all Navy Yards, 15 January 1932, DNI to CinCUS, 22 January 1932, Ellis to Cmndnt 12th ND, 3 March 1932, Box D18, Day File.
23. "League of Nations Security Force, 14 January 1932," *General Board Hearings*, vol. 1, p. 65, GBR; Ellis to Root, 22 March 1932, Ellis to Cmndnt 11th ND, 18 March 1932, Box D18, Day File.
24. Baggaley to Spears, 19 November 1931, Ellis to Pendleton, 5 March 1932, Box D18, Day File.

25. Joslin, *Hoover*, pp. 176–77; Ellis to all NAtts and DIOs, 2 August 1932, Box 3, NAtt Hague.
26. Skoda, in Baggaley to Asst. CofS G–2, 4 March 1932, Caproni, in DNI to NAtt Rome, 22 January 1932, Baggaley to Castleman, 15 January 1932, Box D18, Day File; Corwin to Johnson, 18 September 1929, Box 5, NAtt Hague.

CHAPTER SEVEN   NEW DEAL FOR NAVAL INTELLIGENCE

1. Standley, *Admiral*, p. 26; Yarnell to Puleston, 5 January 1938, Box 4, Harry Yarnell MSS, LC.
2. Standley, *Admiral*, p. 31, FDR to Swanson, 17 December 1934, in Nixon, ed., *Franklin D. Roosevelt and Foreign Affairs*, II, pp. 322–23 (hereafter *FDR&FA*).
3. Roosevelt's Press Conference, 23 May 1934, in *FDR&FA*, II, p. 31; Standley, *Admiral*, p. 33; Davis, *Navy*, pp. 360–62.
4. FDR Memo for Acting SecNav, 16 October 1933, PSF 78, FDRL; *Navy Directory*, 1 January 1936, p. 234; FDR to Swanson, 17 December 1934, 30 May 1935, *FDR&FA*, II, pp. 322–23, 523; Swanson to all Ships, 9 March 1933, Pratt to SecNav, 11 January 1933, Swanson to all Shore Stations, 15 September 1933, GB File 429, GBR; Bullitt to Mariner, 11 November 1933, 121.5551/64, Decimal File.
5. Zacharias, *Secret*, pp. 117, 148; Yarnell to Puleston, 5 January 1938, Box 4, Yarnell MSS; Roskill, *Naval Policy, 1930-1939*, pp. 25–26; Davis, *JCS*, pp. 32–33; McCollum OH, p. 323.
6. ONI Roster, November 1934–February 1935, Box D28, Day File.
7. Standley to SecNav, 11 December 1936, Box D31, Day File; Entry 9 September 1935, pp. 21–22, Name and Subject Index, SNGC 1930–42, RG 80, NA (hereafter SNI); McCollum OH, pp. 257–58; ONIH, pp. 547–49.
8. Puleston to Cmndnt 11th ND, 4 June 1934, Box D25, Puleston to Mayo, 26 January 1935, Box D28, Puleston to Cogswell, 10 March 1937, Box D32, SecNav to Nimmer, 9 February 1934, Box D25, Day File.
9. McCollum OH, p. 142; ONIH, p. 595; Puleston to CBuNav, 17 February 1937, Box D32, Day File; Leahy Memo, 27 August 1937, Box 192, ONIGC.
10. Puleston to Kalbfus, 14 February 1935, Box D28, Puleston to President NWC, 30 April 1937, Box D33; Zacharias to Pence, 31 May 1935, Box D29, Day File.
11. Davis Memo for DNI, 26 January 1935, in Puleston to CNO, 28 January 1935, Puleston to CinCUS, 10 October 1936, Puleston memo for CNO, 6 November 1934, Box D28, Day File; Reminiscences of Rear Admiral Edwin T. Layton, Oral History Transcript, U.S. Naval Institute, 1970, p. 27.
12. Estimate of Situation . . . to Prevent European Nations from Landing Men and Munitions in Brazil, 8 December 1936, Box 40, SPDR; ONIH, p. 595; Puleston to CNO, 22 October 1936, Box D30, Quarterly Report, 19 January 1935, Box D28, Day File; McCollum OH, pp. 141, 251–52.
13. Memo for Beauregard, 6 April 1936, 121.5551/91, Decimal File; Entry 29 April 1937, SNI; DNI to VCNO, 12 October 1943, Box 32, Day File Subseries.
14. Puleston to MajGen Cmndnt USMC, 29 January 1935, Box D28, Day File; Worton OH, pp. 169–71.
15. Pedro del Valle Oral History Transcript, USMCL (hereafter del Valle OH); Standley to SecState, 3 August 1935, 121.5562/64, Decimal File; Puleston to Cogswell, 10 March 1937, Box D32, Day File.
16. Stapler to NAtt Peiping, 27 December 1934, Puleston to MajGen Cmndnt USMC, 9 January 1935, Box D28, Day File; Puleston Memo for CNO, 15 June 1934, GB File 429, GBR.
17. Stapler to ONI, 14 November 1936, Congressional Hearings Data Prepared by ONI, 1934–1941, SPDR; Tate, *Armaments*, pp. 185–96; Swanson to Reed, 31 December 1934, Ingram to McHugh, 3 January 1935, Box D28, Day File.
18. Stapler to Kingman, 9 March 1937, Box D32, Stapler to Mayo, 26 January 1935, Box D28, Day File; History of the 12th Naval District, typescript in NHD.
19. Stapler to Mayo, 26 January 1935, Box D28, Day File; Downes to Puleston, 26 August 1935, Puleston to Downes, 30 August 1935, Box 236, ONI Security-Classified Administrative

Correspondence, 1927–1944, (hereafter ONIAC). A subseries of ONI Administrative Correspondence was processed and opened to researchers by the National Archives too late for inclusion in this book, but a survey of the contents indicates that the new material would change neither interpretaion nor details of this study.

20. McCollum OH, pp. 167, 177–94; History 3rd ND, p. 9; FDR Memo for Leahy, 10 August 1936, Box 89, SPDR.

21. Zacharias, *Secret*, pp. 136, 150ff; Pryor to Cmndt 15th ND, 12 April 1934, Ellis to Cmndt 14th ND, 17 February 1934, Ellis to Baum, 20 February 1934, Ellis to Babcock, 5 April 1934, Box D25, H. Roosevelt to Hull, 24 January 1934, Box D24, Day File.

22. Puleston to Fawell, 5 March 1937, Box D32, Farquhar to Cmndt 1st ND, 11 August 1937, Box D35, Day File; Zacharias, *Secret*, pp. 160ff; McCollum OH, pp. 166–67; Seth, *Secret Servants*, pp. 216–21; Hynd, *Betrayal*, pp. 51ff; LaForet, "Coggins."

23. Hynd, *Betrayal*, pp. 44–51; Seth, *Secret Servants*, pp. 223–31; Puleston to all Bus and Offices, 25 May 1935, Box 33, Confidential Correspondence of the Secretary of the Navy, 1927–1939, RG 80, NA (hereafter SNCC).

24. Leahy to Jenckes, 12 October 1937, Box 33, SNCC.

25. Farago, *Broken Seal*, pp. 83–87; Swanson to SecState, 19 January 1935, Puleston to Cmndt 11th ND, 19 January 1935, Box D28, Day File; Seth, *Secret Servants*, pp. 174–84.

26. Puleston to all Inspectors of Naval Work, October 1934, Box 1, Inspector of Naval Material to DNI, 20 April 1935, Box 2, SNCC.

27. Inspector of Naval Material to DNI, 20 April 1935, Carpenter to DNI, 21 October 1935, Box 2, SNCC.

28. ONIH, pp. 175–76, 222–24, 335; Puleston to Hoover, 15 June 1934, Box D28, Puleston to Hoover, 14 October 1936, Box D30, DNI Confidential Annex to Annual Report for Fiscal Year Ending 30 June 1937, Box D34, Day File.

29. Puleston to McNair, 11 March 1935, Box D29, Puleston to DNC, 21 September 1936, Box D30, Day File.

30. Puleston to McNair, 11 March 1935, Box D29, Day File; Meyers to CNO, 20 February 1936, Box 191, ONIGC.

CHAPTER EIGHT   IN PURSUIT OF DOMESTIC ENEMIES

1. Ellis to Puleston, 23 January 1934, Box D24, Day File; leaks in Box 48, ONIGC; Sadao, "The Japanese Navy and the United States," in Borg and Okamoto, *Pearl Harbor*, pp. 243, 658n81.

2. Shock to Creighton, 21 January 1937, CBuOrd to CNO, 26 August 1936, CBY&D to CNO, 16 May 1936, Box 1, ONIGC; Stapler to Christian, 25 February 1937, Box D30, Puleston to WPD, 17 October 1936, Box D30, Day File.

3. Standley, *Admiral*, p. 35; Pryor to Agnew, 31 January 1934, Nimmer to Cmndt USMC, 27 January 1934, Box D24, Day File; David R. Nimmer Oral History Transcript, pp. 79–81, USMCL; Memo State Dept. to Division of Far Eastern Affairs, 21 April 1930, 121.55/862, Decimal File.

4. Nimmer OH, pp. 79ff; Nimmer to DNI, 10 December 1934, 9 July 1934, 17 November 1934, Stapler to NAtt Moscow, 27 September 1934, Nimmer to DNI, 31 October 1934, Records of U.S. Naval Attaché Moscow, Russia, 1934–35, RG 38, NA (hereafter NAtt Moscow).

5. Standley, *Admiral*, pp. 35, 39–40; IR, 5th ND, 5 July 1934, NAtt Moscow.

6. Puleston, *Mahan*, p. 351; Puleston to CO *Saratoga*, 21 June 1934, Box D25, Day File; Standley, *Admiral*, p. 39.

7. Puleston to CO *Indianapolis*, 20 June 1934, Box D25, Puleston to CBuNav, 4 March 1935, D29, Day File.

8. Lane to SecState, 21 August 1937, 121.5560P/15, Decimal File; Farquhar to Frankel, 26 August, 1937, Box D35, Day File: Reminiscences of Admiral Samuel B. Frankel, Oral History Transcript, U.S. Naval Institute, 1970–74, p. 46 (hereafter Frankel OH).

9. Moore to Woodring to Roosevelt, 11 November 1936, Hull to Roosevelt, 18 September 1936, in *FDR&FA*, II, pp. 431–32, 495–96; CBuAir to all Inspectors, 5 August 1933, Puleston to CNO, 31 March 1936, Memo, 13 May 1936, Box 6, ONIGC.

238   NOTES

10. Fish to Murray, 1 December 1936, Murray to Fish, 4 January 1937, Stevens Memo for Ambassador, 15 January 1937, 121.5541/65–66, Decimal File.
11. del Valle OH, p. 99; Puleston to Cogswell, 10 March 1937, Box D32, Day File; Bullitt to SecState, 12 January 1937, 121.5551/95, Decimal File.
12. Coded telegram to American Embassy Paris, 13 January 1937, Hull to American Embassy, 10 June 1937, 121.5591/95, Decimal File.
13. Cole, *Nye*, pp. 65ff; Navy Dept. to Nye, 21 June 1934, Box D28, Day File.
14. ONIH, pp. 163–65.
15. *Ibid.*, p. 313; Standley to SecState, 26 May 1934, 121.5551/67, Decimal File.
16. Puleston to Cmndnt 6th ND, 8 April 1937, Box D33, Puleston to Cmndnt 12th ND, 16 November 1936, Box D31, Day File; CNO to Cmndnt 9th ND, 14 August 1935, Downes to Puleston, 26 August 1935, Puleston to Downes, 30 August 1935, Collins to Puleston, 27 September 1934, Box 236, ONIAC.
17. Pryor to Newton, 12 February 1934, Box D25, Puleston to CBuNav, 17 February 1937, Box D32, Stapler to Ryan, 18 September 1936, Box D30, Stapler to Cmndnt 14th ND, 23 November 1936, Stapler to Clay, 16 Nov. 1936, Box D31, Day File; ONIH, pp. 598–99.
18. U.S. Congress, House of Representatives, *Hearings*, 74th Cong., 1st Sess. (Washington: GPO, 1935), pp. 81, 774; ONIH, pp. 192–94; Puleston to CNO, 21 September 1936, Box D30, Day File.
19. Yarnell to Puleston, 14 January 1936, Box 9, Harry E. Yarnell MSS, NHD; Puleston Correspondence with the Mahan Family, 1936–1937, William D. Puleston MSS, NHD.
20. Roosevelt to Long, 9 March 1935, *FDR&FA*, II, p. 437; Bennett, *Demagogues*.
21. Sherwood, *Roosevelt and Hopkins*, pp. 128–29; Swing, *Forerunners*, ch. vii; Lewis, *It Can't Happen Here*.
22. Puleston to Cmndnts all NDs, 6 November 1934, Box D28, Day File; File of radicals in Box 272, ONIGC.
23. American Vigilantes, Seattle, Wash., 28 October 1932, Ogan to Kohler, 14 April 1933, Kohler to DNI, 5 April 1933, Cluverius to DNI, 4 May 1933, Box 297, ONIGC.
24. Johnson to St. Clair Smith, 2 October 1938, Box 297, Baldridge to NAtt Berlin, 4 October 1930, Box 202, Campbell to Armstrong, 22 April 1931, Baggaley to Campbell, 7 May 1931, Box 193, ONIGC.
25. Puleston to Walsh, 20 February 1937, Box D32, DNI Confidential Annex to Annual Report, 16 July 1937, Box D34, Day File.
26. Ellis to Dohrman, 12 April 1934, Box D25, Day File; Dohrman to Ellis, 7 April 1934, Dohrman to Ellis, 16 April and 4 May 1934, Box 271, ONIGC.
27. Hoover to Ellis, 21 May 1934, Stapler to Dohrman, 27 July 1934, Box 271, ONIGC.
28. Dohrman to Puleston, 3 September, 26 November 1934, 2 March, 1 June 1935, Box 271, ONIGC.
29. Puleston Memo for CNO, 8 November 1934, D28, Puleston to Cmndnt 4th ND, 15 September 1936, Box D30, Day File; Puleston Memo for CNO, 10 September 1935, Box 127, ONIAC.
30. Puleston to Dohrman, 7 January 1934, Dohrman to Puleston, 9 January 1936, Box 271, ONIGC; Puleston Memo for ASecnav, 5 February 1935, Box D28, Day File.
31. Pryor to Cmndnt 11th ND, 14 April 1934, Leahy to SecState, 11 April 1934, Box D25, Day File.
32. Puleston Memo for CNO, 23 November 1934, CNO to Cmndnt 15th ND, 13 April 1934, Box D25, Day File; Welles to Puleston, 11 December 1934, Box 286, ONIGC.
33. Swanson to McCormack, 6 December 1934, Box D28, Day File; Clement to ASecNav, 18 August 1935, Box 33, OF 18x, FDRL.
34. H. L. Roosevelt to FDR, 8 August 1935, OF 18x, FDRL; Puleston to Cmndnts NDs, 2 March 1937, Box D32, Puleston to Cmndnt 5th ND, 17 September 1936, Box D30, Day File; Ward to FDR, 17 March 1936, FDR to Ward, 23 March 1936, Ward to FDR, 4 April 1936, Box 33, OF 18x, FDRL.
35. ONIH, pp. 189–94; Memo for Acting Director of Budget, 28 December 1936, OF 18x, FDRL.
36. Leahy to All Ships, 17 March 1937, GB File 429, GBR; Confidential Annex to Annual Report B Section, 17 July 1937, Box D34, Day File.
37. Puleston to DWPD, 13 March 1935, Box D29, Day File.

CHAPTER NINE   STRATEGIC STIRRINGS

1. Yarnell to Puleston, 5 January 1938, Box 4, Yarnell MSS, LC.
2. DNI to CNO, 30 October 1933, Box 1, ONIAC.
3. Reminiscences of Captain Stephen Jurika, Jr., USN, (Ret.), Oral History Transcript, U.S. Naval Institute, 1975–76, p. 160 (hereafter Jurika OH); Puleston to NAtt Peiping, 17 March 1937, Box D32, Day File; DNI to CNO, 29 December 1936, Box 191, ONIGC.
4. Hasbrouck to McNamee, 27 July 1922, 22 January 1923, Box 10, ONICC; McNair in, Masland and Rodway, *Soldiers*, p. 131; del Valle OH, p. 95; Puleston to del Valle, 13 March 1937, Box D32, Day File; also, Diggins, *Mussolini*.
5. Dodd to FDR, 19 October 1936, *FDR&FA*, III, pp. 455–56; Furer IR to ONI, 29 April 1936, Impressions on Germany Navy Department, 22 April 1936, James A. Furer MSS, LC; DNI to CNO, 29 December 1936, Box 191, ONIGC.
6. Nimmer to Puleston, 5 February, 15 August 1935, Box 1, NAtt Moscow; Memo of Conversation with Schultz, 1 November 1937, in Memo to State, 4 November 1937, 121.5560P/18, Decimal File.
7. Puleston to Hagemeyer, 31 March 1937, Box D32, Day File; ONIH, p. 587.
8. Jurika OH, p. 308.
9. History 12th ND, p. 4; ONIH, p. 29; Meyers to Holmes, 10 September 1937, Holmes to Yarnell, 13 October 1937, Box 4, Yarnell MSS, LC.
10. IRs 4th Marines, Shanghai, 1 July 1937–September 1938 to Op–16–FE, Box 3, Boone to CO, 8 July 1937, Box 2, Security-Classified Intelligence Reports from Headquarters 4th Marines, Shanghai, China, 1937–1940, RG 38, NA (hereafter IR 4th Marines).
11. McHugh to DNI, 24 April 1938, Box 277, ONIGC; Holmes to CBuOrd, 23 February 1938, Box D47, Day File; McCollum OH, pp. 149–50; Knox to Stimson, 25 November 1942, Box 5, Frank Knox MSS, NHD.
12. Holmes to NAtt Peiping, 24 June 1938, Box D39, Day File; Boone to CO, 8 July 1937, Box 2, IR 4th Marines; atrocities, in Boxes 194–95, ONIGC.
13. Bemis to Yarnell, 26 November 1937, Box 4, Yarnell MSS, LC; Holmes to President NWC, 21 June 1938, Box D39, Day File; Carlson to NAtt Peiping, 13 September 1938, Box 283, ONIGC.
14. Holmes to President NWC, 21 June 1938, Box D39, Day File; Carlson, *Twin Stars of China* (New York: Dodd, Mead, 1940), pp. 27, 33–35, 157ff; reports on Chiang in, Johnson to ONI, 9 March 1937, Bales IR, 12 March 1937, Box 1, Confidential Records Relating to the Sian Revolt and Peiping War, RG 38, NA, (hereafter Sian Revolt).
15. Weekly News Summary Far East, Box 1, Sian Revolt; McCollum OH, p. 150; McHugh to DNI, 24 April 1938, enc. in ONI to Safford, 11 May 1938, Box 277, ONIGC.
16. Perry, *Panay*, pp. 223–24; entry 22 January 1938, p. 32, SNI; Duffield Memo for Forrestal, 25 September 1943, Box 20, James V. Forrestal MSS, Seeley Mudd Manuscript Library, Princeton University.
17. Holmes to JAG, 26 April 1938, Box D39, Day File; Perry, *Panay*, pp. 224, 233.
18. Borg, *Far Eastern Crisis*, pp. 486–503.
19. John Major, "Leahy," in Love, *CNOs*, pp. 101–18.
20. Holmes to CNO, 17 July 1937, Box D34, Day File.
21. Holmes to Cmndnt 3rd ND, 21 December 1937, Box D36, Holmes to Cmndnt 15th ND, 25 February 1938, Box D37, Munroe to Gregory, 20 December 1938, Box D41, Day File.
22. CNO to Gass, 21 November 1938, Box D41, Pryor to DNI, 24 June 1938, Box D39, Day File; ONIH, pp. 1393ff, Appendixes, A and H.
23. CNO to Cmndnts NDs, 28 March 1939, Box D43, Day File.
24. Richardson to DIOs, 14 February 1938, Box D37, Day File; Leahy to all Ships, 12 March 1938, GB File 429, GBR; Leahy to Yates, 18 March 1937, Box D37, Day File.
25. Holmes to CO *Hatfield*, 9 July 1937, Gannon to DNI, 31 August 1938, Box 124, ONIGC; DNI to DWPD, 23 February 1938, DNI to NAtts, 16 February 1938, Box D37, Holmes to Milne, 20 December 1937, Box D36, Holmes to NAtt Buenos Aires, 16 July 1938, Box D39, Day File.
26. Holmes to CNO, 25 May 1938, Box D38, Day File.
27. Holmes to NAtt Rio, 9 March 1938, Box D37, Holmes to CNO, 25 May 1938, Box

D38, Day File; Moffat to Messersmith, 9 February 1938, 121.5556/59, Decimal File.

28. Holmes to NAtt Berlin, 30 November 1938, Box D41, DNI to NAtt Berlin, 15 March 1939, Box D43, Day File.

29. Moffat to Messersmith, 9 February 1938, Messersmith to SecState, 9 and 11 February 1938, 121.5556/59, Decimal File.

30. Holmes to Cogswell, 3 January 1938, Box D36, Day File.

31. Popham to Intelligence Branch, 12 June 1937, Box D34, Day File; Estimates of Potential Military Strength, NAtt London, vol. 1, Docs. 1–77, PSF 196, FDRL.

32. Kelly to Alan [Kirk], 8 December 1938, Box 2, Alan G. Kirk MSS, NHD.

CHAPTER TEN   HEMISPHERIC SECURITY

1. Dallek, *FDR and American Foreign Policy*, pp. 38–39, 86–87.

2. Dorwart, *ONI*, pp. 90ff; bribe in, Goold to SecState, 30 May 1921, 121.55/776, Decimal File.

3. Welles to Van Slyke, 10 February 1919, Box 1, Welles MSS.

4. MajGen Cmndnt USMC to Ellis, 8 December 1919, Ellis File; Coontz to CinCUS Atlantic Fleet, 26 March 1920, Box 2, ONICC; CO *South Carolina* to Long, 23 September 1920, Long MSS; Sayles to Powell, 12 July 1927, File U–2–f, Confidential Naval Attaché Reports, 1900–1945, RG 38, NA.

5. Sellers to DNI, 6 February 1928, Box 5, David Foote Sellers MSS, LC; Sellers to Johnson, 7 June 1928, Box 230, ONIGC.

6. Sellers to Johnson, 26 November 1928, Box 3, Sellers MSS; Kamman, *Search for Stability*, pp. 189–91.

7. U.S. Naval Missions to South America, Box 1, NAtt Tegucigalpa; Niblack Memo to SecNav, 17 May 1920, Box 522, Daniels MSS; Final Report Duties NAtt Rio, 13 December 1922, Box 8, Pratt MSS.

8. Williams Memo to CNO, 30 June 1920, Memo for CNO, 16 June 1920, File 28642–28, SNGC.

9. Henderson to Head Naval Mission Peru, 17 August 1921, Ingersoll to Navy, 25 October 1921, Box 231, ONIGC; Howell to DNI, 13 June 1924, Box 1, NAtt Rio; Reminiscences of Vice Admiral Felix L. Johnson, USN (Ret.), Oral History Transcript, U.S. Naval Institute, 1974, p. 87.

10. Howell to DNI, 13 June 1924, NAtt Rio; also, McCann, *Brazilian-American*.

11. Crowder to SecState, 17 April 1923, 121.5537/17, Decimal File; Walker to DNI, 4 September 1925, Galbraith to Bethlehem Steel, etc., 27 October 1925, Box 2, ONIAC; Morrow to Wilbur, 29 June 1928, 121.5512/15a, Decimal File.

12. Hickey to Bastedo, 13 August 1936, Box 230, ONIGC.

13. Schuyler Memo, 23 January 1923, 121.55/850, Decimal File; Johnson to Sellers, 18 April 1929, Box 5, Sellers MSS.

14. Plan 0-8 TAN, 11 August 1933, Box 147D, SPDR; Baggaley to Church, 23 January 1931, Olsen to ONI, 31 March 1931, Box 285, ONIGC.

15. "Red File," Box 1, NAtt Tegucigalpa; Head of Mission to DNI, 14 March 1932, Irwin to Spears, 27 January 1932, Box 1, NAtt Peru.

16. White Memo to Division Latin American Affairs, 10 June 1931, Thurston to White, 11 June 1931, King to SecState, 23 June 1931, 121.5539/9, Decimal File; *Annual Report of the Navy Department* (1932), p. 15.

17. Wilson to White, 6 May 1933, 121.5515/26, Hanna to White, 19 January 1933, 121.5515/23, Decimal File; Puleston Memo for CNO, 23 November 1934, Welles to Puleston, 11 December 1934, Box 286, ONIGC.

18. Dearing to Roosevelt, 10 March 1936, *FDR&FA*, III, pp. 240–42; John C. Munn Oral History Transcript, p. 39, USMCL; Holmes Memo for DNI, 25 January 1937, Box D31, Day File; Robert Blake Oral History Transcript, p. 76, USMCL.

19. Estimate of the Situation and 0–1 Plan-Blue to Prevent European Nations from Landing Men or Munitions in Brazil, 8 December 1936, Box 40, SPDR; Blake OH, p. 83; Blake Memo to DNI, 9 March 1938, Box 1, ONIAC.

20. Puleston to Maj. Gen. Cmndnt USMC, 31 March 1937, Box D32, Day File; Holmes Telephone Conversation with Duggan, 29 March 1937, 121.5513/4, Blake Memo of Conversation with Duggan, 9 February 1938, 121.5512/49, Leahy to SecState, 11 August 1938, 121.5512/58, Messersmith to Welles, 15 March 1938, 121.5512/49, Decimal File.
21. Hull to Swanson, 12 March 1938, 121.55/912A, *ibid.*
22. ONIH, p. 524; McCann, *Brazilian-American*, pp. 106, 113; Blake OH, pp. 73–74.
23. Blake memo, 5 July 1939, Box 7, Memo for Leahy, 26 June 1937, CNO to DNI, 30 October 1936, Minister Marine to Gill, 25 September 1936, Box 6, ONIGC.
24. McCann, pp. 108–9, 117; ONIH, p. 524; Blake OH, pp. 75–76; Memo, 9 December 1938, 121.5523/20, Decimal File.
25. Holmes Memo for DNI, 25 January 1937, Box D31, Blake memo for DNI, 12 November 1937, Box D36, Day File.

CHAPTER ELEVEN   DOMESTIC SECURITY

1. James to Richardson, 14 August 1940, Jules James MSS, J. Y. Joyner Library, East Carolina University, Greenville, North Carolina.
2. Sherwood, *Roosevelt and Hopkins*, p. 274.
3. Dorwart, "Roosevelt-Astor," pp. 307–22; Carter File, OF 4514, FDRL; Cook, *FBI*, pp. 240–51; Admiral W. S. Anderson, Oral History Transcript, Oral History Office, Columbia University, 1962, p. 230 (hereafter Anderson OH); Roosevelt Memo, 26 June 1939, Box 33, SNCC.
4. Holmes to CBuNav, 6 June 1939, Bryan to Graham, 28 May 1939, Box D44, Day File; Richardson, *Treadmill*, p. 7.
5. Anderson OH, pp. 194–210; Blake OH, p. 77.
6. Anderson to GB, 31 August 1939, Appendix C, ONIH; Nixon Memo for DNI, 28 June 1939, Box D45, Day File; Farago, *Game of Foxes*, pp. 19ff; Anderson to CNO, 16 November 1939, Box 33, SNCC.
7. Anderson, OH, p. 225; Holmes to Messersmith, 10 June 1939, 102.521/251, Decimal File.
8. Anderson OH, p. 230; *also see* The Adolf A. Berle Diary, FDRL.
9. Anderson OH, p. 230; entries 22 April, 28 May, 17 and 29 October 1940, Berle Diary; Nixon to Hoover, 29 June 1940, Box D55, Day File; Minutes of Intelligence Conference, 13 January 1941, Command File, NHD; ONIH, p. 886; Anderson to Cmndnts all NDs, 27 June 1940, Box D55, Day File: Hoover to Anderson, 11 January 1941, Box 2, Kirk MSS.
10. Anderson to Cmndnts 3rd and 12th NDs, 20 June 1939, Anderson to Dashiell, 27 June 1939, Box D45, Day File; Anderson to GB, 31 August 1939, Appendix C, ONIH; Nixon to Zacharias, 24 June 1939, Box D45, Day File.
11. Ickes *Diary*, II, p. 704.
12. CNO to CBuNav, 5 October 1939, Box D47, Day File; ONIH, p. 62; Anderson to Kirk, 30 January 1940, Box 2, Kirk MSS.
13. Memo for Pres., 7 December 1939, OF 1661–A, FDRL; Rood to DNI, 27 June 1940, Box D55, Day File; ONIH, p. 216.
14. Richardson, *Treadmill*, pp. 383–85; entry for April 1940, Berle Diary; Ickes *Diary*, III, p. 197.
15. Anderson to MacFall, 22 July 1940, Box D55, Day File.
16. Nixon to Whitemarsh, 11 October 1939, Box D47, Anderson to Cmndnts NDs, 27 June 1940, Box D55, Day File; *Magic Background of Pearl Harbor*, II, pp. A178–81; DNI to Cmndnts Navy Yards, etc., 12 November 1940, History 1st ND, p. 50.
17. Anderson to Arnold, 22 July 1940, Box D55, Day File; Coggins taped interview, 20 November 1979.
18. Goodman, *Committee*, pp. 56ff; Anderson to CNO, 9 December 1940, Anderson to CBuNav, 21 December 1940, Box D64, Day File.
19. George, *Surreptitious Entry*, p. 84; Munroe to NAtt Cuba, 10 October 1939, Box D47, Day File.
20. Corson, *Armies*, pp. 100–101; Kirk to Anderson, 20 October 1939, Box 2, Kirk MSS.

21. Anderson OH, p. 227; Astor to Roosevelt, 20 April 1941, PSF 116, FDRL; *New York Times*, 15 April 1952, p. 27; Astor to Kirk, 22 April 1941, PSF 116, FDRL; Cassard to CNO, 17 July 1941, Box 2, Kirk MSS.

22. Cassard to CNO, 17 July 1941, Statement of Account of Wallace B. Phillips, July-October 1941, Box 2, Kirk MSS.

23. Anderson to Cmndnts all NDs, DIOs, NAtts, 3 September 1939, Box 31, SNCC.

CHAPTER TWELVE   NEUTRAL OBSERVERS

1. Jacobs to all Bus and Offices, 24 September 1940, GB File 429–4, GBR; Crenshaw to DNI, 5 September 1939, Box 32, SNCC.

2. Anderson to Cmndnts NDs, 3 September 1939, Box 31, SNCC.

3. Anderson to CNO, 12 October 1939, CNO to CO Atlantic Squadron, 3 October 1939, DNI to NAtt Bogota, 7 October 1939, Box D47, Day File; OpNav to ALUSNA Havana, 10 October 1939, Copies of Letters Sent to SecNav, 1918–42, SNGC, RG 80, NA.

4. James to Todd, 29 February 1940, James MSS; OpNav to ALUSNA Buenos Aires, 8 March, 13 April 1940, Letters Sent to SecNav; "Battle of the River Plate," in British Empire Unit to Intelligence Branch, 13 July 1940, Box D55, Day File; ALUSNA Buenos Aires to OpNav, 14 December 1939, GB File 429–4, GBR.

5. Summary of Naval Staff Conversations and Agreements with American Republics, 1940, Box 37, SPDR; Beauregard to CNO, 25 September 1939, Box 3, ONIAC; SecNav to CNO, 27 June 1940, Nimitz to CNO, 12 April 1941, Box 230, Stark to All Ships, 9 July 1940, Box 1 ONIGC; *also, see* McCann, *Brazilian-American Friendship*.

6. Blake Memo for DNI, 11 June 1940, Bode to DNI, 17 June 1940, Box 1, ONIGC.

7, James to Richardson, 14 October 1940, James MSS; James to NAtt Caracas, 5 July 1940, James to NAtt Havana, 29 June 1940, James to NAtt Mexico, 28 June 1940, Box D55, Day File; Munn OH, p. 40; entry 16 May 1940, Berle Diary; Kirk to Anderson, 9 November 1939, Box 2, Kirk MSS.

8. NAtt Berlin to CNO, 29 August 1939, IR, 14 December 1939, 19 January 1940, Selected Naval Attaché Reports Relating to the World Crisis 1937–1943, RG 38, NA, Microfilm Pub. M975 (hereafter SNAR); Kirk to Anderson, 13 December 1939, Box 2, Kirk MSS.

9. Kirk to Anderson, 11 April, 1 and 14 May, 11 June 1940, Box 2, Kirk MSS.

10. Minister to Sweden to SecState, 8 May 1940, Memo for the files, 14 December 1940, 121.5558/41 and 121.5556/82, Decimal File; James to Trammell, 16 May 1940, James MSS.

11. Bullitt, *For the President*, pp. 469–70; Murphy, *Diplomat*, pp. 43ff; Hull to Swanson, 16 May 1939, Memo for Div. of European Affairs, 12 June 1939, 121.5552/57–58, Decimal File.

12. ONIH, p. 667; Anderson OH, p. 227; DNI to DWPD, 16 May 1941, SPDR; African observers, in January 1941, Box D67, Day File.

13. NAtt Berlin to Kirk, 4 February 1941, SNAR; Admiral T. C. Kincaid, Oral History Transcripts, Oral History Office, Columbia University, 1961, pp. 50–57 (hereafter Kinkaid OH); Kirk to Anderson, 13 December 1939, 22 January and 6 February 1940, Box 2, Kirk MSS.

14. Anderson Memo to Greenslade, 9 October 1939, Box D47, Day File.

15. Beehler to DNI, 7 July 1931, Box 3, NAtt Rio; CNO to Cmndnts all NDs, 16 March 1939, in Appendix E, ONIH; Messersmith to SecState, 9 February 1938, 121.5556/59, Decimal File.

16. Anderson OH, p. 227; Bode to DNI, 6 December 1940, Box D64, Day File.

17. Kirk to Anderson, 11 June 1940, Box 2, Kirk MSS; James to DNI, 11 October 1940, James to Trammel, 21 October 1940, James MSS.

18. Johnson to SecState, 18 March, 24 June 1940, 121.5593/152, 159, Decimal File.

19. Johnson to SecState, 5 April 1941, 121.5593/185; Hull to American Embassy Chungking, 12 November 1940, 121.5593/169A, Decimal File.

20. Long to Knox, 2 December 1940, 121.5593/169A, Decimal File; McCollum OH, pp. 263–64; Jurika OH, pp. 355–59.

21. IRs, 20 January 1940, Box 3, 4th Marines Shanghai.

22. Anderson to Miles, 25 September 1939, Box 32, SNCC; CNO to Rickover, 9 October

1939, Box D47, Day File; Tolley to DNI, 16 and 19 January 1940, Box 3, 4th Marines Shanghai.

23. Jurika OH, pp. 313, 328–29, 344.

24. *Ibid.*, p. 409, also 345–46, 387–89, 394–409.

25. "Lessons of the World War, December 1940–January 1941," in Thomason memo for Op–16–F, Box D64, Day File.

26. Murray Memo for the files, 28 November 1940, 121.5583/4, Grant to SecState, 11 December 1940, 121.5592/31, Welles to American Legation Bangkok, 14 November 1940, 121.5592/29, all in Decimal File.

27. Ghormley to Stark, 14 November 1940, Strategic Planning in the U.S. Navy, 1891–1945, microfilm by Scholarly Resources, Wilmington, 1977 (hereafter SP); Anderson OH, p. 229; Messersmith to Davis, 14 June 1939, Holmes to Messersmith, 10 June 1939, 102.521/251, Decimal File; Ghormley to Stark, 6 November 1940, SP.

28. Kimball, *Unsordid Act*, pp. 24–25; Haight, *Aid to France*, p. 234; CNO to Spears, 10 October 1940, Box 1, Letters Sent to Security Section, RG 38, NA.

CHAPTER THIRTEEN   ALUSNA LONDON

1. Roosevelt to Bingham, 11 July 1935, II, pp. 553–54, Davis to Roosevelt, 30 January 1936, III, P. 179, *FDR&FA*.

2. Willson to Kinkaid, 10 May 1938, Box 2, Kirk MSS.

3. Niblack, "Forms of Government in Relation to Their Efficiency for War," *USNIP*, 46 (September 1920), p. 1402; Creighton Memo for McNamee, 2 November 1921, file 21067–3, ONICC; Twining to Knox, 7 December 1921, Box 1, D. Knox MSS; McNamee to GB, in GB Secretary to ONI, 25 November 1925, Box 2, ONIAC.

4. DNI to CinCUS, 27 November 1928, Box 2, ONIAC; Bingham to FDR, 8 March 1934, *FDR&FA*, II, pp. 18–19; Borg, *Far Eastern Crisis*, pp. 496–500; Memo for CNO, 31 December 1937, 5, 7 and 14 January 1938, NAtt London to DNI, 17 January 1938, SP; also, Pratt, "Anglo-American Naval Conversations," pp. 762–63.

5. Leutze, *Bargaining*, pp. 37–38; Kennedy to Kirk, 21 October 1940, Kirk to Anderson, 20 and 28 June, 12 July 1939, Box 2, Kirk MSS.

6. CNO to CinCUS, 2 July 1939, Box 32, SNCC; Anderson to Kirk, 28 June 1939, Box 2, Kirk MSS.

7. Kirk to Anderson, 15 September, 10 October, 3 and 6 November 1939, Box 2, Kirk MSS.

8. Anderson to ALUSNA London, 11 October 1939, SNGC; Anderson to Kirk, 1 April 1940, Kirk to Anderson, 29 March 1940, Box 2, Kirk MSS.

9. Churchill to Roosevelt, 15 May 1940, in Loewenheim, ed., *Roosevelt and Churchill*, pp. 94–95 (hereafter *RC*); Leutze, *Bargaining*, p. 77; Dorwart, "Roosevelt-Astor," pp. 315–16; Ford, *Donovan*, pp. 88–90.

10. Stark to SecTreasury, 6 October 1939, Box D47, Day File; Kirk to Anderson, 21 March, 14 May, 1 June, 14 July 1940, Box 2, Kirk MSS.

11. Kirk to Anderson, 11 June 1940, Box 2, Kirk MSS; compare to Churchill to Roosevelt, 20 May, 15 June 1940, in *RC*, pp. 97, 104–6.

12. Ford, *Donovan*, pp. 90ff; Albion, *Makers*, p. 550.

13. Welles to President, 12 July 1940, PSF, FDRL; Kirk to Anderson, 27 July 1940, Anderson to Callaghan, 8 August 1940, Kirk to Donovan, 14 August 1940, Box 3, Kirk MSS.

14. Historical Narrative Naval Technical Intelligence, unpublished typescript in NHD, pp. 11–13; Stark to CBus, 17 July 1940, Box 89, SPDR; Anderson OH, p. 225; Kirk to Anderson, 14 and 27 July 1940, Box 2, Kirk MSS.

15. Ford, *Donovan*, pp. 91–94; Leutze, *Bargaining*, pp. 94ff.

16. McLachlan, *Room 39*, pp. 216–17; Bailey's Report, 11 September 1940, Ghormley to CNO, 18 September 1940, SP; Leutze, *Bargaining*, pp. 129ff.

17. Ghormley to Stark, 14 November 1940, SP.

18. Sexton to SecNav, 1 July 1940, SP; Matloff and Snell, *Strategic*, pp. 12–13; Leutze, *Bargaining*, pp. 77ff.

19. Matloff and Snell, *Strategic*, pp. 25–28; Leutze, *Bargaining*;, pp. 178–95.
20. Ghormley to Stark, 23 October, 22 November 1940, SP.
21. Churchill to Roosevelt, 7 December 1940, *RC*, pp. 122–25.
22. Roosevelt to Churchill, 11 April 1941, *RC*, p. 137; Minutes of U.S.-U.K. Staff Conversations, January-March 1941, SP.
23. Sherwood, *Roosevelt and Hopkins*, pp. 154–55; Admiral A. G. Kirk, Oral History Transcript, Columbia University, 1962, pp. 174–77 (hereafter Kirk OH).

CHAPTER FOURTEEN   INTERNAL STRUGGLES

1. Entry 5 June 1941, Berle Diary; Pearson, *Fleming*, pp. 99–100; McLachlan, *Room 39*, p. 224.
2. Head Planning Branch to DIOs, 20 February 1941, in ONIH, p. 306.
3. Kirk to Train, 11 March 1941, Box 5, Kirk MSS.
4. Entry, 8 March 1941, Berle Diary; Astor to Kirk, 22 April 1941, PSF 116, FDRL.
5. Kirk OH, p. 177; Kirk to Anderson, 13 December 1939, 9 February 1940, Box 2, Kirk MSS.
6. Roosevelt to Churchill, 29 March, 11 April 1941, *RC*, pp. 136–37; also Bailey and Ryan, *Hitler vs. Roosevelt*.
7. SecNav to GB, 14 June 1941, Rainbow V, 26 May 1941, SP.
8. Kirk OH, p. 182; Kirk pencilled note on back of envelope, 26 March 1941, Box 2, Kirk MSS; Mayfield IR, 15 April 1941, NAtt Havana IR, 24 June 1941, Cmndnt 13th ND to ONI, 2 June 1941, NAtt Mexico City IR, 21 November 1941, MacNulty to ONI, 25 February 1941, Hoover to DNI, 22 July 1941, Keisker to Tamm, 25 August 1941, Box 26, Coastal Information Section Records, RG 38, NA (hereafter CIS).
9. Ingersoll to Farquhar, 27 March 1941, OpNav Telephone Records, Command File, NHD; GNO to CinCUS, Cmndnts NDs, 16 July 1941, Box 24, CIS; History 1st ND, pp. 57ff.
10. George, *Surreptitious Entry*, p. 87, ONIH, pp. 233–34, 269–72.
11. Zacharias to Kirk, 7 March 1941, Box 5, DNI to NAtt London, 16 May 1941, Box 3, Kirk MSS.
12. Kirk to Anderson, 27 March 1941, Box 2, Kirk MSS; Kirk OH, p. 181; ONIH, pp. 78–82, 340.
13. ONIH, pp. 78–82.
14. *Ibid.*, pp. 107–10.
15. Kirk to Anderson, 27 March 1941, Box 2, Kirk MSS.
16. *Pearl Harbor Attack*, part 26, p. 372; "U.S. Naval Air Activity in Europe, 1941–45," Washington: USN, 1945.
17. ONIH, pp. 1254–55; Transcript of John Crawford McQueen Oral History, pp. 47–48, 57, USMCL.
18. Bode to DNI, 26 March 1941, Box D71, Day File; Welles to Stark, 9 June 1941, 121.552/103B, Decimal File.
19. MacMurray to SecState, 15 May 1941, 121.5567/22, Knox to SecState, 15 April 1941, 121.5561/40, Decimal File; Turner Memo for Ingersoll, 4 November 1941, Turner MSS, SPDR; Memo to Mr. Shaw, 29 April 1941, 121.5561/40, Decimal File.
20. Memo of Conversation, 15 May 1941, 121.5561/44, Welles to American Embassy Moscow, 11 July 1941, 121.5561/43A, Decimal File.
21. Thomason to DNI, 20 March 1942, Box 103, Day File; Hooper Memo for DNI, 25 March 1941, GB File 429, GBR; Zacharias, *Secret Missions*, pp. 286–87.
22. Kirk to CinCUS, 5 April 1941, Box D71, Day File; Kirk to DWPD, 12 August 1941, Kirk Memo for File, 14 August 1941, Box 39, SPDR.
23. Minutes of Intelligence Conference, March 1941, Command File; Kirk Circular Letter, 21 May 1941, GB File 429, GBR.
24. Kirk OH, p. 179; Dyer, *Amphibians*, I, pp. 97–98, 103–4, 139.
25. Ghormley to Stark, 23 October 1940, SP: Memo for the President, 15 February 1941, Turner MSS.

26. Stark to All Ships, 15 November 1940, GB File 429, GBR.

27. Callaghan to Forster, 5 February 1941, OF 18x, FDRL; McCollum OH, pp. 311–12; Ingersoll to DNI, 2 January 1941, Box 89, SPDR.

28. Kirk to CNO, July 1941, reply to CNO to DNI, 25 June 1941, McCollum Memo, 8 July 1941, SP.

29. Turner to DNI, 15 July 1941, Box 89, SPDR; Ingersoll to all Cmndnts NDs, 12 August 1941, Box 18, CIS.

30. McCollum OH, p. 320, also 301ff; CNO to DNI, 1 December 1940, Box 89, SPDR.

31. McCollum OH, p. 310; Kirk OH, p. 182.

32. Kirk OH, p. 179.

33. *Ibid.*; McCollum OH, p. 311.

34. Kirk OH, pp. 178, 221.

CHAPTER FIFTEEN   ROOSEVELT'S SPY

1. Carter Memo Concerning Chief of O.N.I. Kirke [sic], 30 July 1941, PSF 122, FDRL.

2. Anderson OH, p. 230; entry 8 March 1941, Berle Diary, FDRL; Murphy, *Diplomat*, p. 70.

3. "Background Data on Origin of Investigations by the Naval Intelligence Service," typescript prepared by Op–16–B–3, in the possession of Clyde J. Roach (hereafter Roach MSS); Dorwart, *ONI*, pp. 104ff.

4. O'Connor to LeHand, 8 December 1939, OF 18x; Martin Confidential Memo, 8 April 1935, OF 6s, FDRL.

5. *New York Times*, 10 June 1943, p. 3; Roosevelt, *Personal Letters*, I, p. 394; *FDR&FA*, I, p. 373, II, pp. 5, 454–55; Dorwart, "Roosevelt-Astor," pp. 307–22.

6. "The Room Membership List," undated, Box 111, Kermit Roosevelt MSS, LC; Dorwart, "Roosevelt-Astor," pp. 309–12.

7. Farquhar to Phillips, 11 May 1937, Box D33, Puleston to Astor, 17 September 1936, Box D30, Day File, Astor to President, 7 January 1933, PPF 40, FDRL; Dearing to FDR, 10 March 1936, *FDR&FA*, III, p. 242.

8. Vincent [Astor] to Franklin [Roosevelt], n.d., 13 January 1938, PSF 116, FDRL.

9. Dorwart, "Roosevelt-Astor," pp. 314–16; Hyde, *Room 3603*, p. 99.

10. Astor to Roosevelt, 20 October ?, 28 November 1939, 18 and 20 April 1940, PSF 116, FDRL; Hyde, *Room 3603*, p. 99.

11. Astor to LeHand, 14 May 1940, Astor to Roosevelt, 1 and 25 June 1940, 20 April 1940, PSF 116, FDRL.

12. Astor to Roosevelt, 25 June 1940, *ibid.*; FDR to Stark, 26 June 1940, OF 18x, FDRL.

13. Astor to LeHand, 31 January 1941, PSF 116, entries 4 and 25 February, 8 March 1941, Berle Diary, FDRL.

14. Kirk to Callaghan, 12 March 1941, Roosevelt to Tully, 19 March 1941, Callaghan Memo for the President, 14 March 1941, PSF 116, DNI to Cmndnt 3rd ND, 28 March 1941, PPF 40, FDRL.

15. Astor to Roosevelt, ? March, 3 April, 9 May 1941, PSF 116, FDRL.

16. Astor to FDR, 20 April 1941, PSF 116, FDRL; Smith, *OSS*, pp. 22–23.

17. Minnie Astor to Roosevelt, 30 October 1941, PSF 116, FDRL.

18. Carter to Roosevelt, 6 January 1934, *FDR&FA*, I, pp. 578–81; also, see PPF 5325, PSF 122, and Papers of Dr. Henry Field, FDRL.

19. Berle Memo for the President, 11 July 1941, Berle Diary; JFC [Carter] Memo for Tully, 1 June 1944, PSF 125, FDRL.

20. Wilkinson to Astor, 30 December 1941, Box D94, Day File; Tully Memos for President, 11 December 1941, 19 February 1942, 1 October 1942, Astor to President, 16 July 1942, Astor to Tully, 14 August 1944, PSF 116, FDRL.

21. Hyde, *Room 3603*, p. 56; Smith, *OSS*.

22. Smith, *OSS*, pp. 41–42; *War Report of the OSS*, p. ix; Murphy, *Diplomat*, p. 92; Kirk to Eddy, 4 November 1941, 121.5583/30, Decimal File.

23. MaLachlan, *Room 39*, pp. 227–32; Corson, *Armies*, p. 146; *War Report OSS*, p. 23; Kirk to Long, 27 October 1941, Hull to Kirk, 28 October 1941, 121.5583/25, Decimal File.

24. Kirk OH, pp. 182–83; Kirk to Murray, 14 November 1941, 121.5583/30; Murphy, *Diplomat*, 66ff; Langer, *Vichy*, pp. 232ff.

25. Berle memo for the president, 11 July 1941, Berle Diary, FDRL.

CHAPTER SIXTEEN   FAILURE OF INTELLIGENCE DOCTRINE

1. Entry 7 December 1941, Berle Diary, FDRL.

2. Dyer, *Amphibians*, I, p. 181; Kinkaid OH, p. 356; Kirk to Wilkinson, November 1941, Box 5, Kirk MSS.

3. Puleston to Hooper, 16 September 1936, Box D30, Day File: CNO to DNI, 6 October 1941, Box 98, SPDR; Corson, *Armies*, pp. 163–65; Wilkinson Biographical File, NHD.

4. Kirk to Wilkinson, 24 September 1941, Box 5, Kirk MSS; Blake OH, p. 79; Wilkinson to CNO, 20 December 1941, Box D93, Day File.

5. U.S. Congress, *Pearl Harbor Attack* part 26, p. 301.

6. *Ibid.*, p. 18; McCollum OH, p. 311.

7. U.S. Congress, *Pearl Harbor Attack*, part 26, pp. 301–2; Baxter to Wilkinson, 12 November 1941, Wilkinson to CNO, 14 November 1941, Bode to DWPD, 23 September 1941, Turner to DNI, 26 September 1941, SPDR; Corson, *Armies*, pp. 163–65.

8. Wyatt to Kirk, 17 September 1941, Box 5, Kirk MSS.

9. Farago, *Broken Seal*, p. 160; U.S. Congress, *Pearl Harbor Attack*, Part 26, p. 226; Minutes of Intelligence Conference, 19 February 1941, Command File; McCollum OH, p. 333.

10. McCollum to Atcheson, 22 Oct. 1941, 121.5593/195, Fish to SecState, 20 Oct. 1941, 121.5553/70, Decimal File.

11. U.S. Congress, *Pearl Harbor Attack*, Part 26, p. 356, part 36, pp. 14–15, 221–23, part 27, p. 748.

12. *Ibid.*, Part 36, pp. 31ff; Part 26, p. 393.

13. McCollum OH, p. 275; Harris, "Magic Leak," p. 93; U.S. Congress, *Pearl Harbor Attack*, Part 26, p. 300.

14. "The Navy School of Oriental Languages," typescript NHD; CNO to CBuNav, 4 July 1940, Box D55, 21 February 1941, Box D68, Day File.

15. U.S. Congress, *Pearl Harbor Attack*, Part 26, pp. 76ff, Part 36, p. 30.

16. Corson, *Armies*, p. 161.

17. Powell memo for the DNI, 26 February 1927, Box 64, SPDR; McCollum OH, pp. 117–18; Puleston to CinCUS, 10 October 1936, Box D38, Day File; WPD to CNO, 16 April 1937, quoted in ONIH, p. 24; entry November 1938, Bemis Diary, SNAR.

18. Basic War Plan ORANGE, SP; Doyle, "War Plan Orange," pp. 49–63.

19. U.S. Congress, *Pearl Harbor Attack*, Part 36, pp. 20, 225.

20. Inglis to Dorwart, 2 February 1980, letter in possession of author; Wohlstetter, *Pearl Harbor*; U.S. Congress, *Pearl Harbor Attack*, Part 36, p. 29.

21. Corson, *Armies*, pp. 157–61; Morton, "Pearl Harbor," 461–68; Ferrell, "Pearl Harbor," pp. 215–33; Melosi, *Shadow*; Inglis to Dorwart, 2 February 1980.

22. Reminiscences of Admiral William J. Sebald, Oral History Transcript, U.S. Naval Institute, 1977, p. 261 (hereafter Sebald OH).

23. U.S. Congress, *Pearl Harbor Attack*, Part 36, p. 233.

24. *Ibid.*, pp. 234–40.

CHAPTER SEVENTEEN   ON THE DEFENSIVE

1. Lockwood Diary, December 1941, Box 1, Charles A. Lockwood MSS, LC; Standley, *Admiral*, pp. 79–80.

2. CNO to Chief of Staff U.S. Army, 11 December 1941, Turner MSS.

3. Buell, *Master*, pp. 162-79; Matloff and Snell, *Strategic*, pp. 97–119; Davis, *JCS*, pp. 553ff, in SP.

4. Guthrie Memo, 17 February 1942, Box 21, CIS; Howell Log, CXXX (1942).

5. Waller to DIO, 15 February 1942, Hoover to Asst Chief of Staff to ONI, 19 December 1941, Donovan to Wilkinson, 25 February 1942, Box 1, CIS.

6. Baldwin to DIO 1st ND, 14 March 1942, Bourgerie to DIO 4th ND, 19 March 1942, Box D103, Day File.

7. Wilkinson Memo for SecNav, 17 March 1942, Box 124, ONIAC; Moore Memo to all Branch and Section Heads, 23 January 1942, Box D97, Day File.

8. Wilkinson to Mayfield, 13 January 1942, Box D96, Day File.

9. Wilkinson to Hoover, 19 February 1942, Box D99, Day File.

10. Entries, 6 and 9 January 1942, Berle Diary.

11. Wilkinson to all Bus, etc., 7 January 1942, Box D95, Wilkinson to Langer, 11 February 1942, Box D99, Wilkinson to Denebrink, 20 December 1941, Box D93, Wilkinson to Donovan, 30 December 1941, Box D94, Day File.

12. Wilkinson to Cmndnt 4th ND, 8 February 1942, Riheldaffer Memo for the Record, 13 February 1942, Box D99, Day File.

13. Turner to CNO, 12 December 1941, Box 98, SPDR.

14. Wilkinson to DWPD, etc., 15 December 1941, *ibid*.

15. Turner to Acting Chief of Staff, 28 January 1942, *ibid*.

16. JFC [Carter] Summary of Preliminary Report on Intelligence Problems, 18 December 1941, PSF 122, FDRL; Foster OH, pp. 245–59; Wilkinson to Astor, 30 December 1941, Wilkinson to Tarrant, 30 December 1941, both in Box D94, and Chandler to Administrative Officer, 17 March 1942, Box D103, all in Day File; George, *Surreptitious Entry*, p. 93.

17. Thomason to Zacharias, 3 February 1942, in Zacharias, *Secret*, p. 287; Wilkinson Memo for Stevenson, 12 March 1942, Box D102, Wilkinson to Walsh, 19 January 1942, Box D96, Day File.

18. King to Cmndnt USMC, 31 March 1942, Box 98, SPDR.

19. Memo of Conference OCNO, 17 January 1942, CNO File, NHD; Turner to Intelligence Staff, 10 April 1942, Box 98, SPDR.

20. Kingman to DNI, 17 January 1942, Box D96, DNI to CNO, 18 December 1941, Box D92, Wilkinson to All Sections of Foreign Intelligence, 13 February 1942, Horne to all Bus, 9 January 1942, DNI to Director Office of Public Relations, 1 January 1942, Box D95, Day File; ONIH, pp. 992–94.

21. Wilkinson to DCD, 9 December 1941, Box D91, Foskett to Chief Office of Procurement and Materials, 13 February 1942, Box D99, Day File; *see*, "Area Economic Program File," Puleston MSS.

22. Westfeldt to Baldwin, 9 June 1942, Box 18, CIS; Entry, 4 April 1942, Berle Diary.

23. Ingersoll to All Divisions of Ops, 18 December 1941, Turner to DNI, 22 December 1941, Box 98, SPDR; Stark to SecNav, 17 February 1942, Box D100, Day File.

24. Heard to Cmndnt 3rd ND, 12 February 1942, Heard to Morse, 12 February 1942, Box D99, Day File; Frank, "Navy v. the *Chicago Tribune*," pp. 284–303; Buell, *Master*, pp. 202–4; Reminiscences of Rear Admiral Harold Cecil Train, Oral History Transcript, Oral History Office, Columbia University, 1966, p. 284 (hereafter Train OH); McCollum OH, p. 473.

25. Thomason to Page, 22 December 1941, Box D93, DNI to DCD, 1 July 1942, Box D116, Op 16x to Op 16D, 17 February 1942, Box D100, Day File.

26. McCollum OH, p. 482.

27. *Ibid*, pp. 445ff.

28. *Ibid*., p. 455; McLachlan, *Room 39*, p. 237; Wilkinson to Holden, 17 March 1942, Box D103, Day File; *see*, Farago, *Tenth Fleet*.

29. Index Card, 1/18/42, SNGC; Delimitation of Investigative Duties, February 9, 1942, in "Brief History B-Section," typescript in Roach MSS.

30. History 3rd ND, p. 157; Campbell, *Luciano Project*, pp. 29, 116; Tripp, *Homosexual Matrix*, pp. 225–26.

31. Wilkinson to MacFall, 2 July 1942, Box 116, Day File: George, *Surreptitious*, p. 116.

32. Wilkinson Biographical File, NHD.

CHAPTER EIGHTEEN   THE MAN WHO WANTED TO BE DNI

1. Zacharias, *Secret*, pp. 83–84, 109.

2. *Ibid*.

3. Nixon to Zacharias, 24 June 1939, Box D45, Day File: Zacharias to Kirk, 7 March 1941, Box 5, Kirk MSS; Zacharias, *Secret*, p. 292; Worton OH, p. 176; Sebald OH, pp. 73, 89; Reminiscences of Captain Henri Smith-Hutton, Oral History Transcript, U.S. Naval Institute, 1973, pp. 96–97 (hereafter Smith-Hutton OH), (by permission Mrs. Smith-Hutton).

4. Zacharias, *Secret*, p. 113; McCollum OH, pp. 86–87; Train OH, pp. 290–91.

5. Train OH, pp. 308–10; Tolley, *Lanikai*, p. 32n.

6. Zacharias, *Secret*, p. 288.

7. Record of Conference, CIS, January 11–15, 1943, Box 24, CIS.

8. Zacharias to CBu Ships, 30 July 1942, Box 124, ONIAC; Zacharias, *Secret*, pp. 304ff; Memo of Conversation, 7 May 1942, entry 18 June 1942, Berle Diary; Zacharias to Clark, 1 August 1942, Box D119, Day File.

9. Zacharias, *Secret*, p. 288; Wilkinson Memo for Stevenson, 12 March 1942, Box D102, Day File.

10. DNI to Director of Budgets and Reports, 27 March 1942, Box 11, Train to all DIOs, 30 March 1943, Box 12, DNI to VCNO, 3 March 1943, Box 8, Day File Subseries; Puleston to DNI, 20 January 1943, Puleston MSS; also, History 3rd ND, pp. 98ff.

11. Sherwood, *Roosevelt and Hopkins*; Major, "Leahy," in Love, ed., *CNOs*, pp. 101–17.

12. ONIH, pp. 987–91; JISC File 334 (7–24–42), JCS Central Decimal File, RG 218, NA; Train OH, pp. 286, 306, 318.

13. Memo, 25 July 1942, Berle Diary.

14. Train OH, pp. 286ff; ONIH, pp. 84, 344; Train to Donovan, 26 July 1942, in Memo of Conversation, 18 August 1942, entry 27 April 1942, Berle Diary.

15. Train Draft Memo for JIC, 19 October 1942, Minutes of Joint Psychological Warfare Committee, 34th Meeting, 9 November 1942, Wilkinson to JCS, 18 and 26 June 1942, File 311.5 (6–18–42), JCS Central Decimal File.

16. Entries, 27 November, 8 December 1942, Berle Diary.

17. DNI to Officer in Charge Caribbean Small Craft Project, 31 March 1943, Box 12, Horne to COMNAVEU, 3 March 1943, Box 8, Day File Subseries; Train to Merrill, 28 October 1942, Merrill to Train, 24 October 1942, Box 53, ONIAC; Train OH, p. 322.

18. Harding to Head Administrative Branch, 8 December 1941, Box D91, Day File.

19. ONIH, pp. 92–95; Lobdell, "Frank Knox," in Coletta, ed., *American Secretaries*, p. 714.

20. Train Memo for Warner, 30 March 1943, Box 12, Day File Subseries; DNI to VCNO, 15 May 1943, quoted in, ONIH, p. 333.

21. Zacharias, *Secret*, p. 306.

22. Kingman to Moore, 13 February 1942, Box D99, Day File; Roetter, *Psychological Warfare*, pp. 140–45; ONIH, pp. 860ff; Scripts of Norden Broadcasts, NHD; Zacharias, *Secret*, pp. 303ff.

23. Record of Conference, January 11–15, 1943, Box 24, CIS.

24. Progress Report, 10th ND, Coastal Intelligence Activities, January 1–31, 1943, Box 18, Memo for the Files, 22 December 1942, Box 24, CIS; COMESTSEAFRON to Comndnt 1st ND, 13 July 1942, in History of 1st ND.

25. Baldwin Memo for Zacharias, 27 January 1943, Box 23, CIS.

26. *Ibid.*

27. ONIH, p. 446.

28. DNI to DIO 7th ND, 4 March 1943, Box 8, Day File Subseries; *Operational Intelligence Notes*, I (July 1945), Command File; ONIH, pp. 770–73, 791; Zacharias to Nixon, 6 April 1943, Box 17, CIS; also, History 12th ND, p. 40; History 1st ND, Appendix X.

29. Baldwin to DNI, 17 April 1943, Box 17, CIS; Pickhardt to Officer in Charge Intelligence Center Pacific Ocean Area, 17 May 1943, Box 124, ONIAC; Sebald OH, p. 280.

30. Zacharias, *Secret*, pp. 315–16; also, *Washington Post*, 6 October 1946, clipping in Zacharias Biographical File, NHD.

31. Train OH, pp. 314–15.

32. ONIH, pp. 830–33; Train to all DIOs, 11 September 1943, Box 30, Pigman to DIOs, etc., 22 October 1943, Box 34, Day File Subseries; Train OH, p. 324.

CHAPTER NINETEEN   GLOBAL AGENTS

1. ONI "Roster," in Train to CinCUS, 4 April 1943, Box 48, Map Room File, FDRL (hereafter MR); List of Equipment for Intelligence Officers, 10 March 1943, Box 18, CIS.

2. Wilkinson to CBuNav, 9 January 1942, Box D95, Day File.

3. Moore to Liaison Officer, 17 December 1941, Box D92, CNO to Cmndnt 15th ND, 27 January 1942, Box D97, Day File.

4. Heard to MajGen Cmndnt USMC, 17 December 1941, Box D92, Day File.

5. Thomason memo for DNI, 11 February 1942, Box D99, VCNO to all NAtts, etc., 30 June 1942, Box D116, Day File, ONIH, pp. 657ff.

6. Heard to Wilson, 12 March 1942, Moore Memo for Liaison Officer, 12 March 1942, Box D102, Moore to Cmndnt 15th ND, 9 January 1942, Box D95, Moore to DNI, 13 December 1941, Box D92, Day File; ONIH, p. 531.

7. White to Barber, 12 March 1943, 121.5537/65, Caffery to SecState, 18 February 1942, 121.5532/79, Decimal File.

8. Westfall to Liaison Officer, 7 May 1943, 121.5525/112, Hurley to SecState, 11 July 1945, 121.5593/7-1145, also 121.5583/65, Decimal File.

9. Entry 12 January 1943, Howell Log; White to Wilson, 2 April 1943, 121.5538/27, Decimal File; Schrader to NLO Valparaiso, 31 March 1943, Box 12, Day File Subseries.

10. Wilkinson to Allen, 4 July 1942, Box D116, Day File; also, 121.5547/17, Decimal File.

11. CNO to CO US 8th Fleet, 12 December 1944, Box 73, DNI to CBuNav, 2 April 1945, Box 85, Day File Subseries; Hayes to SecState, 7 December 1942, 121.5552/129, Harrison to SecState, 2 February 1943, 121.5567/49, Decimal File.

12. Schrader Memo for Wilson, 15 October 1943, Box 33, DNI to NLO Concepcion, 8 October 1943, Box 32, Day File Subseries; Train OH, p. 311.

13. Longyear Memo, 5 August 1944, 121.5551/7-2744, Decimal File; Brawley to NAtt Chungking, 5 February 1943, Navy Group China Records, NHD; Waller Memo for the DNI, 11 February 1942, Box D99, Day File.

14. Miles, *Different Kind of War*, pp. 11ff; Schaller, "SACO," pp. 527–53; Miles to DNI, 24 October 1944, Navy Group China Records; Romanus and Sunderland, *Time Runs Out*, pp. 18, 160, 385.

15. Hitch in, 2 July 1942, Box D116, Day File; Miles, *Different*, pp. 342–43; Bales, "Chinese Communists—Their Potential in Allied War Effort," 18 January 1945, carton 332H3C–2, Secret Naval Attaché Reports, RG 38, NA.

16. History of Naval Attaché London, pp. 28–36; History of Naval Air Europe, pp. 67ff, NHD.

17. Heard to NAtt Guatemala City, 10 June 1942, Box D95, Day File; White to DNI, 15 June 1942, Box 98, SPDR; Dorwart, *ONI*, p. 128; Hayes to SecState, 30 December 1942, 121.5552/129, Foster Memo, 15 March 1943, 121.5552/129½.

18. Cabot to Bonsall, 10 December 1943, Long to Bonsall, 2 December 1943, Bonsall to Long, 14 December 1943, 121.5514/63, Decimal File.

19. Tait to SecState, 15 April 1943, 121.5551/193, Hayes to SecState, 15 July 1942, 121.5552/107, Memo for Central Division, 3 March 1942, 102.502, Hull to Knox, 14 March 1944, 121.5594/99A, also, 121.5594/93, Decimal File; McCollum OH, pp. 448–53; Smith-Hutton OH, pp. 377–85.

20. Train OH, pp. 319–21; Hull to American Embassy London, 8 October 1943, 121.5561/187, Dunn to Smith, 8 September 1943, 121.5561/183D, Decimal File; Standley, *Admiral*, pp. 424–26; 470–71; Henderson to SecState, 25 November 1942, 121.5561/121, Decimal File.

21. Naval Observer Basra to ONI, 7 February 1945, Carton 332h3C–2, Secret NAtt Reports; also 121.5561/61, Decimal File.

CHAPTER TWENTY   DEFINING THE NAVAL INTEREST

1. Entry, 28 April 1942, Berle Diary; also, Berle and Jacobs, eds., *Navigating*, pp. 260ff.

2. ONIH, p. 580.

3. Furer, *Administrative History*, p. 157; Farago, *Tenth Fleet*, pp. 214ff; Sebald OH, pp. 270ff; Smith-Hutton OH, p. 393ff.

4. History 12th ND, p. 7; DIO Conference, in ONIH, p. 343; Train to DIOs, 1 September 1943, Box 29, Day File Subseries.

5. Westfeldt to Smith, 14 August 1942, Box 18, CIS.

6. DNI to DIOs, 25 February 1944, in History 1st ND.

7. Carter Memo, 13 September 1943, OF 18x, FDRL; ONIH, p. 757.

8. DNI to DIOs, 25 February 1944, in History 1st ND; also, Dorwart, *ONI*, pp. 12–20.

9. Pash, *ALSOS*; Schuirmann to Schade, 13 August 1944, in History Naval Technical Mission in Europe, p. 150, NHD; Smith-Hutton OH, p. 489.

10. Naval Technical Mission, pp. 1, 77, 150–52; also, Pash, *ALSOS*.

11. DNI to all Branches, 22 November 1944, Box 72, Day File Subseries; Naval Technical Mission, p. 27; Mission to Japan, microfilm, NHD.

12. ONIH, pp. 834–40; Heard to Morton, 27 November 1944, Box 72, Heard to Coordinator R&D, 13 November 1944, Box 71, Thebaud to LeBreton, 14 April 1945, Box 85, Day File Subseries.

13. Zacharias, *Secret*, pp. 335ff; Diary Entry, July 1945, Box 10, Ferdinand Eberstadt MSS, Seeley Mudd Manuscript Library, Princeton University.

14. King to DNI, 13 February 1945, in History 3rd ND, Appendix T; DNI to DIOs, 26 October 1944, Box 70, Thebaud to BuPers, 17 November 1944, Box 71, Morton to OpIntel Officers, 9 December 1944, Box 73, Day File Subseries; also, "Navy Oriental Language School History," pp. 29–31, NHD; Thebaud to all DIOs, 30 April 1945, Box 86, Day File Subseries.

15. Forrestal to Price, 13 November 1944, Box 71, CNO to Joint Army-Navy Experimental Testing Board, 9 April 1945, CNO to Advance Intelligence Center, 3 April 1945 Box 84; DNI to NAtt Capetown, 28 June 1945, Box 91, Thebaud to Division of Naval Intelligence, 22 November 1944, Box 72, Day File Subseries; Thebaud Memo for the JCS, 9 December 1944, Box 164, MR, FDRL.

16. Thebaud Memo for VCNO, dict. by Souers, 7 December 1944, Box 73, Day File Subseries; several weeks later Admiral Leahy opposed as "premature" the centralization of intelligence, Leahy Memo for President, 6 March 1945, Box 163, MR, FDRL.

17. Thebaud Memo for the DCD, 10 April 1945, Wharton to DIO 1st ND, 28 April 1945, Box 86, Day File Subseries.

18. Wharton to CinCUS Atlantic Fleet, etc., 11 November 1944, Box 71, Day File Subseries.

19. Thebaud to Distribution List 6, 26 June 1945, Box 91, Wharton to DIO 1st ND, 28 April 1945, Box 86, *ibid.*

20. Caskey, in ONIH, p. 455; also, CNO to SecNav, 29 December 1941, Box 94, Waller Memo for the DNI, 12 March 1942, Box 102, Day File Subseries.

21. *New York Times*, 4 June 1946, p. 6.

22. Wylie to Op–16–F, 13 December 1944, Box 195, SPDR; Wylie Memo on Postwar Aims of the Soviet Navy and Merchant Marine, 24 October 1944, GB File 429, GBR; Sebald OH, pp. 295–96; ONIH, pp. 694, 703.

23. *New York Times*, 17 September 1946, p. 2; *see Amerasia Papers*.

24. Wharton to DIO 1st ND, 28 April 1945, Box 86, DNI to Cmndnts all NDs, 26 June 1945, Box 91, Day File Subseries.

25. Keisker Memo for the DNI, 17 August 1945, in "Background Data on Origin of Investigations by Naval Intelligence Service," Roach MSS.

26. Inglis Memo, December 1945, Text of Remarks Made by Inglis Before the General Planning Group, 1 August 1946, Box 106, SPDR.

SELECTED BIBLIOGRAPHY

Albion, Robert Greenhalgh. *Makers of Naval Policy, 1798–1947*. Annapolis: Naval Institute Press, 1980.

The Amerasia Papers: A Clue to the Catastrophe in China, 2 vols. Washington: Government Printing Office, 1970.

Bailey, Thomas A. and Ryan, Paul B. *Hitler vs. Roosevelt: The Undeclared Naval War*. New York: Free Press, 1979.

Bennett, David H. *Demagogues in the Depression: American Radicals and the Union Party, 1932–1936*. New Brunswick: Rutgers University Press, 1969.

Berle, Beatrice Bishop and Jacobs, Travis Beal, eds. *Navigating the Rapids, 1918–1971: From the Papers of Adolf A. Berle*. New York: Harcourt Brace Jovanovich, 1973.

Borg, Dorothy. *The United States and the Far Eastern Crisis of 1933–1938*. Cambridge: Harvard University Press, 1964.

Borg, Dorothy and Okamoto, Shumpei, eds. *Pearl Harbor as History: Japanese-American Relations, 1931–1941*. New York: Columbia University Press, 1973.

Braisted, William Reynolds. *The United States Navy in the Pacific, 1909–1922*. Austin: University of Texas Press, 1971.

Buell, Thomas B. *Master of Sea Power: A Biography of Fleet Admiral Ernest J. King*. Boston: Little, Brown, 1980.

Bullitt, Orville H., ed. *For the President, Personal and Secret: Correspondence Between Franklin D. Roosevelt and William C. Bullitt*. Boston: Houghton Mifflin, 1972.

Bywater, Hector. *Sea Power in the Pacific: A Study of the American-Japanese Naval Problem*. New York: Constable, 1934.

Campbell, Rodney. *The Luciano Project: The Secret Wartime Collaboration of the Mafia and the United States Navy*. New York: McGraw-Hill, 1977.

Challener, Richard D., ed. *United States Military Intelligence, 1917–1927*, 30 vols. New York: Garland, 1977.

Cole, Wayne S. *Senator Gerald P. Nye and American Foreign Relations*. Minneapolis: University of Minnesota Press, 1962.

Coletta, Paolo E., ed. *American Secretaries of the Navy*, 2 vols. Annapolis: Naval Institute Press, 1980.

Cook, Fred J. *The FBI Nobody Knows*. New York: Macmillan, 1964.

Corson, William R. *The Armies of Ignorance: The Rise of the American Intelligence Empire*. New York: Dial Press, 1977.

Costello, Commander Joseph Daniel. "Planning for War: A History of the General Board of the Navy, 1900–1914. Ph.D. dissertation, Tufts University, 1969.

Cronon, E. David, ed. *The Cabinet Diaries of Josephus Daniels, 1913–1921*. Lincoln: University of Nebraska Press, 1963.

Dallek, Robert. *Franklin D. Roosevelt and American Foreign Policy, 1932–1945*. New York: Oxford University Press, 1979.

Davis, George T. *A Navy Second to None: The Development of American Naval Policy*. New York: Harcourt Brace, 1940.

Davis, Vernon E. *History of the Joint Chiefs of Staff in World War II*, 2 vols. Washington: JCS Historical Section, 1953.

Diggins, John P. *Mussolini and Fascism: The View from America*. Princeton: Princeton University Press, 1972.

Dingman, Roger. *Power in the Pacific: The Origin of Naval Arms Limitation, 1914–1922*. Chicago: University of Chicago Press, 1976.

Donner, Frank. *The Age of Surveillance: The Aims and Methods of America's Political Intelligence System*. New York: Alfred A. Knopf, 1980.

Dorwart, Jeffery M. *The Office of Naval Intelligence: The Birth of America's First Intelligence Agency, 1865–1918*. Annapolis: Naval Institute Press, 1979.

Dorwart, Jeffery M. "The Roosevelt-Astor Espionage Ring." *New York History*, 62 (July 1981): 307–22.

Doyle, Michael K. "The U.S. Navy and War Plan Orange, 1933–1940: Making Necessity a Virtue," *Naval War College Review* (May-June 1980) 46–63.

Dulles, Allen. *The Craft of Intelligence*. New York: New American Library, 1963.

Dyer, Vice Admiral George Carroll. *The Amphibians Came to Conquer: The Story of Admiral Richmond Kelly Turner*, 2 vols. Washington: Government Printing Office, 1971.

Farago, Ladislas. *The Broken Seal: The Story of "Operation Magic" and the Pearl Harbor Disaster*. New York: Random House, 1967.

———. *The Game of the Foxes: The Untold Story of German Espionage in the United States and Great Britain during World War II*. New York: David McKay Co., 1971.

———. *The Tenth Fleet*. New York: Ivan Obolensky, 1962.

Ferrell, Robert H. "Pearl Harbor and the Revisionists." *The Historian*, 17 (1955): 215–33.

Ford, Corey. *Donovan of OSS*. Boston: Little, Brown, 1970.

Frank, Larry J. "The U.S. Navy v. the *Chicago Tribune*."*The Historian*, (Feb. 1980): 284–303.

Furer, Rear Admiral Julius Augustus. *Administration of the Navy Department in World War II*. Washington: Naval History Division, 1959.

George, Willis. *Surreptitious Entry*. New York: Appleton-Century, 1946.

Goodman, Walter. *The Committee: The Extraordinary Career of the House Committee on Un-American Activities*. New York: Farrar, Straus and Giroux, 1968.

Haight, John McVickar, Jr. *American Aid to France, 1938–1940*. New York: Atheneum, 1970.

Hamill, John. *The Strange Career of Mr. Hoover Under Two Flags*. New York: William Faro, 1931.

Harris, Ruth R. "The 'Magic' Leak of 1941 and Japanese-American Relations," *Pacific Historical Review*, 50 (Feb. 1981): 77–96.

Herzog, James H. *Closing the Open Door: American-Japanese Diplomatic Negotiations, 1936–1941*. Annapolis: Naval Institute Press, 1973.

Holmes, W. J. *Double-Edged Secrets: U.S. Naval Intelligence Operations in the Pacific during World War II*. Annapolis: Naval Institute Press, 1979.

Hyde, H. Montgomery. *Room 3603: The Story of the British Intelligence Center in New York during World War II*. New York: Farrar, Straus, 1963.

Hynd, Alan. *Betrayal from the East: The Inside Story of Japanese Spies in America*. New York: McBride, 1943.

Ickes, Harold L. *The Secret Diary of Harold L. Ickes*, 3 vols. New York: Simon and Schuster, 1953–54.

Jeffreys-Jones, Rhodri. *American Espionage From Secret Service to CIA*. New York: Free Press, 1977.

Joslin, Theodore G. *Hoover off the Record*. Garden City: Doubleday, Doran, 1934.

Kahn, David. *The Codebreakers*. New York: Macmillan, 1967.

Kamman, William. *A Search for Stability: United States Diplomacy Toward Nicaragua, 1925–1933*. Notre Dame: University of Notre Dame Press, 1968.

Kimball, Warren F. *The Most Unsordid Act: Lend-Lease, 1939–41*. Baltimore: The Johns Hopkins Press, 1969.

Knox, Captain Dudley W. *The Eclipse of American Sea Power*. New York: American Army & Navy Journal, 1922.

Laforet, Eugene G., MD. "Cecil Coggins and the War in the Shadows." *Journal of the American Medical Association*, 243 (April 25, 1980): 1653–55.

Langer, William L. *Our Vichy Gamble*. New York: Alfred A. Knopf, 1947.

Leutze, James R. *Bargaining for Supremacy: Anglo-American Naval Collaboration, 1937–1941*. Chapel Hill: University of North Carolina Press, 1977.

Loewenheim, Francis, et al., eds. *Roosevelt and Churchill: Their Secret Wartime Correspondence*. New York: Saturday Review Press, 1975.

Love, Robert William, Jr. *The Chiefs of Naval Operations*. Annapolis: Naval Institute Press, 1980.

McCann, Frank D., Jr. *The Brazilian-American Alliance, 1937–1945*. Princeton: Princeton University Press, 1973.

McLachlan, Donald. *Room 39: A Study in Naval Intelligence*. New York: Atheneum, 1968.

The "Magic" Background of Pearl Harbor, 8 vols. Washington: Department of Defense, Government Printing Office, 1977.

Mashbir, Sidney. *I Was an American Spy*. New York: Vantage, 1953.

Masland, J. W. and Rodway, L. I. *Soldiers and Scholars*. Princeton: Princeton University Press, 1957.

Matloff, Maurice and Snell, Edwin M. *Strategic Planning for Coalition Warfare, 1941–1942*. Washington: Department of the Army, 1953.

Melosi, Martin V. *The Shadow of Pearl Harbor: Political Controversy over the Surprise Attack, 1941–1946*. College Station: Texas A&M University Press, 1977.

Miles, Vice Admiral Milton E. *A Different Kind of War: The Little-Known Story of the Combined Guerrilla Forces Created in China by the U.S. Navy and the Chinese during World War II*. Garden City: Doubleday, 1967.

Morison, Elting E. *Admiral Sims and the Modern American Navy*. Boston: Houghton Mifflin, 1942.

Morton, Louis. "Pearl Harbor in Perspective: A Bibliographical Survey." U.S. Naval Institute *Proceedings*, 81 (April 1955): 461–68.

Murphy, Paul L. *World War I and the Origin of Civil Liberties in the United States*. New York: W. W. Norton, 1979.

Murphy, Robert. *Diplomat Among Warriors*. Garden City: Doubleday, 1964.

Murphy, Walter F. *Wiretapping on Trial: A Case Study in the Judicial Process*. New York: Random House, 1965.

Murray, Robert K. *Red Scare: A Study in National Hysteria, 1919–1920*. Minneapolis: University of Minnesota Press, 1955.

Niblack, Rear Admiral A. P. *The History and Aims of the Office of Naval Intelligence*. Washington: Government Printing Office, 1920.

Nixon, Edgar B., ed. *Franklin D. Roosevelt and Foreign Affairs*, 3 vols. Cambridge: Harvard University Press, 1969.

Pash, Boris T. *The ALSOS Mission*. New York: Award House, 1969.

Pearson, John. *The Life of Ian Fleming*. New York: McGraw-Hill, 1966.

Pelz, Stephen E. *Race to Pearl Harbor: The Failure of the Second London Naval Conference and the Onset of World War II*. Cambridge: Harvard University Press, 1974.

Perry, Hamilton Darby. *The Panay Incident, Prelude to Pearl Harbor*. New York: Macmillan, 1969.

Pratt, Lawrence. "Anglo-American Naval Conversations on the Far East of January 1938." *International Affairs*, XLVII (Oct. 1972): 745–63.

Preston, William, Jr. *Aliens and Dissenters: Federal Suppression of Radicals, 1903–1933*. Cambridge: Harvard University Press, 1963.

Puleston, Captain William D. *Mahan: The Life and Work of Captain Alfred Thayer Mahan, U.S.N.* New Haven: Yale University Press, 1939.

Pusey, Merlo J. *Charles Evans Hughes*, 2 vols. New York: Macmillan, 1951.

Reber, Lieutenant Colonel John J. "Pete Ellis: Amphibious Warfare Prophet." U.S. Naval Institute *Proceedings*, 103 (Nov. 1977): 53–64.

Richardson, Admiral James O. *On the Treadmill to Pearl Harbor: The Memoirs of Admiral J. O. Richardson*. Washington: Government Printing Office, 1973.

Roetter, Charles. *The Art of Psychological Warfare, 1914–1945*. New York: Stein and Day, 1974.

Romanus, Charles F. and Sunderland, Riley. *Time Runs Out in CBI*. Washington: Office of Chief of Military History, 1959.

Roosevelt, Kermit, introduction. *War Report of the OSS*. New York: Walker, 1976.

Roskill, Stephen. *Naval Policy Between the Wars, 1919–1929*. New York: Walker, 1969.

————. *Naval Policy Between the Wars, 1930–1939*. Annapolis: Naval Institute Press, 1976.

Schaller, Michael. "SACO! The United States Navy's Secret War in China." *Pacific Historical Review*, 44 (Nov. 1975): 527–53.

Seth, Ronald S. *Secret Servants: A History of Japanese Espionage*. New York: Farrar, 1957.

Sherwood, Robert E. *Roosevelt and Hopkins, An Intimate History*. New York: Harper & Bros., 1948.

Smith, R. Harris. *OSS: The Secret History of America's First Central Intelligence Agency*. Berkeley: University of California Press, 1972.

Spector, Ronald. *Professors of War: The Naval War College and the Development of the Naval Profession*. Newport: Naval War College, 1977.

Sprout, Harold and Margaret. *Toward a New Order of Sea Power: American Naval Policy and the World Scene, 1918–1922*. Princeton: Princeton University Press, 1946.

Standley, William H. and Ageton, Arthur A. *Admiral Ambassador to Russia*. Chicago: Henry Regnery, 1955.

Stimson, Henry L. and Bundy, McGeorge. *On Active Service in Peace and War*. New York: Harper & Brothers, 1947–48.

Swing, Raymond Gram. *Forerunners of American Fascism*. New York: Julian Messner, 1935.

Tate, Merze. *The United States and Armaments*. New York: Russell & Russell, 1948.

Taylor, Teleford. *Two Studies in Constitutional Interpretation: Search, Seizure, Surveillance and Fair Trial and Free Press*. Columbus: Ohio State University Press, 1969.

Theoharis, Athan G. *Spying on Americans: Political Surveillance from Hoover to the Huston Plan*. Philadelphia: Temple University Press, 1978.

Tolley, Kemp. *Cruise of the Lanikai: Incitement to War*. Annapolis: Naval Institute Press, 1973.

Trask, David F. *Captains and Cabinets: Anglo-American Naval Relations, 1917–1918*. Columbia: University of Missouri Press, 1972.

Tripp, C.A. *The Homosexual Matrix*. New York: McGraw-Hill, 1975.

U.S. Congress, Joint Select Committee. *Hearings on the Pearl Harbor Attack*, 39 vols. Washington: Government Printing Office, 1946.

U.S. Congress, Senate. *Naval Investigation: Hearing Before a SubCommittee on Naval Affairs*, 2 vols. Washington: Government Printing Office, 1921.

Wheeler, Gerald E. *Admiral William Veazie Pratt, U.S. Navy: A Sailor's Life*. Washington: Naval History Division, 1974.

————. *Prelude to Pearl Harbor: The United States and the Far East 1921–1931*. Columbia: University of Missouri Press, 1963.

Wohlstetter, Roberta. *Pearl Harbor: Warning and Decision*. Stanford: Stanford University Press, 1962.

Zacharias, Captain Ellis M. *Secret Missions: The Story of an Intelligence Officer*. New York: G. P. Putnam's, 1946.

INDEX